The Wealth Explosion

The Wealth Explosion:

The Nature and Origins of Modernity

Stephen Davies

Head of Education at the Institute of Economic Affairs, London, and Senior Academic Fellow at the John Locke Institute; formerly program officer at the Institute for Humane Studies, George Mason University, Virginia; Senior Lecturer, Department of History and Economic History, Manchester Metropolitan University, and a Visiting Scholar at the Social Philosophy and Policy Center, Bowling Green State University, Ohio.

EER

Edward Everett Root, Publishers, Brighton, 2019,
In association with the Institute of Economic Affairs, London

EER

Edward Everett Root, Publishers, Co. Ltd.,
30 New Road, Brighton, Sussex, BN1 1BN, England.

www.eerpublishing.com
edwardeverettroot@yahoo.co.uk

Details of our overseas agents are on our website.

Stephen Davies, *The Wealth Explosion. The Nature and Origins of Modernity*

First published in Great Britain in 2019.

© Stephen Davies 2019.

This edition © Edward Everett Root 2019.

ISBN 9781912224593 Paperback
ISBN 9781912224586 Hardback
ISBN 9781912224609 eBook

Cover pictures:
Gathering Pumpkins - an October Scene in New England, 1867, John Whetten Ehninger, (Alamy)
BASF Werk Ludwigshafen, 1881, Robert Friedrich Stieler, (Alamy)

Production by Head & Heart Book Design
Printed in Great Britain by TJI Limited, Padstow, Cornwall.

Contents

Introduction

THE life that almost all human beings live today is different in kind from the ones our ancestors lived, from the advent of agriculture until comparatively recently. This is because of a process of transformation that has changed the human world ever more rapidly and continues to do so. The process is one that could have started in a number of places and at different times but which first became established and sustained in one, in many ways marginal, part of the world about two hundred and fifty years ago. How and why this happened is one of the biggest questions in history and several other fields of enquiry, perhaps the largest.

At various times all of us pause for reflection and ask ourselves big, important questions about ourselves, and the world we live in. One of these is the subject of this book, the question of how and why the contemporary world, our world, is different in a profound way from that of even our recent ancestors and how and why this dramatic transformation came about. Hopefully in answering that question we will have a better understanding of our current situation and how we arrived there and of what further questions to explore if we are to see more clearly where we may go in the future. The aim of this book is thus both ambitious and modest. It is ambitious because it addresses one of the biggest questions in history and the social sciences, that of what modernity is and how and why it came about in the fashion and location that it did. In other words it tries to identify the distinctive features of the human world in which we now live and how, where and when the process of transformation that produced that world and continues to form it began. This is clearly a huge topic and some may think it is too large and complex to be tackled with any hope of success.

However my goal is also modest and limited in several ways. Much of the argument is tentative, reflecting the reality that this is an area of rapidly moving research and investigation, where our knowledge and understanding of these issues is steadily growing. Most importantly this is not a work of original research and any contribution that it may make to the debates on these questions is not the result of new primary research. My goal is rather that of synthesis, of taking the work produced by many scholars and trying to see what kind of picture has begun to emerge from their arguments, debate and research. What I hope to do is to employ the work of these many scholars to create a coherent explanation and narrative of the origin, development and essential features of the condition of modernity, in which all human beings now live. My purpose is to present that picture in an accessible and understandable form and so to make the work and insights of many scholars available to a wider audience.

The starting point or initial insight is to realise that the experienced life of human beings today has a truly novel quality. Human beings today, in all parts of the world, live in a way that is truly unprecedented. In other words it is not a matter of there being more of what has been before or better or faster versions of things that were known to our forebears. Rather the experiences and reasonable expectations of anyone born in the last hundred years are so different from those of the vast majority in all previous epochs that we can say quite definitely that they are genuinely novel. There has been a fundamental change in the quality and nature of human life and experience. Moreover this change is continuing and accelerating, so that the gap between the experience of those now living and the people of the past is becoming ever greater. The extent and profundity of the novelty of the modern world is something that is often not grasped, because we take for granted so much of what we have around us, and because we are in some sense a part of this and so need an exercise of self-conscious introspection to be aware of it. Historical and philosophical perspective is what we lack. When we apply these however, it becomes clear that we and the two or three generations before us, are all part of a huge discontinuity in human affairs, comparable only to the advent of agriculture and settled civilisation, or the taming of fire and the discovery of complex tools.

Naturally, there are many who deny this, not least among professional historians. The *deformation professionelle* of the historian is indeed to see only continuity and to downplay the reality or extent of change. Even the historical profession though has a majority view that there is a clear break between the modern world and what came before it. As time passes and the transformation of both the human and physical worlds becomes more marked it becomes ever more difficult to make the case for continuity. However, agreement that there is a degree of novelty about the modern condition and even about the main elements of that novelty, do not mean that there is general agreement about other matters. There has been a distinct lack of consensus over even the apparently simple matter of when to date the appearance of modernity and its main features. Even more profound are the arguments over exactly how and why the phenomena that we collectively call modernity came about and why they appeared when and where they did. It is these disagreements that have inspired a host of studies and research with much, often warm, debate. The outcome is that our knowledge and understanding of these issues has increased significantly in the last thirty years and we can see the first signs of broad agreement (over such matters as chronology for example).

The other side of the debates over how modernity came about, and what it is, is a growing understanding of the shared nature of most of the societies and human experience of the world before modernity. When we look at the story of the past, of the rise and fall of empires and kingdoms, the appearance, spread and transformations of religions and cultures, and the development and flourishing of human knowledge and technology, the initial impression is of inexhaustible variety and constant change. However, when we look below the surface, at the structures of everyday life and economic conditions rather than at politics and culture it is continuity and sameness that becomes more apparent. As historians such as Fernand Braudel have noted, the material conditions of life for most human beings in most places have remained the same for very long periods of time and have been much the same, apart from variations produced by geography, across the world. This is even more apparent when you compare the life of the past to that of the present and recent past. At this point the variety of institutions and cultures becomes less prominent than the commonalities in these areas. As Patricia Crone for example has argued there are certain practices, institutions, and social structures that are common to almost all traditional (i.e. pre modern) societies, at least those where agriculture is the basic economic activity. (Clearly there are significant differences between agricultural societies and pastoral ones or those where hunter-gathering remained the predominant way of life).

The basic reality confronting our ancestors that leads to this fundamental sameness is that they all lived in a Malthusian world. That is, they lived in a world of radical scarcity. Ever since the appearance of agriculture (maybe even before then) human beings lived in a world where there were structural, natural constraints on how much could be produced at any given time and place. This meant that social and economic life had an almost zero-sum quality, in which it was very difficult to increase the total size of the 'pie' of useful production so that for one person to become better off somebody else had to become worse off. (Almost rather than absolutely because wealth increasing and value adding activity did take place. However it was limited and tended to have effects that did not last). In response to this situation all kinds of social institutions developed, from norms of conduct to political institutions to worked out intellectual and religious systems. These worked to enable complex forms of human life and to protect people as much as was possible against the vagaries of misfortune, given that this was a world in which the overwhelming majority lived at a subsistence or near subsistence level. One central part of these institutions was profound hostility towards and suspicion of, innovation. If modern societies are in some sense neophiliac we can truly say that almost all societies before the modern were neo-phobic.

Of course innovation did happen. However, when compared with what has happened since the later seventeenth century it was patchy, limited and above all was not sustained. There were episodes of intense innovation (and one in particular deserves notice) but these did not last. The crucial difference between our world, the modern world, and that of our ancestors is that we have escaped from the Malthusian cage, through sustained and ever more intensive innovation. This is an observation that has been made many times by many authors but it bears repeating and further exploration. Whether this will continue or rather prove to be a single and almost certainly unrepeatable episode in human history is another big question, which we currently cannot answer.

However thinking about the contrast between the modern world and the traditional world, and about how the one became the other does throw up a series of questions. Scholars from several disciplines have addressed these over the years. Recently however the focus on these questions has sharpened and new perspectives and methodologies have come to be employed. This has led to new insights and understandings. The obvious first question is that of whether there is actually such a big difference between the modern world and what went before. Here the majority of opinion is that there is a profound distinction but there is a vigorous and thoughtfully argued minority position that denies this. Wide agreement has also emerged about the nature and content of that difference. Apart from the details the shared perception is that modernity is best understood not so much as a set of conditions but as a particular kind of process that produces those conditions, and which is still continuing.

At this point however consensus and agreement end. Another obvious question is that of when and where the process of transformation that we call modernity began. Although there is increasing agreement here, to the effect that the process got going in North-West Europe in the middle to later eighteenth century, there is still a lot of argument and debate about this. There is even less agreement about why (if that is the case) the process began in that particular time and place. Why not somewhere else or at some other time? Here there are a whole series of competing accounts, explanations, and perspectives. In particular there is warm disagreement about what kind of perspective or metanarrative to use. Should the focus be on the history of something called western civilisation (since that is seen as the dynamic agent of change) or should we take a global or world history perspective? Should the centre of attention be politics, economics, institutions, ideas, or some combination of these? How important are things such as social relations (particularly class), technology, or natural phenomena such as geography and climate? Finally there is the issue of which disciplinary perspective yields the most insight. Economics, sociology, cultural studies, and geography all have their supporters (as do other disciplines such as biology or anthropology). In the event it is the empirical and inevitably eclectic discipline of history that has taken centre stage. This book is part of that but tries to use the insights that other disciplines bring, particularly economics and sociology.

Given all this, the actual content of this book works in the following way. In the first place it argues that the modern world is distinctive, and came into existence towards the very end of the eighteenth century. It is broadly globalist, inasmuch as it rejects arguments for European distinctiveness, at least before the seventeenth century and in many ways before the eighteenth or even the nineteenth. This account gives a central explanatory role to economic institutions and the part played by trade and exchange, which are seen as broadly benign and as opposed and contrasted to political power. It is argued that capitalism is not the same as a market and property based economy (which has existed for thousands of years in almost every part of the world) but is a specific and peculiar kind of market economy that only becomes established in the early to mid nineteenth century.

However, it also argues that while the breakthrough to modernity could have happened in several parts of the world and could have (and nearly did) happen before the eighteenth century, the fact is that it first took place in Europe, primarily because of particular events in the political and intellectual history of the world in the sixteenth and seventeenth centuries which worked out differently in Europe as compared to elsewhere. This was however not predetermined or even a consequence of earlier developments but to a great degree something contingent, the result of specific events and the thoughts, desires, and actions of actual historical persons. This means that the narrative put forward in this book is neither stadial nor teleological. It does not see the modern world as a telos or goal toward which all previous history was working and so does not see the past mainly in terms of those parts of it that can be seen as being in some way forerunners or anticipations of the present. Nor does it present the history of the world or some part of it as being made up of a series of stages, with each one a development or advance from the previous one and therefore in some sense 'higher'. It also argues that the crucial feature of the process that starts in eighteenth century western Europe is that it is sustained, because of the outcomes of specific political conflicts and because of the behaviour of elites, who were responding to incentives created by the changes and events mentioned above.

In terms of the structural detail the book is organised in the following way. The first chapter looks at what exactly is distinctive about modernity and the way we live now and explicitly compares and contrasts this to the common, structural, features of the world of our ancestors. It also sets out the key idea of innovation (understood to refer to both economic and intellectual innovation) and the way this brings about change, and the way in which the human social world before the modern had all kinds of barriers to this, whether legal, political, social or cultural. The second chapter goes on to give a survey and account of the main debates and arguments taking place around the key questions identified above and sets out the particular perspective that I am following in the book and my agreements and disagreements with the authors surveyed. Those who want to simply go straight to the action can jump this chapter but it does locate the rest of the book relative to other ones.

One of the crucial arguments is that the possibility of escaping the Malthusian cage of traditional society was around for a long time before it actually happened, and that it came close to happening on several occasions. The third chapter looks at the most striking such instance of an 'aborted modernisation', which took place in Medieval China, under the Song dynasty and its reversal and suppression under the subsequent dynasties of the Ming and Qing. This is interesting in itself but it also casts light on the historical barriers to innovation and the way in which it could be deliberately and systematically rolled back.

Chapters four and five focus on one of the two key turning points that this account identifies. This was the way that military and political institutions were transformed throughout the world by what historians call 'the military revolution' (sometimes the 'gunpowder revolution'). The key argument made here, through a narrative, is that this had one kind of outcome in most of the world in terms of the politics and social relations it produced but a very different one in Europe. The European outcome is argued to have been largely contingent and even low probability. However, the argument goes, it led to a marked change in the incentives facing all members of European societies, but above all those facing the political and economic elites, which in turn led to a series of changes in their behaviour and thinking.

The sixth chapter looks at the intellectual and cultural upheaval that took place in seventeenth century Europe and which is usually (but rather misleadingly) called the 'scientific revolution'. This was related to and connected to the political and social shift described in the previous chapter but was, it is argued, an independent phenomenon, hence its getting a chapter of its own. As with the military and political transformations described in chapters four and five, the argument is that what we have here is in a significant sense a global phenomenon that happened to take a particular course and form in Europe (and also in this case, in Japan).

The seventh chapter looks at how these transformations in Europe and Japan worked out when the world came to face a Malthusian crunch at the end of the eighteenth century (there had been many such crises before, including a global one in the fourteenth century and arguably another in the seventeenth). The chapter looks at the way in which the pressure of the crisis on certain European societies led to a response that became the process of transformation that produced and continues to produce the state of affairs described in the first chapter, which we call modernity. It also analyses how the process was sustained rather than being choked off as in earlier episodes, because of the outcome of certain intellectual and political conflicts as well as the incentives facing the wealthy and powerful. A further point is to look at how the world that came out of the process had certain qualities and features that we may describe as modern (because they only appear with modernity) but which were not essential or necessary features of the modern world because the outcome of certain processes and conflicts could have been different without destroying the main process of change. The disappearance of slavery as a widespread and important institution is one example but there are others.

This is further explored in the eighth chapter, which brings the story up to the present day and looks at both the nature of the contemporary economic and political world and its likely prospects. Two big issues touched on here are those of whether the process of modernity will continue or will prove to be only the longest and most dramatic episode of innovation and growth in human history after which the world will revert to its previous long-standing norm, and secondly that of whether the modern world going forward will continue to have the same features that it currently has or will evolve into something significantly different.

Finally, the story and analysis presented in this book raises the question explored in the postscript, that of how to understand our own historical situation and how we should locate it in the overall sweep of history. One common way of seeing the advent of modernity is, as said, to see it as 'the triumph of the West', the spread and diffusion of a distinctively Western civilisation and its supplanting or transformation of other civilisations. This makes modernisation the same as Westernisation and means that eventually, should things continue on their present course, the entire world will belong to one, essentially Western, culture and civilisation.

   The narrative and analysis presented in this book casts doubt on this. If modernity marks a decisive break from the past and is the outcome of events that happened in historical Western Christian civilisation but could have happened elsewhere then two things follow. The first is that modernity represents a break or discontinuity with <u>all</u> traditional civilisations, including the Western Christian one. This means that in a very real sense we are no longer living in Western civilisation, that the historic Western civilisation based on Christianity and the inheritance of the classical world no longer exists as a living entity but has been supplanted by a new civilisation, the modern one. The second conclusion is that this modern civilisation will inherit a good deal from its historical Western predecessor but will also increasingly draw upon the heritage of other historic civilisations, in an increasingly eclectic fashion. The outcome (for reasons of technology) is indeed likely to be a single world civilisation but not one that is clearly or decisively shaped by any one of the historical societies of the Old World. Rather it will be something truly new.

   One final point is that I have eschewed the extensive use of references unless these are for specific points rather than general arguments. Instead a bibliographical essay that suggests further reading to explore the themes and arguments of the main text follows each chapter.

Acknowledgements

THIS book has been the product of much reading and many conversations, so there are many people who have contributed to it, maybe without realising they had done so. The first suggestion that I should undertake this project came from Tom G. Palmer and he and the Cato Institute subsequently provided support and arranged for assistance from the Earhart Foundation, without which this would not have been possible. So in the first place I thank Tom Palmer, and David Boaz for their support and encouragement and the Cato Institute and the Earhart Foundation for their support. I have also had support and encouragement from my colleagues at the Institute of Economic Affairs, most notably Professor Philip Booth. The intellectual debts are so many that I cannot list all of them but I have gained particular benefit from conversations with Jacob T. Levy (who will recognise the tripartite model of modern political discussion as coming from him), Mark Pennington, Peter Mentzel, Steve Horwitz, Sarah Squire, Jared Rubin, Eric Schliesser, Peter Ryley, Pierre Garello, Douglas Rasmussen and Deirdre McCloskey. Joel Mokyr, Andre Gunder Frank, and Patricia Ebrey all had a great influence on my thinking through their writing. A crucial influence (which will be apparent to anyone who reads the central chapters of this book) is the work of Geoffrey Parker and before then his teaching at St Andrews. Indeed, the subject and argument of this book is in many ways the product of the experience of taking his Early Modern European course there in the 1970s. Last but not least is the support and encouragement I have had from Liz who truly made this possible.

The Wealth Explosion:

The Nature and Origins of Modernity

CHAPTER I

The Way We Once Lived and The Way We Live Now

Change and Continuity in Human Experience

PEOPLE alive today, even the poor, are the luckiest people in human history. Compared to their ancestors – even their recent ancestors – they are by any objective standard amazingly well off and fortunate. They will on average live far longer and be much less likely to suffer from serious illness or accident. The great majority will not experience the loss of a parent or sibling from natural causes before they reach adulthood. Most will experience levels of comfort and convenience that were once available only to the wealthy – and often not even to them. Not only will their lives be less marked by tragedy and loss than those of most human beings for most of recorded history, they will have a range of opportunities open to them that were never available to any but the most privileged in earlier times. In addition they will have possibilities open to them that even past kings and emperors could only imagine – if that. Quite simply the kinds of constraints and limits that defined the lives of most human beings for the greater part of history will not apply to them. The only people who may enjoy even greater fortune are our possible descendants, who could enjoy an even higher level of comfort and opportunity and escape even constraints that still contain us.

Why though is our experience – and that of our parents and grandparents – so different from that of our more distant ancestors? This is because we are living and participating in a process of complete transformative change. This process began some two hundred or more years ago and has already changed the way human beings live far more radically than many realise. Moreover, it is continuing, at an accelerating rate, and many will argue that the greatest changes are yet to come. The results of this process are many but the central one is a fundamental change in the essential conditions of human life. In other words, there has been a change in the structures and patterns of everyday life and in the expectations and experiences of ordinary people. How to evaluate these changes is a matter of continuing disagreement but most people if asked would find them enormously positive and would react with horror to any idea of reversing them. We are part of an explosive growth above all in the capacity of human beings to control material resources and make them useful – what we may call without exaggeration a 'wealth explosion'

Change as transformative as this has only happened a few times in human history. When the layman or woman looks at the past they see what looks like a story of constant change and alteration. Rulers and dynasties come and go, there are changes, often dramatic in culture and religion, politics and government see repeated shifts and changes of course while wars, revolutions and the movement of peoples sweep away old arrangements. The trained eye of the historian however sees continuity as more important than change in most cases. Things that appear to be novel often turn out to be nothing of the kind or even revivals of older forms. A dynasty may change, there may be a change of rulers, even a revolution or conquest but on closer examination the structure of government remains much the same and alters very slowly, if at all. Even apparently dramatic changes such as the Reformation or the rise of Islam turn out to be much slower and more gradual events than one might suppose. Moreover, even in cases such as these the deep underlying structure of daily life and experience does not change very much or does so at a glacial pace. To use the theatre as a metaphor, there may be changes in detail or in the cast of characters but the play and its basic structure remains the same while the layout of the theatre itself is constant regardless of which play is being performed. Thus, there are different kings or dynasties but the monarchical form of government persists, there may be significant alterations in religious doctrine and observance but the institution of religion itself persists and its details in practice change much less than we might imagine.

The point to grasp is that not all areas of human life are as mutable and unstable as, say, political affairs. While some aspects of human life change frequently and rapidly others have historically only altered slowly, taking several generations for a true shift to take place. Others hardly change at all and remain constant for thousands of years. These are the structures that limit and determine human existence and experience, the basic facts and realities of everyday life that persist as the unchanging backdrop to the rapidly changing scenes and acts of politics, and intellectual and religious life.

The French historian Fernand Braudel captured this division, through the metaphor of the ocean. The surface, which corresponds to the visible and dramatic events of politics, is unstable and changes swiftly and dramatically. Below this is the level of currents, of slow and gradual ebb and flow, which corresponds to areas such as culture, trade and commerce, art and science where change happens, but slowly over several lifetimes. The bulk of the ocean however, and in this metaphor the greater part of actual human experience, consists of what he calls the 'structures of everyday life', the basic human activities that make up most of human life, and the way that these are organised. These hardly change at all over time but rather remain broadly stable and constant. If they do change, it is so gradual as to be only perceptible after the passage of centuries or even thousands of years. This is partly because these deep structures of social organisation and ways of living are shaped and defined by factors such as biology, geography and the nature of the physical world, which are beyond mere human will or choice,

There are difficulties with Braudel's metaphor, especially the implication that the events of the higher levels are somehow determined by those of the deeper structural one and so no more than consequential epiphenomena. However, it captures an important fact about historical human experience, which is one reason why so many historians find it compelling. If we look at the lives of ordinary people in particular as opposed to those of the elites we cannot help but be struck by the continuity of experience and patterns of life that we discover. The everyday life of a peasant farmer in Roman Gaul was not that different from that of his descendants in the middle ages or the seventeenth century. Details change but the pattern of existence and its content remains much the same. Even at the level of the elite change proves to be less than we might imagine.

The Major Shifts in Human Experience

However, there are times in history when even the fundamental structures of life change. These are episodes that mark a move from one form of human existence to another. As such they are very rare and in fact only three such transformations are generally recognised. The first occurred some 50,000 years ago with the transition from the Middle to the Upper Palaeolithic. At this time the number and variety of tools made and used by our ancestors suddenly expanded. This led to a dramatic rise in the number of humans and the much more intensive hunting and exploitation of the planet's megafauna. Humans went from being only one species among many to being the dominant one on the planet. The same period also saw the appearance of art in the form of cave paintings and carvings and possibly the first forms of religious practice and belief (although this is less clear). Towards the end of this period we find the first signs of the domestication of animals and of trade and exchange, often over considerable distances

The second major shift in human affairs followed on from this and was of course the advent of trade and agriculture, leading to the appearance of settled civilisations, which first took place about 10,000 years ago. The kinds of change involved this time included, alongside the appearance of agriculture as the main means of human subsistence, the creation of cities and of government and organised religion, as well as writing. (It was once thought that cities were a consequence of the advent of agriculture but recent evidence supports the thesis first put forward by Jane Jacobs that trade and cities came first, with agriculture a response to the problems and opportunities this created). Later on came the use of metal for tools rather than stone and bone. The traditional world that we know about from history and archaeology is the one created by this transformation. The changes that happened in the Neolithic transition and the rise of settled, complex societies defined the parameters within which all historical societies since then have operated – until very recently. The modern world, the one we all now inhabit, is as different in kind from the world inhabited by all of our ancestors since the invention of agriculture as theirs was from the world of our pre-agricultural hunter-gatherer ancestors. It is the product of the third such basic shift in human life and experience.

All three of these transitions have a number of common features. They all involve a radical shift in technology (defined in the broadest sense to include social technique as well as tools). In each case there was a clear increase in human population and in the number of human beings that could be supported by the planet (in its carrying capacity). This rise in population is not just a consequence of the other changes but also a cause. All three transitions see human societies becoming more complex, with the number and variety of social relations and interactions increasing dramatically. This is connected to a basic change in social structure and organisation and the way most people live. Alongside these material changes there is a profound alteration in culture and ultimately in the sensibility of humans and the way they think about and understand both themselves and the physical world.

Interestingly, all three started in certain particular places. That is they did not appear all over the inhabited world at roughly the same time. Instead they first manifested in a specific area or areas of the planet's surface and then occurred later elsewhere. The first happened initially in Africa, the second first happened in the Old World in the Middle East and North China, while occurring independently and later in Mesoamerica, Peru and North America. The third, which we are presently experiencing, first began in North-West Europe and also independently in Japan. One common way of understanding this is through diffusionism, the notion that something starts in one place and then spreads from that point to the rest of the world, either through contact (including conquest) or emulation. For some phenomena such as epidemic disease or religion this is clearly true but it is not clear that this is the best way to think of these three world transformations. It could be that in addition to expansion and contagion there was also independent but later emergence, or a more complex process in which the growth of the new form of human life simply made older forms unviable by (metaphorically or literally) denying them space. There is considerable room for argument in all three cases about whether the change could have happened earlier and whether it could have started elsewhere. The other big question is that of whether any of these changes was inevitable, in the sense that it was bound to happen eventually, or rather was the product of other changes that were ultimately driven by chance or uncontrollable natural factors, such as climate.

The point, that the modern world is different in kind from traditional, agricultural societies in a profound or basic way, has been made many times. Typically, this is coupled with the observation that the change that has brought about this rupture in historical continuity is both abrupt and rapid, and relatively recent. There is also growing agreement about roughly when and where this transformative process really got going with the overwhelming consensus locating it in Northwest Europe during the 'long nineteenth century' of 1780 to 1914. John Maynard Keynes gave one account of this change in 1919. He pointed out how much the world had changed in the course of that 'long century' and elsewhere observed that George Washington had more in common with a Roman centurion in terms of his experiences and the way he lived than he did with an American born in 1900. In other words, there had been more change, of a more profound nature, between 1776 and 1914 than there had been during the previous two thousand years. Keynes also identified some of the central features of this change, above all the much greater interconnectedness of the various parts of the world and their inhabitants and a dramatic and unprecedented rise in the average standard of living for a large part of the world's population. These are indeed central features but not exhaustive, as we shall see.

The view of Keynes, that the years since the later eighteenth century had seen a fundamental rupture in historical continuity, has subsequently been articulated by a whole host of scholars and thinkers, from a wide range of positions. Nor was Keynes saying something dramatically novel even then. Today we tend to see the nineteenth century as a period of calm and stability but that was not how those who lived through it saw things. Rather they were struck by the unprecedented rapidity and extent of change, and felt themselves to be living in an age of transformation and dissolution of old certainties, which some found exhilarating and others alarming.

The Old World and Its Ways

What though were the structural, persistent features of the world that agriculture made, which persisted until recently and are only now passing away (if indeed they are)? To reiterate an earlier point, the sheer variety of the human past may seem to make this a meaningless question or one that can only be answered at a level of abstraction so high as to make the answer effectively meaningless. However just as the detail of a landscape viewed from ground level is flattened out and homogenised by being seen from an aeroplane, so our own historical location enables us to see commonalities to almost all of the societies that have existed since agriculture became widespread. Increasingly, it is the similarities that strike us rather than the detailed variations, precisely because these are some of the features that are changed or radically diminished in our own experience.

A Malthusian World

The single most important persistent feature of the world before modernity is that for human beings it was one of radical constraint. This was because of the condition of fundamental and (more importantly) unshiftable scarcity that confronted most of them for most of the time. That we live in a world of scarcity is of course one of the foundational commonplaces of economics. We do not live in a world of abundance where no matter how much we want or consume individually and collectively there is always plenty remaining of as good quality as we have consumed. Rather there are limits to resources of all kinds and it takes effort (the use of other resources, above all time) to acquire and use the resources that do exist. We cannot have our cake and eat it. However, the intensity of scarcity, the degree to which this condition limits human life and its options, has been much more severe for most of history than it is in the modern world. Moreover, for most of recorded human history there was seldom any easy way to escape this.

That resources were limited was a commonplace throughout history. Revealingly this was recognised as much in folk sayings as in learned discourse: so for example the Chinese saying "The land is scarce and the people are many". The reality was that all human beings, even many of the wealthy, were always living on the edge of dearth and famine. Typically they were only one failed harvest away from serious hunger and shortage. If the harvest failed two or more years in succession (as it did every twenty years on average) the result was famine and starvation. Because there was little or no cushion or reserve, natural disasters such as droughts, floods, or volcanic eruptions had much more pronounced effects than they now do in much wealthier modern societies. It was not only crops and food that were in short supply. The other products of human labour such as clothes and household goods were also limited. Most people had two sets of clothes at most and leather boots or shoes were so valuable that they could be mentioned in wills. More fundamentally, as the Chinese saying recognised, essential resources such as land and water were often not enough for the demands of the human population.

All of this was recognised and theorised in 1798 by the English clergyman and economist Thomas Malthus. Malthus' *Essay on Population* (which was essentially a thought experiment directed at the utopian arguments of people like Godwin) argued that while the output of products (particularly food) could only grow arithmetically (2-4-6-8....), human population would grow geometrically (2-4-8-16…) unless subject to checks. The gloomy conclusion was that unless the natural growth of human population could be constrained in a sustained way, human beings would always tend to increase in number until population reached the maximum that could be supported by existing and available resources, which would be a state of affairs where the majority were living at the edge of subsistence. This was of course the reality in Malthus's own time, and had been the case since the advent of agriculture, if not before then.

Malthus proved to be one of the worst prophets ever, given the way things have worked out from his own time to our own. (This may prove to be a temporary embarrassment but that remains to be seen). However, he was one of the greatest historical sociologists. His insight is crucial for understanding the world created by agriculture, which our ancestors lived in. In essence it was a Malthusian world in which over the longer term things worked out exactly as his model predicted.

In the first place this was a world where poverty was the normal default condition for most people. One of the last things Jesus told his disciples was "The poor you will always have with you". (He meant that this was a permanent and lasting state of affairs, unlike his physical presence in the world, which was not). This reflected something that everyone took for granted: most people everywhere were poor and this was not going to change. Everyday life for most people was shaped by this reality.

This poverty sprang in turn from another feature of the Malthusian world: the productivity of human work (labour) and of the other 'factors of production' (land and capital) was low and increased very slowly, if at all. A related feature of life was that even when resources were being used to their maximum capacity (given things such as the level of technology and the organisation of production) many resources remained idle. In particular, for most of history underemployment of labour was the norm: while people were poor they did not necessarily work continuously or as much as many do today. There was often an increase in total output, what we would now call economic growth. However, this was what economists now call 'extensive growth', it was more output achieved through more input such as a rise in population or a growth in the amount of time that people worked. Because there was, ultimately, no increase in output per capita in the first case or in output per hour worked in the second, there was no rise in living standards.

Another feature of this world was that the primary and overwhelmingly dominant economic activity was agriculture. (As a direct result most people lived in rural environments). As the British historian E. A. Wrigley has pointed out, all pre-modern societies had to have at least 80% of their adult population engaged in agriculture. The alternative was failure to produce enough food, and hence starvation. This was also one of the principal reasons for chronic underemployment because the 80% in question were only fully employed by agriculture for two periods of the year (planting and harvest). So the normal life experience was to be primarily a peasant farmer or agricultural worker, or to work in a trade that was directly connected to farming. It also meant that the pattern of daily life was driven by the cycle of farming and its demands, as well as being shaped by the seasons and the rising and setting of the sun to a degree that we have now forgotten. (Wrigley, 1987)

All of this in turn reflected another basic structural feature of human life in traditional societies. This was a low use of energy compared to what we find in the modern world. Although wind and waterpower were used from an early date the main source of energy for work of every kind was biological, the muscle power of humans and animals. This in turn derived ultimately from the solar energy converted by the process of photosynthesis. The significant aspect was that this use of energy did not increase: the energy input into most productive processes did not increase with time and the total amount of usable energy used and available did not rise relative to population, even over very long periods of time.

What this meant was that traditional society also lacked the degree of social complexity that even underdeveloped ones have today. The idea of social and economic complexity is an old one, going back to the Scottish Enlightenment. In economic terms it refers to two things. The first is the phenomenon of the division of labour, in which a productive process (such as the making of pins in Adam Smith's famous example) is broken up into a series of discrete tasks, each undertaken by a different person rather than being done entirely by one single individual. The second is that of the 'roundaboutness' of the productive process, an idea first formulated by the Austrian economist Eugen Von Bohm-Bawerk. This is best explained by the example of fishing. In its simplest form the fisherman catches fish directly with his hands. A more roundabout way of achieving the same end is to first make nets or a fishing rod and then catch fish. A yet more roundabout method is to make a boat as well as nets and tackle. More roundabout methods take longer and require capital investment (which is forgone leisure and consumption) but yield greater output. The greater the degree of both division of labour and roundaboutness of production in an economy, the more complex it is. Social complexity refers to a number of things, such as the number and frequency of social interactions between people, the number and diversity of social roles, and the complexity and elaboration of social institutions.

More complex societies are typically wealthier and have greater capacity to do things (to manipulate, alter, and control the environment) than less complex ones. Pre-modern societies were all much less complex in all senses than are modern ones, even those that are underdeveloped. The reason was their structurally limited use of energy, which meant their ability to control their environment was limited in turn. This meant that division of labour and roundaboutness of production or social and institutional complexity could not get past a certain point because to go beyond that point required a significant increase in the use of energy. This point has been theorised by the American historian Ian Morris, in his social development index. One of the striking findings is that the modern world (since 1750) has a much higher social development index than any past society. (Morris, 2013)

So all past societies before the modern era were marked by endemic poverty, low or non-existent growth (as we experience it), low levels of energy use and capture, and low levels of social and economic complexity. All this meant that our ancestors inhabited a world that was indeed a zero sum game for most people most of the time. That is, it was very hard to grow the real size of the 'pie' of goods and services more rapidly than population over a prolonged period. This in turn meant that it was hard for any person or group to become better off without making some other person or group worse off, because we are speaking of the division of a fixed 'pie'. This had rather dark implications for many human social relations at both the personal and higher social levels, meaning that they often had a predatory or exploitative aspect.

Moral Economy

However, this situation also produced a cooperative response from most people. This was a set of social institutions and practices found (in varying forms of course) in all pre-modern societies. They are often referred to as the 'moral economy' a term first used by the historian E P Thompson but given wider applicability by the anthropologist James Scott. What Scott and Thompson mean are a series of social practices that taken collectively served to ensure that marginal groups were protected against the adverse effects of change or accidents. In concrete terms this meant things like the sharing of access to key resources such as water or seed or tools, the rotation of access to good land through things like the medieval European open field system, restrictions on arbitrage and the free movement of prices, and controls on technology and training by institutions such as guilds and fraternities. The aim was to ensure a floor below which people could not fall except in the case of disaster in which case if one starved all did.

The paradoxical effect of these kinds of social institution however was that while they gave society a quality of robustness and security that it would otherwise have lacked, they also inhibited innovation. All traditional societies were to some degree neophobic – the novel was regarded with suspicion and assumed to be harmful until strong evidence showed otherwise. This outlook has a paradoxical quality because it is actually sustained innovation of all kinds that has enabled our species to escape the Malthusian constraints. However our ancestors were not simply foolish in being sceptical of or even hostile towards innovation. The reality is that innovation of any kind is risky. Most innovations fail and in failing they have negative effects and consume valuable resources. The effects of the innovative process in general outweigh this (the minority of 'hits' produce much greater benefits than the losses caused by the majority of 'misses') but this is not obvious. Moreover, in a world where most people are on the edge of subsistence innovation will naturally (and for many people correctly) be seen as simply too dangerous.

The need for security also explains another universal feature of pre-modern societies, the central place of the household. Households were the foundational institutions of economic, social, and political life. This has only changed within what is still just about living memory (and has still not changed in many parts of the world) and yet this is the area where popular incomprehension of the past and its difference from the present is most marked. Today, if most people (in the developed world at least) were asked what the basic unit of society is they would say it was the individual person. The model this reveals is that of a society made up of interconnected individuals and defined by the relations between them. By contrast our ancestors all thought of society as consisting of households. Individuals not part of a household were aberrant, and either pitied or feared and seen as dangerous. All larger and intermediate social units were assemblages of households. In fact the household was seen as society as a whole in miniature and larger society as the household writ large. The natural type of authority and governance was thought to be the same in both cases. All this reflected reality. Almost everyone did live in a household and to live as a single person on one ones own for any length of time was very rare. This was because, even for the wealthy, survival on ones own was extremely difficult. Being part of a household was thus a practical as well as a social necessity.

At this point many readers may object. Surely the pre-modern world was not as static and uniform as this implies. At one level this is obviously true, there was a great deal of change in areas like cultural and intellectual life or politics but this did not affect the structural features described here. There are aspects of life where there was quite profound change over long periods, one of the most striking being a long run tendency for societies to become less violent but that went along with even slower or non-existent change in the areas we have described. What we can discern are episodes where it seems that these structural constants were indeed going to give way. These episodes or 'eflorescences', as one historian has called them, were periods that did see significant social and technological innovation and consequent modern style growth. There are also, usually simultaneously, periods that we may describe as 'ages of reason', when intellectual life and enquiry becomes more extensive and open. The crucial point though is that these episodes do not last and so do not lead to a sustained transformation of the conditions of life. Instead there is a reversion to the conditions just described. Very often such episodes of dynamism conclude in a process of simplification in which complex societies and economies collapse and revert to a much simpler and less dynamic and productive form. (The term collapse should not lead us to think of such episodes as cataclysmic – in fact they actually took between sixty and a hundred and fifty years). This is because such societies are unable in the last analysis to escape from the Malthusian constraints of limited resources.

Ruling Classes and Industrious Classes

The final feature of traditional societies is closely related to this last point, as we shall see. There was a basic social division found in all societies after the advent of agriculture. This was between those who produced wealth by production or exchange on the one hand and those who acquired it through the use of force or fraud on the other. The first category included peasant farmers (the great majority) as well as artisans, merchants, and traders of all kinds. The second category were those who controlled not the means of production but what we may call the means of predation – organised force or systematic mystification in other words. These were the ruling classes of society such as aristocrats and clergy. The second group often did come to control and own great wealth and much productive resources, such as land for example, but this was a consequence of their privileged position rather than the cause of it. That position derived in the first instance from their greater access to the means of violence. They were not however simply parasitical because, partly for their own advantage, they came to provide what economists call 'public goods' such as defence against other human predators (bandits, criminals, or members of other tribes and political communities), or a means of settling disputes peacefully (so a legal system).

These ruling groups were the primary subjects of historical accounts until very recently. There is a good reason for this, quite apart from the practical point that most of the surviving sources are concerned with them, which is that they were the primary active force in human history. It was rulers and elites who had the power to actually make things happen. They were the ones with agency in other words. In addition, as Peter Laslett famously argued, they were the only social class in society with true class-consciousness, a self-conscious awareness of their own group interest. (Laslett, 2015) This and their nature meant that their relation to innovation and activities that actually changed the world in a positive way was ambivalent. On the one hand, to the extent that innovation led to actual growth in productivity, that meant more resources for them to extract from the productive part of society. On the other hand if it went on for a long enough time it would tend to weaken their position and increase the capacity of other social groups for effective action. Another aspect of the ruling classes historical role was the way that successful groups tended to expand the area of the planet that they controlled and so create an empire. Empires produced internal peace and so although they were created using (often) savage violence, once established they brought social peace to a large part of the planet's surface. However this also meant an even stronger incentive for the successful group to keep things the same.

Arguments For and Against The Idea of a Radical Discontinuity

The authors who argue that the modern world is somehow different in kind from what has gone before in human history make many claims and identify many aspects of the modern world as truly novel when compared to the past. However, these apparently multitudinous claims can be put into three broad categories. The first is a set of arguments to the effect that the material conditions of life have been transformed for most of the world's inhabitants by a combination of economic growth and scientific and technological innovation. As a result, what were once the luxuries enjoyed by potentates have now become the common expectation and necessities of the masses. Consequently, the typical daily experience and life story of the average person is hugely different from what it would have been less than two hundred years ago. Nor is this just a matter of greater wealth and comfort. Technological innovation has made things possible for ordinary people that existed only in the realms of imagination before, even for the wealthy, such as being able to communicate instantaneously with someone on the other side of the world or to travel great distances swiftly and in relative comfort and safety or to listen to a particular musical performance at any time. In addition, changes in medicine and public health mean that what were once near universal experiences of illness, pain and mortality are now much reduced or even eliminated.

The second set of arguments identifies and defines a more gradual but still definite change in human consciousness and character. In essence the argument is that human beings are more restrained, more socialised and more civilised than before in their manners and behaviour and that this reflects a more fundamental alteration in their social consciousness, in the way that they understand and perceive both themselves and others and their relations with other people. Again the argument is that this change has come about recently and comparatively suddenly.

The final set of analyses focus on a number of changes in social organisation, in the way human beings live together and in the kind of institutions that their interactions produce. The argument here is that the kind of social order that we inhabit is novel, as well as the daily life that we enjoy and the way we understand our position and ourselves. These kinds of argument were made almost since the very start of the process they identify and describe. Thus, some of the earliest accounts come from the Scottish Enlightenment of the later eighteenth century or from that movement's intellectual descendants, such as the English historian T. B. Macaulay.

However not everyone shares this view, to put it mildly. There is a strong counter argument put by an equally diverse and varied body of authors. The rival position holds that while the modern world is indeed different from the past, that this is a difference of degree rather than of kind. To put it another way, they argue that the main elements of the changes that mark the modern world and the institutions and practices that have brought them about are simply continuations or intensifications of processes and practices that have been around for a long time, maybe even thousands of years, at least in some parts of the world. They also argue that while the changes of the nineteenth and twentieth centuries were indeed far-reaching and dramatic they were no more profound or sweeping than those of other periods in history that featured change of equal significance. Two points of comparison that are made are the period now commonly described as Late Antiquity (roughly CE 300 to 700) which saw the worldwide collapse and replacement of the major civilisations of the ancient world, and the so-called 'Axial Age' between 800 and 200 BC that saw the appearance of the major old world religions.

In one sense, this criticism is correct. The transformation we are talking about did not arrive out of the blue, without any real connection to what had gone before. Thus it did not happen via some *deus ex machina* such as a self-generated event or series of events that had no connection to what had gone before or to the specific historical locations in which they occurred. What we may say is that the transformation that produced the modern world, as in the two previous episodes of systemic change, was the product of a slow accumulation of things, such as knowledge, that had been going on for a long time but had reached a kind of critical mass. This would mean that the breakthrough could not have happened earlier unless some key variable had changed or reached a particular level earlier. Alternatively it could have happened sooner but something prevented this from happening and eventually at some time and place these barriers were no longer effective.

However these qualifications do not substantially affect the case for the modern world being significantly different from the past. There are two rejoinders to the argument for continuity and persistence. The first is that the changes in a number of indicators are so massive compared with what had gone before that we are clearly talking about a qualitative change rather than a merely quantitative one – it is a case of something quite new rather than merely a lot more of what we had before. Moreover, as Friedrich Engels pointed out, a quantitative change that is sufficiently large, or is sustained for a long enough time, becomes a qualitative one. In that case, even if each increment of change is small and the process is continuous, so long as the change is cumulative there comes a point where the change and its effects become radical, that is they change the nature of the object of the change.

However, it is the second rejoinder that is really telling. In some areas, such as economic integration and productive capacity the element of continuity and progressive change is marked. However, there are several crucial areas where the changes are not only large and significant but also abrupt and sudden. These include such matters as life expectancy, average living standards, degree of urbanisation, rate of technological innovation, and speed and ease of travel and communication. Not only is the modern world qualitatively different from earlier periods by a whole range of measures, research shows that in many cases the change over the last hundred and fifty years is so much swifter than at earlier times that comparing this period to earlier ones produces a picture of rapid change contrasted with one of relative stasis. This is most clear when we examine things such as material well being and consumption but is also true of matters such as the total body of knowledge, both theoretical and practical. It is most difficult to establish in areas such as culture and belief, where quantitative measurement is much more difficult if not impossible. We can point to several examples of radical and abrupt alteration even here though.

The Main Features of Modernity

What though are the main elements of this change, which makes the modern world so different from that of our ancestors? To put it more formally, what are the main features of modernity? Historians have given it a number of labels, often reflecting their own emphases. Thus for Eric Jones we are speaking of 'modern growth' while for Julian Simon it is 'sudden modern progress'. All of the authors though agree on the main elements. As indicated earlier, these can be grouped under three main heads.

Changes in Physical Circumstances and Conditions

Number One: More People

In the first and primary place are a set of interconnected changes in the physical conditions of human life and existence. The most basic is simply the number of people and the rate at which population has grown since about 1800. Between the discovery of agriculture and 1800 total world population had never exceeded one billion and for most of the time got nowhere near that figure. It had approached this level during the later thirteenth century and had again come close during the eighteenth century but the evidence we have suggests that before then somewhere less than one billion was the maximum number of human beings that the planet and traditional agriculture could support, its carrying capacity. Throughout recorded history the total number of people was kept in check, mostly well below the one billion figure, by 'natural checks' of the kind that Thomas Malthus identified almost two hundred years ago, above all disease, and malnutrition or outright starvation.

According to the United Nations, after slightly more than a century of steady growth total world population reached one billion around 1830. It then doubled to two billion by 1930 and then doubled again by 1975. The point of course is that not only is the world's population much larger now than at any time in the past but the rate at which population has increased has accelerated dramatically. It took one hundred years to go from one to two billion (1830 to 1930), thirty years to go from two billion to three billion (1930 to 1960) and only fifteen years to go from three billion to four (1960 to 1975). It then took just thirty-six years to reach seven billion in 2011. Before the late eighteenth and early nineteenth century, population growth was slow and subject to sharp reverses such as that experienced in the fourteenth century. Moreover, there was often considerable variation with some parts of the world experiencing stagnant or declining population at the same time that others saw rapid increase. (So for example Northern Europe saw a rise in population in the first part of the seventeenth century while Southern Europe saw a decline). In the modern world there has been growth in all parts of the world, this has been sustained and, until very recently, has proceeded at an accelerating rate. (There are strong indications now that the rate of increase has fallen sharply and that world population will stabilise, although this will not happen until the 2050s).

This historically unprecedented rise in population has consequences beyond the obvious. There is a connection between rising population and economic dynamism and growth. Although population is commonly seen as a drag or burden on economic growth, it is in fact quite the opposite. More people means more demand and stimulates productive economic activity in response. At the most basic level it means more labour for production of all kinds. More living human beings at any one time means more creativity and ideas hence more opportunities for innovation. Higher population typically means higher density of population in the habitable parts of the planet. This reduces the cost and difficulty of human interaction and leads to a much richer and denser network of social interaction and human institutions, both formal and informal. Ideas arise in much greater numbers from this increased interaction. In a word human life in general becomes much more sociable and the range and variety of human contacts tends to increase.

The immediate cause of this dramatic population explosion was a steady and rapid decline in death rates. In the pre-modern world death was omnipresent and an everyday reality. You had to be extremely fortunate to reach twenty without losing a close relative, either a parent or a sibling. On average, you had a one in four chance of dying before your first birthday, rising to one in three if you were born in a town or city. If you made it to the age of ten then you could expect on average to live for a further forty to fifty years. From the parents' point of view, it was simply unheard of to have children and not lose at least one in infancy or childhood. This was true for even the very wealthy and powerful, as any study of the family trees of royal families will show. By contrast, in the modern world, even the poor can expect to live beyond seventy and life expectancy is rising steadily, causing increasing panic among actuaries and pension fund trustees. The death of a child, once a tragic but commonplace event, has now become so unusual as to seem a true tragedy, a perverse departure from the normal course of life.

Number Two: Transformed Physical Conditions Through Intensive Growth

This increase in life expectancy is intimately connected to the second material aspect of the modern world, the one that receives pride of place in most accounts. This is the phenomenon of sustained intensive growth. We take this so much for granted that we no longer realise how historically unusual this is, nor how dramatic and extensive its effects are over time. Economic growth simply means an increase in the total amount or value of useful services and products over a given period. The essential thing to grasp is that there are two kinds of economic growth, extensive and intensive. The first is the one described earlier, producing more output with higher input. This extensive growth, as it is called, can lead to a rise in living standards through windfall gains, as for example, when new land is brought under the plough or discoveries make new land and resources available. However, in the end this peters out because there is no sustained increase in output for each unit of resource used, and the number of people tends to rise in response to the gain in output until the ratio of production to head of population is where it was before the windfall gain. So there is a step change but no sustained rise in productivity.

In the case of intensive growth there is a continuing increase in output per unit of input, in other words there is an increase in the productivity of the factors of production such as land, capital, labour or raw material and energy. Above all, there is an increase in output per head of population. In the medium to longer term there is actually more output from less input, so fewer people, resources, land and capital are required to produce a greater amount and value of products and services. This is why, despite what is popularly believed, raw materials and even land are actually less scarce now after more than two hundred years of intensive growth than they were before. (Simon, 1990) The increases in productivity of the various factors and above all of labour means that intensive growth results in a sustained rise in living standards.

There are a number of ways to measure this rise in living standards. The simplest is to look at income, adjusting this for inflation. Today according to the World Bank, less than 10% of the world's population have to survive on an income of less than $1.25 per day. This is the level the World Bank uses for absolute poverty and destitution, living on bare subsistence. In 1820, our best estimates suggest that 80% of the world's population were subsisting on an equivalent income. Almost all of the rest got by on the equivalent of four to six hundred dollars a year. In 1919, Keynes estimated that there had been a fourfold rise in the average real income in Europe since 1800. We now know that he was too cautious and the real rise was six fold. Since then real incomes in Europe and North America have increased further so that they are now more than sixteen times what they were in 1800 in real terms. Nor is this rise in real incomes confined to Europe and North America. (McCloskey, 2016) In recent years, there has been a dramatic decline in the number of people living in absolute poverty by the World Bank's measure, particularly in China and India but with significant improvement in other parts of the world, including Africa.

In reality, a rise in income is only a rough way of estimating the rise in living standards brought about by intensive growth. A much more accurate way is to see how long people on average incomes have to work in order to buy certain products and commodities, or how much they have to pay for comparable products. In 1999 the Encyclopaedia Brittanica took a list of a hundred products that were identical then to what they had been when produced in 1900, a list that included such household names as Jacob's Cream Crackers. Of the one hundred products, ninety-eight cost less in real terms. Moreover this real decline in the cost of products goes along with a rise in real wages and a decline in working hours so that the number of hours worked on average or median earnings to buy a product such as a durable consumer good such as a car or fridge is only a fraction of what it was twenty years ago. Of course many products that we now take for granted and could not imagine living without were not even thought of, much less available, even thirty years ago, never mind a hundred. In addition the quality of products constantly improves relative to their real cost. Thus, a digital camera today with a memory of ten megapixels will cost about four hundred dollars whereas only five or six years ago you would have paid around six hundred for just one and a half megapixels.

However, statistics such as these, however dramatic, give us only a partial idea of how life has been transformed by more than two hundred years of intensive growth. The conditions of life for ordinary people have changed so much that a time traveller from 1800 would find the way we live now almost paradisiacal. The essential reality is that poor people today now live more luxuriously and in greater comfort than rich people two hundred or even a hundred years ago. This is partly due to another aspect of modernity, the incessant stream of innovation and new products, but it also reflects economic growth and the way it transforms luxuries into necessities. Economic growth also makes things possible that were only imaginable before (if that), simply because of the greater amount of accumulated wealth that is available. It is this that is at the heart of the modern world and all that is novel about it. If in traditional society growth and hence wealth was radically constrained, what we have had since the later eighteenth century is a wealth explosion, a bursting of those constraints and a huge expansion in the quantity of wealth (stuff ultimately) and the opportunities this creates.

For all of these results growth does not have to be particularly rapid. It simply has to be intensive, as described earlier, and sustained. In other words, even slow rates of intensive growth by modern standards will have dramatic results if they are sustained for long enough. This also means that the cumulative effect of even small changes in the underlying rate of economic growth can be huge, given enough time. What is particularly thought provoking is to use simple mathematics to work out what the average real income of our descendants will be, should growth continue in the future as it has in the past. One person who has done this is the 'Armchair Economist' Steven Landsburg. As he points out, assuming just the historic rate of long term income growth over the course of the last fifty years means that if you earn fifty thousand dollars a year now then in twenty five years your children will be earning the inflation adjusted equivalent of eighty nine thousand dollars while your grandchildren in fifty years time will be earning the equivalent of one hundred and fifty eight thousand in today's money. (Landsburg, 2012)

Of course, we should not just assume that current trends will continue in this way. The point is that it is now conceivable and not merely fanciful to think in this way. Back in any time before the nineteenth century you simply did not consider whether people in general would be better off after a given number of years because in the majority of cases (i.e. for the population as a whole) it did not happen or did so slowly as to be unnoticeable unless you thought in terms of centuries rather than decades or even generations. A popular notion is that this kind of growth cannot continue because of constraints such as the finite supply of raw materials and the impact upon the planet of such high levels of production.

In fact, the opposite is the case, provided that the source of this growth continues. (As we shall see there is now broad agreement as to the immediate source of intensive growth). The nature of intensive growth means that as it continues raw materials become more abundant rather than less and the impact of human beings and their activities on the natural environment actually diminishes rather than increasing. What is no longer possible is to stand still and maintain the current level and volume of productive activity and human population with no further growth or innovation. That is because the consumption of resources does raise their opportunity cost, i.e. the amount of other resources that have to be employed to make them useful, above all energy. It is this that makes continuing innovation essential.

A crucial point is the novel nature of economic growth in modernity. Although as said before, there were episodes of intensive growth in the past, these were not sustained. Just as the population growth of the modern age is unprecedented so is the phenomenon of sustained, year-on-year intensive growth. In addition, just as the rate of population growth accelerated during the course of the nineteenth and twentieth centuries, so the rates of intensive growth experienced in various parts of the world have tended to increase over the last two hundred years. Thus at the start of the modern process of intensive growth in North West Europe we are talking about growth of about one per cent per annum. By the early nineteenth century, this had increased to about two per cent in Britain. There was a move to a significantly higher level after about 1860, during the so-called 'Belle Epoque', with growth rates of five per cent or more being recorded for the first time while rates of as high as ten per cent have been experienced since 1945. A world with the standard of living, conditions of life and quantity of accumulated capital produced by more than two hundred years of sustained intensive growth is truly novel, just as a world containing six billion people is.

Number Three: Urbanisation

Economic growth is connected in turn to the third distinctive aspect of material life in the modern world. This is the great move from the countryside to the city. Before the nineteenth century there was no society where more than twenty per cent of the population lived in large urban settlements, whether towns or cities. In general the figure was much less than this and in most cases no more than ten per cent of the population was urban. The overwhelming majority of human beings lived in the countryside, in small rural settlements; the village was the normal environment for most people at most times. In 1851, the British census revealed that for the first time in human history this was no longer the case; a majority of the British population in that year lived in towns with a population of more than fifty thousand. Since then this become the case in one part of the world after another and, just as with population growth and economic growth, the process has accelerated. The United Nations now estimates that sometime in 2006 the majority of the world's population was urbanised for the first time in human history.

Again, this has implications beyond the obvious ones. Many things that are possible in the city are not in the small town or village and so the quality and nature of urban life are radically different from those of the countryside. The presence of a large number of people in a relatively confined space creates, via high population density, all kinds of opportunities for human interaction at relatively lower cost in terms of time and effort than elsewhere. This means that the opportunity for economic specialisation and enhanced division of labour is much greater. This in turn means that social life and human relations are more complex and varied and ways of living can flourish that are not possible in a smaller community simply because of the lack of people with specific interests or tastes or skills within a reachable geographical area.

The proximity of large numbers of people with varied skills and tastes does not only enhance productive specialisation and output and the creation of a much denser and richer civil society. It also makes possible a much more diverse and varied pattern of consumption because the costs of meeting peculiar or minority tastes and demands are much less. The wealth and opportunities brought about by city life and the trade relations that connect flourishing cities to other, often distant, parts of the world mean that they attract incomers from a wide range of ethnic, geographical and religious backgrounds and have a diverse and varied population. (One of the signs of a city's decline is that its population becomes more homogeneous – this is both a cause and an effect of that decline). Most strikingly the city offers something that is absent from life in the smaller rural community. This is privacy and anonymity, the possibility of maintaining a substantially private and personal area of life that is not known to or accessible to all of one's neighbours. Clearly there are costs as well as gains – some things and ways of life that are possible in the countryside cannot be realised in the town or city – but the evidence of people's actual choices over the last two hundred years is that on balance most prefer the city.

Number Four: Sustained and Rapid Technological Innovation

The final physical aspect of modernity that commentators have noticed is the effect of technology or, to be more precise, of continuous and accelerating technological innovation. This has been the central observation of a number of authors, notably Joel Mokyr and Peter Drucker. In one sense, there is nothing new about technology or technical innovation. The capacity of human beings to use tools to alter the environment is one of the defining characteristics of our species. The Middle Ages and the ancient world saw many inventions and significant technical and engineering achievements. The work of Joseph Needham and his collaborators reveals the extent of technological innovation in China throughout the history of that civilisation. This should remind us that our ancestors were no less intelligent and inventive than we are.

Despite this however, they did not experience the kind of technological innovation and development that we increasingly take for granted. In historic societies innovations were haphazard and occasional. They were often abandoned or not widely adopted. When they were, the adoption of the new technology and its geographical diffusion were usually very slow and patchy, with frequent retrogression. Above all, there was no real connection between technical knowledge and expertise on the one hand and abstract, theoretical knowledge on the other and so there was no real connection between the more general understanding of the universe and its nature that was held by the educated and the kinds of technology used in everyday life and production. There were periods when innovation became more frequent in certain places, as in China under the Song, Europe during the high Middle Ages, and the Middle East under the early Abbasids, but as with intensive growth, these episodes were not sustained. Moreover, even at their height they did not come near to the level and rate of innovation and its diffusion seen since 1800.

By contrast, since the later eighteenth century technological innovation has become frequent, systematic, increasingly rapid as regards its application and diffusion, and clearly connected to systematic theoretical knowledge. A listing of innovations in any area of technology would show that the great majority have come about since 1800. Not only that but several entirely new technologies have come into being since then and others, such as chemistry and medicine, have gone from a condition of rudimentary knowledge to a state of such sophistication by comparison with what has gone before that we may rightly regard them also as novel.

Innovation in all areas of technology is now the product not so much of ad hoc individual invention as of organised and systematic research which is intended to produce new products and technologies or to refine and improve existing ones. The gap between the initial invention and its widespread use has now shrunk to less than a decade in most cases. Thus, mobile telephone networks first appeared in 1981 and the cell phone had become an almost universal accessory within five years, the compact disc was first sold by Phillips in 1982 and had almost completely supplanted the vinyl record by the mid-1980s, the DVD took less than a decade to make the video cassette a historical curiosity. By contrast, it took almost forty years for the telephone to become a near universal appliance in the United States and even longer in other parts of the world. Such developments and those in areas such as materials, chemistry, and biological technology all derive from the application of discoveries made in theoretical science.

All of this has contributed significantly to the phenomenon of intensive growth by helping to increase productivity. It also helped in the transformation of the material conditions of everyday life. The discoveries of people such as Faraday, Edison, Tesla, and James Clark Maxwell have utterly changed the way people live. Living as we do in a world of electrical lighting, we find it hard to imagine one where candles and lamps were the only means of keeping darkness at bay and daily life was regulated by the movements of the sun. Television and radio and the recording of music have made a range of experiences immediately available when in earlier times they would have not have been experienced more than a few times in a lifetime for the majority of the population.

Medicine has been transformed since the mid-nineteenth century from one of the hazards of life to a principal factor in the decline in death rates and increase in longevity alluded to earlier. The average speed of travel has shot up dramatically since 1800 – before then for the whole of history the fastest way of travelling on land was on the back of a galloping horse. The cost of travel has also fallen dramatically, both in money terms and in terms of the time it takes, so that journeys that would have been major once in a lifetime undertakings for our ancestors are now an everyday commonplace. Again, all of this innovation is different in quality to what was the norm in earlier historical periods and there has been an abrupt surge in its frequency and rapidity since the middle of the eighteenth century, with the rate accelerating even further since then.

Psychological and Cultural Changes

Such physical changes in the life of humanity are relatively easy to observe and lend themselves to quantitative measurement and comparison. As such they have attracted the most attention. However, there are also another series of distinctive features of the modern world that are equally important, although more difficult to pin down and define. They have not escaped notice however, not least because these were the elements of the modern that attracted the most attention, when it was actually in its infancy and only just becoming apparent. These are a series of changes in the mental life of humanity, both intellectual and emotional. As with the physical changes set out earlier, there were earlier intimations of these changes in various times and places but they did not become fully established and self-sustaining until the later eighteenth century, in Western Europe and North America. It was at that time that they were first identified and analysed, by a number of thinkers but particularly by those associated with the Scottish Enlightenment. Since then they have been analysed by philosophers and historians of ideas among others, with sociologists exploring their concrete manifestations.

Number One: Critical Rationalism

The most important by far, and correspondingly the one that has attracted most notice, is the domination of intellectual life by what is generally called 'critical rationalism'. Just as there are periods or episodes of intensive economic growth and technological innovation, so we can also discern what we may call 'ages of reason', periods marked by wide ranging intellectual discussion that see a marked development of philosophical enquiry, in the widest sense of that term. In these particular times and places ideas that would normally lead to their authors being silenced one way or another find free expression, theses and arguments are pushed to their conclusions, and orthodox and accepted modes of thought are subjected to critical scrutiny while a wide variety of approaches to intellectual questions and knowledge find an outlet.

Such episodes of philosophical enquiry tend to produce what David Hume called 'melancholy and delirium'. That is, either an exaggerated and unreasonable certainty of having found the ultimate truth about everything or a profound scepticism and despair of ever actually knowing anything. Faced with the destructive effects and implications of radical scepticism, and the questioning of established institutions, beliefs and ways of life that it and the existence of many competing schools of thought bring about, one response is to abandon philosophy altogether or to clamp down on its manifestations and enforce an orthodoxy. Another is to assert the superior claims of faith, and tradition or revelation as sources of knowledge and to reduce intellectual debate to exegesis and hermeneutic. Such reactions tend to bring 'ages of reason' to an end, sometimes permanently.

The result of this is that for most of history, in complex societies, intellectual life is dominated by two kinds of systematic thought, magic and religion. These differ in many ways but share some common features, above all a reliance upon authority (often in the form of a specific text) and tradition as sources of authoritative knowledge, that is knowledge that is appealed to in order to settle intellectual disputes when no other means can be found or which trumps other kinds of evidence. The other significant shared element is the notion that ultimately there is a systematic and organised body of knowledge that describes all that can be known about everything that exists and which while incredibly large, is still finite as well as structured. That is, our knowledge of one part or aspect of the universe and existence is part of a larger systematic whole and as such intimately connected to our knowledge of those other parts. Thus, in the medieval Christian and Islamic system of thought there was a clear and direct connection between knowledge of the stars and the larger cosmos and knowledge about the human body and its functioning.

In contrast to this, critical rationalism does not have either of these qualities. Rather it is an approach to knowledge and thinking about the world that has the following elements. Our knowledge of the world depends either upon physical sensory experience of it, or some kind of ultimately certain foundational proposition from which we can deduce conclusions about the world. We can reject radical scepticism and relativism, inasmuch as we can make statements about the world that we can reasonably describe as true, and we have a set of methods by which we can try to distinguish between competing or incompatible statements and establish their relative accuracy. Statements about the world are made and held to be true in a tentative way, that is they are always open to question and thus to revision or outright refutation.

However, the degree of tentativeness varies, from the purely formal to the considerable. Belief and faith, no matter how passionate, are therefore not the same as knowledge. While we can only hold statements about the world to be true in a tentative fashion, we *can* be certain in some cases about the untruth of statements. There is a process, of logical reasoning or material investigation, by which statements about the world can be subjected to scrutiny and testing. This reduces the degree of tentativeness with which some statements are held to be true and generates new statements, often in place of others now shown to be untrue. This process of conversation and discussion generates a body of knowledge that is growing and theoretically infinite, rather than ultimately finite however large. It is open ended rather than closed. This body of knowledge, while it has many interconnections, does not have the kind of systematic structure found in the pre-modern or traditional world picture. Thus, there is no direct and necessary connection between medicine or biochemistry and astronomy for example.

This way of thinking about the world has far reaching implications and effects and insofar as it has become the predominant way of thinking about and understanding the world in the modern age, so those effects have become noticeable features of modernity. It leads to a steady growth in the sum of human knowledge, far more rapid and extensive than anything experienced in the past, not least because the knowledge it generates is cumulative so that we know more about a given subject than our ancestors did, rather than just knowing or understanding it differently. There is a direct connection between this way of thinking and the swift technological innovation of the modern world, because of the way it links practical and theoretical knowledge, making each one dependent upon the other. In practice, it also has destructive implications for other, traditional ways of thinking about the world and experience suggests it has an ultimately corrosive effect upon traditional ways of thinking and living and of justifying them. It also generates a very distinctive way of thinking about the world, our place in it, and the nature of the self. In particular, it leads to a questioning of authority and a particular notion of selfhood and personal identity.

There are intimations of this way of thinking at various times and places in human history but, as said, these do not survive and in some cases we know of the existence of such thinking only because of the survival of works written to rebut it. However in the later seventeenth and eighteenth centuries one such episode was able to persist and go on to become the dominant way of thinking in a significant part of the world (although this took a long time and its victory is still contested and partial). The result is that in the modern world we have for the first time a civilisation in which critical rationalism is the most practically influential way of thinking about the world, rather than at most a minority view. The other distinctive intellectual features of the modern are closely connected to, or even derived from, this main one.

Number Two: Secularism and a Transformation of Religious Experience

One of these is a transformation in the nature and experience of religion. This is intensely controversial, inasmuch as many deny even the existence of this change and it is still by no means complete, although more advanced than many suppose. It is also controversial in itself, with some welcoming it while others deplore it. We should be clear what it is that we are talking about here. At one time, many thought that a prominent aspect of the modern was a process of secularisation, and a corresponding decline in the importance and even the existence of religious belief. This is clearly not the case, as a brief study of present day news headlines will show. However, the form, nature and influence of religion and the religious experience in the modern world are all radically different from what they have been throughout recorded history for the overwhelming majority of men and women. It is important to realise in this context that what many call 'fundamentalism' is not traditional religious thought, belief and observance or a reassertion of these in the face of the challenge of modernity but is itself a modern phenomenon and is increasingly the form that the religious impulse takes under modern conditions.

For the greater part of human history, religion held a special and privileged position as the source of answers to ultimate questions of ethics, and the origin, meaning, and purpose of existence and human life. This is no longer the case, to put it mildly. Many of the traditional beliefs and propositions derived from religion based answers to such questions (such as the existence of a particular kind of afterlife with implications for the here and now) do not command widespread acceptance in the way they once did, that is they are no longer seen as providing authoritative guidance in these areas. More generally the world has become 'disenchanted', as Max Weber put it, it is no longer perceived and understood by almost everyone through the prisms of magic and religion or thought of as being explicable only by reference to the transcendent. In the modern world fully-fledged and explicit atheism and rejection of religion is now possible and widespread, which has never been the case before.

This is not just a matter of atheism no longer attracting censure and punishment. In previous periods, scepticism concerning matters of religious belief was actually easier for, and consequently more widespread among, the uneducated. For an educated person it was very difficult because of the central place held by religious thought and belief in the structured knowledge system that explained the world and humanity's place within it. For an educated person in sixteenth century Europe for example the entire body of belief about the world and its workings rested upon and presumed the existence of God. If one were to adopt atheism then none of this made sense and it all fell to pieces. This is one reason why scepticism led to nihilism and despair of any kind of knowledge or meaning, and a flight for refuge in convention or authority. This no longer the case and the presumption of a religious doctrine (whether theistic or not) is no longer needed to make sense of the world or to explain it.

Perhaps the most dramatic change is that in most of the world organised religious belief and practice is no longer connected to or a central part of political power (despite the efforts of some who would make this the case).

Appeal to religion is no longer the basis of political legitimacy, even in regimes that claim it is. Above all, religious belief and observance are no longer a central part of the function of most governments. Rather, they have moved from the public to the private sphere so that they are no more the concern of political authority than one's choice of underwear. It is hard to overemphasise how profound a change this is, compared to the past. This would have dumbfounded most of our ancestors as for them the support of true religion was perhaps the central and primary function of political authority, the neglect of which was bound to bring all sorts of disasters in its train.

Perhaps the most profound change however and the most truly novel, is in the lived experience of the religious believer. It is clearly not the case that religious belief and experience have ceased or even diminished. The number of believers is in absolute terms larger than it has ever been (because of the population growth alluded to earlier) while if current demographic trends continue they will form an ever larger part of the total population. What has changed is the nature of the predominant religious experience. For all of pre-modern history religion for the great majority was something that was lived, experienced and practiced in everyday life and ritual, rather than being a matter of conscious, explicit intellectual belief. Although there were creeds, for most religion was something one did rather than a set of explicit intellectual ideas and beliefs. In the modern world, although practice is obviously still important, for all believers religion has become a matter primarily of belief and doctrine rather than concrete lived experience, with the latter following from and being determined by the former. This makes religious belief more fervent in many cases but also more brittle and vulnerable because more conscious and explicit and therefore more susceptible to criticism and doubt. Moreover the rise of critical rationalism means that religious perceptions and beliefs are not the universal and shared mental framework that they once were.

Number Three: The Growth of Sympathy

Another significant change that marks out the cultural and mental world of the modern as compared to what went before is one that attracted much attention from an early date. This was the growth of what eighteenth and early nineteenth century authors termed 'sympathy' and 'sensibility'. As defined by authors such as Adam Smith and Lord Kames this meant the capacity to put oneself in the position of another person and feel an intimation of what that person felt or experienced. This was associated with a general 'softening' or 'polishing' of manners and behaviour. In other words, there was a tendency for people to be gentler, less aggressive, more self-conscious and controlled, less impulsive, more sensitive to the suffering or hardship of others. This was seen as being connected to the growth of trade and commerce and what they called 'luxury' and we would call affluence or comfort. In other words, as people became more connected to others, often distant, by the connections of trade and by social intercourse, and as their lives became more comfortable and less harsh so their psychology changed and they became gentler, less violent and aggressive and more controlled and 'refined' (to use a key term) in their way of behaving. In the language of the time this meant that the 'passions' as they were called, that is strong and natural human desires and feelings, came to be tamed and made milder and less fierce and powerful or even subject to the check of reason and calculation.

This may seem to be simply a reflection of eighteenth century rationalism and optimism but in fact there is a lot of evidence for the view that the modern world has indeed seen such a change. Again, people such as Smith, Hume and Kames thought that the change was gradual (although they were struck by the extent and rapidity of change in their own country and lifetime) but very soon after their own lifetimes the change in this aspect of human life also underwent an abrupt acceleration. At this point, many people will simply find the argument implausible. Given the terrible political events of the last hundred years and the widespread evidence of cruelty, violence and aggression that fill the daily news, how can anyone think that over that period human beings in many parts of the world have become less passionate, gentler and more in sympathy with the suffering of others?

One point to make is that the attention given to such matters and the horror they inspire are because there has been such a change. Things that were seen as unexceptional and normal in the past, even if regrettable, are now regarded as egregious and horrible precisely because they are less common. Clearly something as intangible yet profound as a widespread or even general shift in the way most people feel or in their psychology is hard to measure or demonstrate. However, there are a number of indicators, some of which can actually be quantified. One is the evidence of delinquent behaviour as captured in the records of the criminal justice system. The evidence here is that over the last two to three hundred years there has been a long term secular decline in interpersonal violence. Three hundred years ago the bulk of the cases brought before criminal courts were crimes of violence. They now make up only a small proportion of the courts' business. In addition the actual incidence of such crimes on a per capita basis has also declined so that they are a much less frequent part of experience.

There are several other prominent indicators. One is the change in the functioning of the criminal justice system, with a pronounced shift away from harsh and brutal or sadistic physical punishment such as public execution, flogging or branding. Another is the transformation that we can trace in popular attitudes towards children and animals. In very recent times historically what we would regard as brutal and cruel treatment was widespread or even normal for both whereas now this arouses revulsion and disgust. Literature and personal writings such as diaries and correspondence are another kind of evidence, which again shows a significant alteration in popular psychology, at both an individual and a collective level. Finally, there is the evidence of manners, where we can clearly trace what one author calls the 'civilising process' by which ways of speaking and behaving become steadily more controlled and moderate.

Looking at this evidence we can say firstly that there has been a radical change in what historians call the 'collective mentality' of modern men and women, that is the common mental assumptions, habits and ways of thinking, feeling and behaving that they share. The second thing we can say is that this change became much more rapid and widespread among all levels of society at some point in the early nineteenth century. Here we can draw the analogy and connection with trade and economic development. In the case of trade and economic development, we can indeed trace a very gradual process of increasing trade and economic integration between different parts of the world and a slow corresponding rise in the level of economic development and standards of living. After the later eighteenth century, this process becomes so much more rapid and extensive that both it and its effects are wholly different order of magnitude – explosive in fact.

Similarly, there is clearly a long-term trend in the direction just described with respect to human mentality and ways of behaving. Thus, there is a very long term trend for inter-personal violence to decline. Our Stone Age ancestors lived in a society that was unbelievably violent by contemporary standards (as do many more recent hunter-gatherers) and we can trace a decline in levels of violence since that time. However, as with trade, the process while of long standing underwent a dramatic breakthrough or acceleration after the later eighteenth century so that, as in the economic sphere, there was a greater change in popular psychology and ways of behaving between 1800 and 1900 than for several centuries at least before then.

Number Four: Ethical Universalism and Cosmopolitanism

One particular aspect of this change in attitudes and ways of thinking that is worthy of notice is the widespread acceptance of ethical universalism, not just at the level of theory but of feeling and sentiment. This is the idea that all human beings everywhere not only share certain basic common qualities and characteristics but are also a common community of rights and sentiments. This has several aspects. One is the notion of rights that are universal, that is all human beings everywhere have them or can claim them, simply by virtue of their being biological humans. Again, this is nowadays a belief that does not strike people as absurd even though they may have philosophical problems with it. By contrast, the historically normal way of thinking about this, even in cultures where the idea of rights was known, was that rights were specific and particular claims that applied to particular groups of people, whether a social group or rank or the members of a particular political community. Thus, there were the rights of freemen or of aristocrats or the clergy but not of men in general (much less women) or of Englishmen or Frenchmen or the inhabitants of a particular place or town but not the rights of man in general. The idea of universal rights that apply to all human beings everywhere appears in the eighteenth century and has since been generalised by a series of political campaigns that have applied the notion to groups previously not included notably slaves and women.

This by itself is rather dry for many. What gives ethical universalism its novel power is the notion that one should and could feel a common sentiment or sympathy for a person who has no direct connection to you other than a shared humanity. Although most accept that people will have stronger feelings and attachments towards those who are physically or biologically closer, these feelings are no longer thought to be exclusive or exhaustive. An early and arresting example of this sentiment was the anti-slavery medallion produced by Josiah Wedgwood, showing a kneeling slave with chains on his arms and the slogan "Am I not a Man and a Brother?" Certainly religious leaders and philosophers in all of the world's civilisations had made a case for ethical universalism from a very early date (in fact from the 'Axial Age' alluded to earlier) but this was not reflected in general sentiment or belief.

Moreover, there was a wealth of argument that defined the bounds of sentiment more narrowly and confined it to the tribe or community or family or particular religious group. The idea that one should be concerned and moved by the fate of people who were not connected to you struck most people before the eighteenth century as bizarre or even improper. Once again, there was a dramatic shift from the later eighteenth century onwards and what has happened since then has been a spread of the idea. Of course, it is still often honoured more in the breach but the sentiment itself has come to command ever-wider assent. Connected to this is the wide acceptance of the idea that all people are in some sense of equal moral worth and standing. Again, this may be honoured more in the breach but it was not even thought of by most people in most traditional societies: ancient Romans or Medieval Europeans or Chinese would mostly have been baffled by it for example.

Number Five: Individualism and Materialism

The last major observable alteration in the mental life of humanity that has marked modernity is the dramatic rise of individualism and an associated materialism. This does not mean a rise of individuality and non-conformity. In fact, paradoxically the growth of individualism in the modern world has gone along with a rise in conformity as observers such as J. S. Mill and Alexis de Tocqueville noted in the nineteenth century. The point rather is this. Today it is taken for granted by most people that society is composed of individual men and women, and that the individual person is the basic unit out of which larger social wholes are made. (This is regardless of whether the individuals in question are seen as self-defined in some sense or as being socially defined – the point is that in either case it is individuals that are the subjects of argument and analysis). In marked contrast, our ancestors (and many people even today) simply did not think in this way about either society or the place and life of particular men and women in this way.

Rather as we have seen, they saw the wider social order as being composed of smaller social units, above all that of the household or family, which they thought of as a kind of miniature political and social order, a microcosm of the macrocosm of society as a whole. The practice therefore was for people to define their personal identity through their social attachments as the spouse, parent, child or relative of other people, something reflected even in the names they bore.

By contrast, in the modern world, while people are obviously still very much aware of such close social connections, there is a strongly held notion of a core personal identity that is independent of all of them and derives ultimately from a sense of self-awareness and self-consciousness. In many cases this means that social relations, including even close ones of an ultimately biological nature, are felt to have a kind of instrumental quality, as existing to serve the persons concerned rather than being a fact or part of their existence. This means that the course of life is believed to be in great part a product of choice in the part of the actor whose life it is. Thus, identity becomes something shaped by actions and choices or by outside circumstances but is not simply something given by a web of relations into which one is born. It also means that the aim of life is commonly taken to be the physical well being and mental flourishing and development of this self or person, however it has been defined or come into being.

The novelty of this way of thinking about the self is striking. For most of history, existence is seen fatalistically, as being highly determined, and the aim of life is to live in a way that is appropriate to ones nature and being, as so defined. The predominant idea in the so-called 'axial' religions is that real fulfilment comes only after death or in some other condition of existence rather than in the physical mundane life. What this change means is that in the modern world the notion of identity becomes increasingly troubled and problematic, as it also becomes more individualised and takes on an increasingly plastic quality. At the same time, the purpose of both public policy and individual action is to maximise well being and happiness in the here and now. Again what we have here is a dramatic shift in the way of thinking of most people, one that has earlier intimations and expressions in many times and places but does not ever become predominant in the way that it has in the modern world.

Changes in Social Structure and Organisation

Number One: The Emancipation of Women and the Transformation of the Household

In addition to these changes in both material life and general psychology and feelings the way we live now is also marked by radical transformation of basic forms of social organisation. One of the most radical, which is still like all the others very much in progress, is a change in the position of women. Quite simply women in the modern world have a legal status and social and economic position that is unprecedented in terms of the independence that they have. This is partly a matter of changes in ideology and mental perception but is even more due to the economic transformation described earlier, along with innovations brought about by the technological revolution, above all effective contraception. As with some of the other changes, we are now more aware of the limits and shortcomings of this change than we are of the degree to which things are radically different from what they were in the past. What this actually shows however is the extent to which we now take these changes for granted and assume them to be normal when in fact they are novel.

The change in the legal and social status of women in the modern world is closely connected to another fundamental alteration of basic social structure, which is the replacement of the household as the basic unit of almost every area of human life. The reason why our ancestors almost all thought of society as a federation or collection of households was that for most purposes that *was* exactly what it was. The household was the essential unit for all economic life, including both production and consumption. It was the location of most social functions and activity including education and most forms of leisure and entertainment. It was also the institution through which the function of government was exercised – royal government in every part of the world was essentially household government, even after the reforms of the Renaissance period. The overwhelming majority of people lived all or almost all of their lives as members of a household of one kind or another, even if they were not biologically related to its other members. That is they did not live alone or in non-household based collectives (which is why the institution of domestic service was such a central and important one in many places).

The relations that existed between the various members of the household, above all those between parents and children and the father and children in particular were the models for all other social relations, which were thought of as based upon them or as simply another form of them. The only major exceptions were friendship and religious fellowship or associations. (Organised religious institutions such as the Christian church or Buddhist monasticism were also the main exception to the predominance of the household and even here, the actual institutions were modelled upon household ones). In the modern world, the household has increasingly lost most of its functions apart from those of consumption and child rearing and even the latter is now shared with other institutions, which are taking an ever-larger role in this area. Social relations are no longer seen as actual or metaphorical biological household relations but are understood rather in terms of such kinds of relations as contract or association. In public life, the role of the household is now vestigial and declining. Alongside this has gone the progressive attenuation of more extended familial relations such as those of the kin-group or tribe, which were fundamental for traditional society in many parts of the world.

Number Two: The Rise of Large Institutions

Instead, large, structured and impersonal institutions now carry out the functions once performed by households and extended family structures. This is the aspect of modernity most noticed by authors such as Peter Drucker. The institutions include things such as the factory, the prison, the asylum, the hospital, and the university. Some of these have earlier origins or manifestations but the size and form they have assumed in the modern world are again unprecedented. The three most significant institutions are the military, government, and the modern business corporation and these have done more to shape the modern world than any others. All of these institutions, however different their purposes, share certain common features.

The most important is a hierarchical and functional organisation, and the institutional practice of what we now call 'management', a form of administration and purposive use of resources that is conducted by a distinct class of technically skilled personnel. This is separate from such things as family ties, inasmuch as it is conducted in a neutral and impersonal manner and is not subject to such constraints as family loyalty and obligation or ties of clientage. As with all of the other features of modernity, there are intimations of these institutions in earlier periods but they do not become the fully realised and dominant entities that they now are before the nineteenth century. Their rise to dominance in almost every area of life however is rapid and takes place over a period of no more than fifty to eighty years, between roughly the 1860s and the 1920s.

Number Three: The Appearance of Modern Government

This is a central part of another change, which is the transformation of government. The modern state is again a truly new institution in a number of ways apart from its unprecedented size. In particular, its organisation and quality are different from those of states or governments in the past. The main novel feature is not such procedural features as democracy but rather a new conception of what the nature and purpose of government actually is. This is connected to a change in the organisation and functioning of government, particularly the disappearance of household government and the huge decline in a system of public administration that depends upon personal relations between people with power, above all the relation between client and patron, which is the basis of most administration in historic traditional societies. Alongside this goes the appearance of the modern Weberian bureaucracy in which government is conducted by professional and full time civil servants according to impersonal and binding rules.

Finally, modern governments have a markedly different set of functions. Historically the principal role of government as measured by expenditure is overwhelmingly that of warfare, with the administration of justice coming in a poor second. By contrast, in the modern world the largest and most important functions of government are those associated with what the early theorists of the modern state called the 'general welfare'. Again, there are earlier intimations of this and indeed the theory of the modern state is first developed in the sixteenth and seventeenth centuries but the actuality of it is not realised until the early nineteenth century when, once again, the change proves to be both unprecedentedly profound and very rapid.

Number Four: A New Kind of Ruling Class

Taken together, the rise of institutions and the transformation of government and commerce in particular mean that while traditional social hierarchy and divisions have declined or even vanished, new ones have taken their place. As pointed out earlier, in the traditional societies that grew out of the appearance of agriculture there was a social hierarchy with a definite ruling class or classes, based upon the differential control of organised violence. All societies had a distinction between those who gained income from production and exchange and interacted with other human beings primarily through consensual or biological relations and those who gained income by the use of force (whether actual or institutional) and interacted primarily through relations based on power.

In most societies, these ruling groups were landlords, usually in actuality or origin warrior aristocrats, and clergy, along with in a few cases public officials and wealthier merchants. Other commonly recognised groups were peasant farmers (who made up the great bulk of society), artisans and craftsmen, merchants and social out groups such as slaves or people regarded as ritually unclean. This social hierarchy was reflected not only in social mores and culture but in the law and administration with all sorts of detailed rules to govern social interactions between people of different social rank, some of them merely social while others had the full force of legal sanction. In the modern world, the traditional hierarchical model of law and society has been swept away. We can truly say that in some ways we are all egalitarians now – we disagree only about how far equality should go or what form it should take. The kind of fundamental defence of inequality of status and degree as it was called, that was once commonplace (and made by Shakespeare for example) would now be unthinkable.

However, power still exists although it is exercised in a new way and the consequence is the emergence of a new kind of ruling group. This is a managerial elite, based upon expertise and knowledge and recognised not by things such as coats of arms and badges but rather by certifications and paper qualifications. (Perkin, 2002). This new elite justifies its position as being a meritocracy rather than aristocracy. (Whether this is a valid defence is another matter, the point is that the argument used is different in kind). The modern world has also seen the dramatic expansion in recent years of what one author calls the 'creative class', which formerly only existed as a very small and marginal group of artists and scholars. (Florida, 2014). Here again there has been a radical and rapid change, with forms of social relation and hierarchy that had continued in one form or another for thousands of years being replaced in less than two hundred, not by a society with no forms of inequality of status and power, but by a distinctively new kind of ruling group and social formation with a completely different basis.

Number Five: The Abolition of Slavery

It is not only the ruling class that has changed dramatically. Another very striking feature of the modern world that marks it out from its predecessors is the almost complete disappearance of slavery, along with most other kinds of unfree labour such as serfdom, peonage and indenture. Slavery was a near universal feature of the pre-modern world. In some times and places it was a central institution in others a marginal or minor one but it was found almost everywhere. Many thinkers defended it as a necessary or benign institution and although others saw it as regrettable, they regarded it as inevitable and necessary. For most it was not problematic at all, its existence and utility were simply taken for granted. Then, in just over a hundred years between the 1770s and the 1880s slavery and the slave trade were effectively abolished. Once again, this marked a fundamental break with the past and the disappearance of an institution and practice that had existed for millennia. In addition, the very idea of slavery has become indefensible and nobody now dares to defend it, much less openly advocate it.

Did All of This Have A Cause – and if So What?

So if there is a process that started around two hundred and fifty years ago and which is continuing to transform the human world, what then is the core of that transformative process? We have identified and described the main elements of that change and it is worth pointing out that most of these are currently dynamic in the sense that they are still going on – global population is still rising, the world continues to become more urbanised, economic growth is still with us, and (despite what many think) human beings in general are responding more to the better angels of our nature. The obvious question is what has caused all of this? As we shall see scholars have given many answers to that question and are far from agreement. A common reaction is to say that one of the elements or aspects of modernity described above is the cause of all the rest. For this to be the case it would have to be exogenous, something independent of the rest and in some sense outside them. Each of the features described has been presented as being that force by at least one writer and sometimes by many. Alternatively all of the features described could be mutually reinforcing aspects of a complex phenomenon that has some other ultimate cause. Others have suggested this with the proposed cause ranging from social conflicts arising from the evolution of productive forces (Marx) to the influence of ideas and beliefs (many thinkers) to institutions or to the processes of economic exchange themselves (many economists). This is far from being an exhaustive list, as we shall see. However the most persuasive argument is that the key factor is innovation and social experimentation. This is a wider category than purely scientific or technological innovation. It also includes novelty and innovation in other areas such as the organisation of aspects of life including the economic, political and intellectual, of ideas and their expression, and ultimately in ways of living. The question then becomes one of finding out why human beings became increasingly innovative at a certain point in history (assuming as we should that there was no sudden change in human nature at that time).

The Questions – How to Explain This?

The modern world, the way we live now, is thus fundamentally different from the way people have lived for several thousands of years earlier. The material conditions and limits of human experience have been and are being transformed by population growth, urbanisation, and unceasing technological innovation and, above all, by sustained intensive economic growth. The common psychology and sense of self of most people and the cultural and intellectual order have also adopted novel and unprecedented forms. The same is true of important forms of social and political organisation, most notably government and commerce, while there have been significant changes in the forms of social hierarchy. There have been radical alterations to the status of women and in the role of the household or family. All of this amounts to a true revolution in human affairs. The various changes are all interconnected and to a great degree mutually reinforcing. It may be that one of the changes is exogenous, that is it is independent of the rest and the one that ultimately causes all of them. Economic growth, population, and critical rationalism have all been candidates for this role, along with unprecedented access to energy via the use of fossil fuels. However, it seems more likely that no one part of the process is the prime mover of the rest in this way, even if we ascribe more importance to some than to others. The key factor that we can identify is innovation but to say that only raises the question of how this happens and why it has only become so prominent since the early eighteenth century.

Not only has there been a profound change, but also all of the evidence suggests that it happened very swiftly and comparatively recently. Essentially, we are talking about a process that begins in the later part of the eighteenth century, accelerates markedly after the mid-nineteenth century, and is continuing. What we have here therefore is not just a transformation in human experience but a sharp discontinuity. It does not make sense to think of this as just the latest stage of a long, continuous and homogeneous process that can be traced back into the distant past and represented as a single smooth curve or line. This is not to deny the continuing influence of the past upon the present but to emphasise the abrupt and sudden way the various changes have taken place, often in less than a generation in many parts of the world.

Why the Later Eighteenth Century? Why Europe?

This however raises profound questions. In particular, it raises the questions of why these changes happened at all and why they did so when and where they did. Why did they start to occur in the later eighteenth and early nineteenth century and not before (although as we shall see some historians believe they did start to happen earlier before being stopped)? In addition, the 'revolution of modernity' as we may call it, did not suddenly burst out all over the world at once. Rather it first happened in a very particular place, which is North-West Europe. Subsequently it also began to happen in other parts of the world, while there was a largely independent breakthrough in Japan at almost the same time as Europe. The pattern is similar to that of the earlier agricultural revolution, which also first appeared in particular places, notably the Middle East, before happening elsewhere. Why though did the changes of modernity first appear in Europe rather than, for example, China? This is a puzzling question, given that for most of history Europe is a relatively unimportant backwater compared to the other major civilisations, in terms of both economic and intellectual activity. Somehow, after the later seventeenth century Europe came to surpass all of the other major civilisations by most measures. To put it another way, it abruptly manifested the first signs of 'sudden modern progress' (to use Julian Simon's terminology).

Since as far back as the early to mid nineteenth century scholars from many disciplines have been concerned with and exercised by these questions. This concern has taken a number of new directions in the last thirty years, with the rise (or more properly reappearance) of world history as a field of study. What though are the arguments and theses that have been put forward and can we make sense of their variety and complexity?

Further Reading and Bibliographical Essay

The commonalities and ultimate similarity of pre-modern agricultural societies is set out in Patricia Crone, *Pre-Industrial Societies: Anatomy of the Pre-Modern World* (Oneworld Publications, 2015). The classic study of the everyday life (particularly the domestic structure) of pre-modern Europe is Peter Laslett, *The World We Have Lost: Further Explored* 4th ed. (Routledge, 2004). The structural analysis and distinctions pioneered by Fernand Braudel and the scholars of the so-called Annales School of French historians are hugely important here as they introduce the idea of the continuity of forms and patterns of everyday life over very long periods. This is a major theme in all of Braudel's work but the most relevant here is his three volume magnum opus *Material Civilisation and Capitalism, 15th to 18th Century, Vol. I: The Structures of Everyday Life; Vol. II: The Wheels of Commerce; Vol. III: The Perspective of the World* (University of California Press, 1992; 1st published 1982).

With Malthus there is no alternative to reading the man himself. Fortunately there are many excellent editions of the famous Essay, which explain its context and set out the differences between the first edition of 1798 and later ones (in which Malthus amended his initially grim thought experiment). One of the best is Thomas R. Malthus & Geoffrey Gilbert (ed.), *An Essay on the Principle of Population* (Oxford University Press, 2008). A recent work which radically shifts our understanding of the context of Malthus's work and the thinking behind it is Alison Bashford & Joyce Chaplin, *The New Worlds of Thomas Robert Malthus: Rereading the 'Principle of Population'* (Princeton University Press, 2016). This should be supplemented by Robert J. Mayhew (ed.), *New Perspectives on Malthus* (Cambridge University Press, 2016). The way the arguments set out by Malthus can be understood as referring to a condition or situation that is still with us is the subject of Paul Neurath, *From Malthus to the Club of Rome and Back: Problems of Limits to Growth, Population Control, and Migrations* (Routledge, 1994). An example of the works that point out how the prophecies have not been realised – so far – is Donald O. Mithchell, Merlinda D. Ingco & Ronald C. Duncan, *The World Food Outlook* (Cambridge University Press, 1997). The great anti-Malthus work is Julian Simon, *The Ultimate Resource2* (Princeton University Press, 1996). Two books that apply Malthusian understanding to history and look at the question of how we managed to escape the Malthusian constraint are Alan Macfarlane, *The Savage Wars of Peace: England, Japan, and the Malthusian Trap* (Wiley-Blackwell, 1997) and Alan Macfarlane, *Thomas Malthus and the Making of the Modern World* (Amazon, 2014).

The notion of a 'moral economy', meaning a range of practices and institutions that enabled the population of the pre-modern world to cope with Malthusian constraints while at the same time preventing the kind of sustained innovation that would lead to escape from them is found in two great works in particular, James C. Scott, *The Moral Economy of the Peasant: Rebellion and Subsistence in Southeast Asia* (Princeton University Press, 1976), and Edward P. Thompson *Customs in Common: Studies in Traditional Popular Culture* (New Press, 1993) as well as Thompson's original essay "The Moral Economy of the English Crowd in the 18th Century", *Past & Present*, 50, (1971), pp. 76-136. The connection between this and the wider questions looked at here is explored in my own essay "Economic History, Scarcity, and Morality" in Elena Leontjeva, Aneta Vaine, Marija Vysniauskaite (eds.), *The Phenomenon of Scarcity: Being, Man, and Society* (Lithuanian Free Market Institute, 2016), pp. 201 – 225.

The phenomenon of complexity and its declining payoffs and the way that pre-modern civilisations periodically experience relatively abrupt collapses or periods of simplification is definitively set out in Joseph Tainter, *The Collapse of Complex Societies* (Cambridge University Press, 1988). Also important are the studies collected in Norman Yoffee and George L. Cowgill (eds.), *The Collapse of Ancient States and Civilisations* (University of Arizona Press, 1991). An argument that we have not escaped the Malthusian trap and the cycle of collapse but are in fact about to experience it again, as well as a mathematical model of how the process works, can be found in John Michael Greer, *The Long Descent: A Users Guide to the End of the Industrial Age* (New Society Publishers, 2008).

The idea of a social division between ruling classes that gained income from predation and protection rackets (or more benignly, supplying public goods) and productive or industrious classes that acquired it by trade and production was a commonplace of nineteenth century thought, as the regular use of phrases such as 'the industrious classes' reveals. The major modern work that expounds this and connects it with a wider account of the contrast between free relations between human beings and those based upon power (and so ultimately dominance and submission) is Alexander Rustow, *Freedom and Domination: A Historical Critique of Civilisation* (Princeton University Press, 2014; 1st published 1980). (This is a one volume summation of the three volume German work published between 1950 and 1957). This kind of class analysis is associated with what is usually called the 'conquest theory' of the origins of government, the state, and structural social inequality. Two works that set this out and apply it are Franz Oppenheimer, *The State: Its History and Development Viewed Sociologically* (Perennial Press, 2018; 1st published 1908) and Charles Tilly, *Durable Inequality* (University of California Press, 1999). Another well known essay is Charles Tilly "War Making and State Making as Organised Crime" in Peter Evans, Dietrich Rueschemeyer & Theda Skocpol (eds.), *Bringing The State Back In* (Cambridge

University Press, 1985) pp. 161 – 191. Tilly's *Coercion, Capital, and European States, AD 990 – 1992* (Wiley-Blackwell, 1992) uses this kind of analysis to explain the formation of states in Europe and points out that the form this finally took was only one of several available. A benign view of the historical role of both ruling classes and large empires in particular is the theme of Ian Morris, *War! What is It Good For? Conflict and the Progress of Civilisation From Primates to Robots* (Farrar, Strauss, and Giroux, 2014) but see my review of this in "Blood and Leviathan" *Reason Magazine*, July 2015.

It is the sociologists who for historical reasons have been the most systematic and clear in defining what modernity is and what its main features are. One classic exposition is Peter L. Berger, *The Capitalist Revolution: Fifty Propositions About Prosperity, Equality, and Liberty* (Basic Books, 1986). The work of another scholar in this area is set out in Michael Lessnoff, *Ernest Gellner and Modernity* (University of Wales Press, 2002). Other useful introductions are the classic Marshall Berman, *All That is Solid Melts Into Air: The Experience of Modernity* (Penguin, 1988), Stuart Hall & David Held, *Modernity: An Introduction to Modern Societies* (Wiley Blackwell, 1996), Anthony Giddens, *The Consequences of Modernity* (Polity, 2013), and Hartmut Rosa, *Social Acceleration: A New Theory of Modernity* (Columbia University Press, 2013). The transformation of the idea of the self and of self-consciousness is described in Dror Wahrman, *The Making of the Modern Self: Identity and Culture in Eighteenth Century England* (Yale University Press, 2004) while Anthony Giddens, *Modernity and Self-Identity: Self and Society in the Late Modern Age* (Stanford University Press, 1991) brings the same theme up to the present. A good example of the many critical views of modernity is Augusto del Noce, *The Crisis of Modernity* (MQUP, 2014) while an early example of this that comes from the point in time where the notion of modernity was being clearly formulated is Charles Baudouin, *The Myth of Modernity* (Routledge, 2015; 1st published 1950).

The economic wealth and sustained growth that are the central aspects of modernity are discussed by all of the economic historians mentioned here. The detailed figures for average income can be found most easily by going to the websites of the World Bank and the OECD, the World Bank in particular has a regular annual report and a series of statistical estimates going back to the 1800s. The OECD was for many years the employer of the man who did more to put definite figures to economic transformation that anyone else. This was the late Angus Maddison whose achievement can be found in his many published books and the continued work of his colleagues at https://www.rug.nl/ggdc/historicaldevelopment/maddison/. Some of his main works are: *The World Economy: Historical Statistics* (OECD, 2003), *Contours of the World Economy 1-2030 AD: Essays in Macroeconomic History* (Oxford University Press, 2007), and *The World Economy: A Millenial Perspective* (OECD, 2001).

There are several specific aspects of modernity mentioned here that should be explored. The most important is the practice and idea of critical rationalism. As a term critical rationalism was first formulated by Karl Popper in the middle part of the twentieth century but the essential argument had been developed earlier by philosophers such as Charles Sanders Pierce and William James. They in turn had amended the earlier arguments of rationalists such as Descartes and empiricists such as Bacon, crucially by moving away from the idea that that the validity of a truth claim depended on how it was justified (by deduction from first principles in the Cartesian case, by appeal to the evidence of the senses in the empiricist one). Instead they introduced the idea of the tentativeness of truth claims. Popper's additional element was the idea that the way that knowledge (less tentativeness) progressed was through a dialogue in which claims were subjected to attempts to disprove them. This was a case however, where the formulations of the philosophers had caught up with the practice of investigators, from the seventeenth century onwards (not overlooking earlier episodes as in the Hellenic era, ninth century Baghdad or thirteenth and seventeenth century China). The best introduction to this is W. W. Bartley, *Retreat to Commitment* (Open Court, 1999) and a hard line version of the approach is given in David Miller, *Critical Rationalism: A Restatement and Defence* (Open Court, 2015).

The topic of secularism is one that has attracted much attention recently, for obvious reasons. Two good introductions are Andrew Copson, *Secularism: Politics, Religion, and Freedom* (Oxford University Press, 2017), and Graeme Smith, *A Short History of Secularism* (I. B. Tauris, 2007). A good examination of the theoretical issues that the concept raises is Gordon Graham, "Religion, Secularisation, and Modernity" *Philosophy* 67 (1992) pp. 183 – 197. The modernity and novelty of fundamentalisms is set out in Oliver Roy, *Secularism Confronts Islam* (Columbia University press, 2007). The extreme difficulty of an educated person's adhering to atheism before the eighteenth century was classically set out in Lucien Febvre, *The Problem of Unbelief in the Sixteenth Century: The Religion of Francois Rabelais* (Harvard University Press, 1985; 1st published 1942).

The nature and development of the 'civilising process' is the subject of the classic works by Norbert Elias, *The Civilising Process: Sociogenetic and Psychogenetic Investigations* (Blackwell, 2008), and *The Society of Individuals* (Continuum, 2001). The current state of knowledge on this subject is summarised in Steven Pinker, *The Better Angels of Our Nature: Why Violence Has Declined* (Penguin, 2011). The idea of cosmopolitanism and the issues it raises are clearly set out by one of its leading contemporary exponents in Kwame Anthony Appiah, *Cosmopolitanism: Ethics in a World of Strangers* (Norton, 2010). The ways that this sensibility developed in different contexts but in a related way has been the subject of a number of recent studies. Two of the best are Margaret C. Jacob, *Strangers Nowhere in the World: The Rise of Cosmopolitanism in Early Modern Europe* (University of Pennsylvania Press, 2016), and Seema Alavi, *Muslim Cosmopolitanism in the Age of Empire*

(Harvard University Press, 2015). The notion of an 'axial age' in which the main religious traditions of the world first appeared was originally formulated by the German philosopher Karl Jaspers. Good introductions to the idea and its implications are Karen Armstrong, *The Great Transformation: The Beginning of Our Religious Traditions* (Random House, 2006), and Robert N. Bellah & Hans Joas (eds.), *The Axial Age and its Consequences* (Harvard University Press, 2012). A sharp critique of the whole notion can be found in Iain Provan, *Convenient Myths: the Axial Age, Dark Green Religion, and the World That Never Was.* (Baylor University Press, 2013)

Historical demography and the history of both households and families has become a growth industry since the 1970s. Two books that summarise much of what is now known as regards Europe are David I. Kirtzer & Marzio Barbagli (eds.), *The History of the European Family. Vol. I: Family Life in Early Modern Times, 1500 – 1789* (Yale University Press, 2001), and *The History of the European Family. Vol. II: Family Life in the Long Nineteenth Century (1789 – 1913)* (Yale University Press, 2002). A very useful essay is E. A. Wrigley, "Reflections on the History of the Family" *The Family* 106 (1997) pp. 71 – 85. An economic analysis of the history of families and households that complements the analysis given in this book is Steven Horwitz, *Hayek's Modern Family: Classical Liberalism and the Evolution of Social Institutions* (Palgrave Macmillan, 2015).

Large institutions and their transformation in the modern world are analysed in the works of Peter F. Drucker, in particular in *The Age of Discontinuity* (Harper Row, 1969) and *The New Realities: in Government and Politics, in Economics and Business, in Society and World View* (Harper Row, 1989). Drucker also treats the way that this leads to a new kind of social formation, and ultimately a new dominant social group. The outstanding work of social history on this topic is Harold Perkin, *The Rise of Professional Society: England Since 1880* (Routledge, 2002) and his *The Third Revolution: Professional Elites in the Modern World* (Routledge, 1996).

Both historians and sociologists cover the history of the modern state in a number of places. A classic work that argues against my position is Joseph R. Strayer, *On the Medieval Origins of the Modern State* (Princeton University Press, 2005; 1st published 1970). The classic account of the modern state that connects it to military change is Martin Van Creveld, *The Rise and Decline of the State* (Cambridge University Press, 1999). The common perception is that large modern states appeared by 1648 but Scott F. Abramson, "The Economic Origins of the Territorial State" *International Organisation* 71 (2017) pp. 97 – 130 convincingly argues that the tendency up to 1800 was for increased fragmentation or the continued existence of large empires rather than the appearance of modern territorial states with their typical forms of governance. The way that this process spread after 1800 is described in Andreas Wimmer & Yuval Feinstein, "The Rise of the Nation-State Across the World, 1816 – 2001" *American Sociological Review* 75 (2010) pp. 764 – 790. The case for the modern state being only one of the possible kinds of polity that could have appeared is made by Charles Tilly in the work cited earlier and also by Hendrik Spruyt, *The Sovereign State and Its Competitors* (Princeton University Press, 1994) and his earlier "The Origins, Development, and Possible Decline of the Modern State" *Annual Review of Political Science* 5 (2002) pp. 127 – 149.

CHAPTER II

Historiography and Theory

THE transformation of the human world described in the previous chapter is obviously the central fact of the last three hundred years of world history, and one of the two or three great divisions in the entire history of the world. As such it has attracted attention and led to much argument, in almost all academic disciplines. Many of those disciplines have only come into existence as coherent bodies of study since the advent of modernity and some, notably economics and sociology, came about because of the need to respond to the changes of modernity and to understand them. Given this, there are many questions to be asked, all of which have been the subject of warm and continuing debate.

Is Modernity Different?

The most fundamental question is the one discussed in the previous chapter, that of whether the sharp division argued for in the previous chapter is real or illusory. Is the world of the last 250 to 300 years truly profoundly different from what came earlier or is it only a continuation of what came before but possibly with some things more prominent? A number of prominent scholars have argued the latter case. The German-American sociologist and historian Andre Gunder Frank argued towards the end of his life that there was no real difference between the modern world and earlier periods of history and that what we could observe in the last few centuries was simply the continued development and unfolding of a world-system that had become established no later than 4,000 BC. The changes we can observe, he argued, were simply ones of degree and scale rather than kind and simply reflected the steady growth of human knowledge and capacity and the intensification of certain process such as global economic integration over that very long time period. Consequently he rejected the idea of a teleological or clear pattern of movement towards an end state in world history and came to explicitly reject the notions of stages in world history and distinct and successive modes of production for each one.

Another sceptic, coming from a very different political standpoint but arriving at similar kinds of conclusion is the British historian J. C. D. Clark. He has argued for an essential continuity in human history in his essay collection *Our Shadowed Present* and has argued (as have several economic historians) that the idea of a radical economic transformation in late eighteenth and early nineteenth century Britain (an 'Industrial Revolution') is incoherent, with the reality one of much slower and more gradual change. Other historians of the Middle Ages such as Lynn White have made the case that the technological innovation of the modern world is not unprecedented and that there was just as much during the high Middle Ages of the twelfth and thirteenth centuries. This is significant, because an account of the British Industrial Revolution is at the heart of most descriptions of a relatively rapid movement from traditional societies to the world of the modern, with Britain usually seen as the vanguard of this change.

In fact it is historians of all types who are most cautious and sceptical about the idea that the contemporary and recent world is in some way profoundly different from most of the human past. This reflects the belief of most historians that *nihil novi sub sole*, nothing is truly new in history. However other disciplines, particularly economics and sociology, are much more persuaded that the difference is real and can produce solid argument of the kind outlined earlier to show this. The decisive fact is that the most dramatic change has taken place in everyday conditions of life, and that these had on all the evidence remained fairly constant for most people over a very long period before suddenly being transformed over the space of about six generations at most.

What Is Modernity?

The second big question is the one examined in the previous chapter, of what it is that marks out the modern world from the previous traditional and Malthusian world. Again it is the sociologists and the economists who have set this out most clearly, with help from economic and social historians. Authors such as Anthony Giddens have given very clear and succinct accounts of this. Some things are obvious and widely acknowledged, such as the dramatic rise in population or the increase in urbanisation. Others are generally known but their precise nature is frequently not grasped. This is particularly true for the two central aspects of modernity, sustained and intensive economic growth and the explosive growth in both theoretical and applied knowledge. It is agreed by most that these are the central and most visible aspects of modernity and that many others are consequences of these two. (This does not stop scholars arguing that both are consequences of something else even more basic, as we shall see). The centrality of intensive economic growth and the resulting dramatic increase in wealth (the wealth explosion or 'great enrichment') means that many accounts focus narrowly on changes in economic life, production and distribution, with the changes first observed in later eighteenth century Britain given pride of place.

In addition there are some phenomena that are recognised as being peculiar to modernity, that is they are not found before the modern period (however that is defined) but which are not agreed as being essential to it. That is to say there are some aspects of the modern world that define its very nature and constitute what makes it different from the past – if they had not come about then modernity would not have – while there are other phenomena that are part of the modern world but which would not be had the course taken by political history been different. We can imagine feasible and possible worlds in which there is modernity (sustained intensive growth, large scale urbanisation etc) but without these features. Examples of this might include the virtual disappearance of slavery and the transformation of the status of women. Finally, there are others that are contested, in the sense that some scholars think a change has taken place, while others deny that there has been a change. Secularisation (or a change in the nature and status of religion) is one, as is a change in the consciousness and sense of identity of people in general. Here again it is the sociologists who are most certain that there has been a radical shift.

The modern world, the way we live now, is thus fundamentally different from the way people have lived for several thousands of years earlier. The material conditions and limits of human experience have been and are being transformed by population growth, urbanisation, and unceasing technological innovation and, above all, by sustained intensive economic growth. The common psychology and sense of self of most people and the cultural and intellectual order have also adopted novel and unprecedented forms. The same is true of important forms of social and political organisation; most notably government and commerce, while there have been significant changes in the forms of social hierarchy. There have been radical alterations to the status of women and in the role of the household or family. All of this amounts to a true revolution in human affairs.

Not only has there been a profound change but also all of the evidence suggests that it happened very swiftly and comparatively recently. What we have here therefore is not just a transformation in human experience but a sharp discontinuity. It does not make sense to think of this as just the latest stage of a long, continuous and homogeneous process that can be traced back into the distant past and represented as a single smooth curve or line. This is not to deny the continuing influence of the past upon the present but to emphasise the abrupt and sudden way the various changes have taken place, often in less than a generation in many parts of the world.

However all of this is only the start of the argument. If we accept that there has been a radical change, and agree on what its main features and elements have been, there are still a whole series of questions to consider. The first is the one already mentioned, that of whether we can identify a particular process that is the cause or origin of the changes described in the previous chapter and above. The further ones that are the centre of argument are when and where the processes that we collectively call 'modernity' came into being, and why it was in that particular time and place.

When Did Modernity Start?

As has already been said, this not a simple matter. There is little argument about the location, which is the lands around the North Atlantic, particularly North-Western Europe. The date is more problematic and suggestions range from the fourteenth to the mid-nineteenth centuries. This is reflected in the conventional periodisation that is familiar to anyone who has done a history degree, in which the ancient world is succeeded by the Medieval which then passes around 1450 to 1550 into 'Early Modern', to be succeeded by 'Modern' around 1750 and 'Late Modern' around 1900 (with a venture into something called 'post-modernity' for the more daring). Here again we can discern a difference between the predominant views of the various disciplines. Historians (and also political theorists) tend on the whole to locate the start of modernity at an earlier period. The sixteenth century, or even the mid-fifteenth are still popular while many opt for the seventeenth century and particularly its central decades. There is reason for this in terms of ideas (with the first appearance of the modern ideas of sovereignty and the establishment of the modern system of international relations at Westphalia in 1648) and in culture with both the scientific revolution and the first appearance of a strongly favourable view of commerce and exchange (in the Dutch Republic). In addition it is the second half of the seventeenth century that sees European powers become clearly militarily superior to non-European ones, with the single exception of China.

However while some economists also locate the start of modernity in the seventeenth century most of them, and the overwhelming majority of sociologists and anthropologists, locate it much later in the later eighteenth century at the earliest. There is also a significant and growing minority of historians who fix on that time. In addition recent work suggests that the processes at the heart of the modern (innovation and sustained intensive growth) went to a new level after roughly 1850 to 1865. Literary critics and scholars of cultural and intellectual history also tend to focus on the later nineteenth century as the period of dramatic change. Consequently, we can say that there is a growing agreement that the distinctive features of modernity appear around the middle of the eighteenth century and become both dominant and firmly established by the middle of the nineteenth, so that full blown modernity comes into being in the years after 1850. A notion that has been much bruited recently is that we have now moved beyond the modern into the post-modern. This is popular with the scholars of cultural forms such as literature and architecture and probably reflects the decline or recession of aggressive modernism in these fields but again the overwhelming majority of sociologists, political scientists and historians reject this. The view here is that we are either still in full blown modernity or that we are in at most a later phase of that process – liquid modernity as Zygmunt Bauman calls it. All this suggests that we should rethink the conventional periodisation set out above, with the period from 1450 to 1850 becoming 'Late Western' and 1850 to around 1950 becoming Early Modern. Given all this the big questions for scholars are those of why the changes we have described first happened when and where the emerging consensus says they did.

The Questions – How to Explain This?

There are a multitude of theories that take one aspect of modernity as the cause of the rest or, more significantly, argue that one factor is the primary cause of the transformation. The main candidate for being the central element that causes all of the rest is intensive economic growth. Not surprisingly it is economists who are most keen on this. A large subset of the scholars who advocate this sees industrialisation as the key factor. The problem with that argument is that if it were correct then places such as Denmark or Australia would count as not yet modern, because they have not industrialised (the status of France would also be questionable). Clearly economic modernisation is not the same as industrialisation (the appearance of a large, industrial manufacturing sector) as there are other routes to that condition. (This means that the extensive debate over why industrialisation was 'delayed' in much of nineteenth century Europe is, quite simply, a waste of time).

The problem with making sustained economic growth the cause of everything else in modernity rather than just the central element is that several of the other prominent features are either not clearly connected to it or appeared at an earlier stage. In particular this is the case with some of the intellectual and cultural aspects of modernity, such as sceptical rationalism, individualism, and new ideas about both economic life and religion. That might suggest that these were the cause of the other parts of modernity.

In fact it makes more sense to think of all the various changes as interconnected and to a great degree mutually reinforcing. It is very difficult to show that one of the changes is exogenous, that is it is independent of the rest and the one that ultimately causes all of them. Economic growth, population, and critical rationalism have all been candidates for this role. However, it seems more likely that no one part of the process is the prime mover of the rest in this way, even if we ascribe more importance to some than to others. What we can argue about with more certainty however is whether there was a particular set of circumstances at a certain time that began the change or a change in the working of traditional society that made them possible if not inevitable.

Institutions

Scholars from several disciplines have made arguments for some particular factor that lies behind the eruption of modernity. These are varied but can be grouped under six broad headings. The first, and by far the most popular is that of institutions. Institutions in this sense means authoritative and culturally embedded practices and social norms. These include such things as property rights, money, markets, financial institutions such as banking and credit, the law in general and more widely the 'rule of law' (a state of affairs in which power is exercised according to rules known in advance to all rather than in an arbitrary and wilful fashion), free speech, accepted rules of research and investigation, the modern company or firm, and intellectual property such as patents and copyright. As the (far from exhaustive) list just given shows it is economists who have particularly emphasised this kind of argument. The late Douglass North was one of many to argue that it was secure and tradable property rights along with the rule of law that were at the root of modernity. The legal scholar Harold Berman argued that the rule of law and a state of legal pluralism, in which there was more than one source of authoritative law (which he saw as arising in twelfth century Europe) was critical. Other economists, such as Joel Rosenberg, have made the case for the invention of the company as a way of organising business activity, along with widely accepted standards of accounting, above all double entry bookkeeping. Yet others have argued for the creation of modern finance in the later seventeenth century or the appearance of the limited liability joint stock company in the middle of the nineteenth century. In addition to all of these there is another whole constellation of authors who argue the case for the sovereign territorial state as being the progenitor.

For these arguments to work, their authors have to show not only that the institution in question is a necessary condition of modernity (that it could not have arisen without it or that it shaped it in a decisive way) but also that it did not exist either long before modernity began or in places where it did not initially appear. Instead they have to show that this factor came into existence for the first time only in the part of the world where modernity first appeared and not too long before it started. If they cannot do that, then the causal connection cannot be shown. North explicitly made this case, arguing that the required combination of secure and transferable property rights with constitutionally limited government and the rule of law only came into being with the Glorious Revolution in Britain in 1688-90. Rosenberg and Birdzell, and Berman, make a similar case for the institutional innovations they identify as crucial but argue that they appeared in Europe during the Middle Ages. The problem with almost all arguments of this kind is simple. In some cases the supposedly key institution existed in other places where modernity did not arise spontaneously once they had appeared. The combination of property rights and the rule of law for example was found in many parts of Europe apart from the British Isles and also in other parts of the world at various times without the phenomena of modernity arising. Alternatively the institutions in question come into existence several centuries before even the first twinklings of modernity. In that case, if they are the cause of it, why did they take so long to have an impact? The obvious conclusion in that case is that these institutions are a necessary condition of modernity but not a sufficient one.

In other cases, such as that of the limited liability joint stock company, although invented by the Dutch in the early seventeenth century, it only became widespread after 1860, long after the time when most people think modernity first began, so it cannot be a cause. This is also the problem with the argument for the sovereign territorial state being the key factor. True modern administration and government did not appear until after the other elements of modernity or at the very most alongside them so it is hard to make the case for this being the crucial factor on its own.

Trade and Investment

A related but distinct set of arguments emphasise not so much institutions as activities. The most favoured is trade, and particularly long distance trade. Another is capital accumulation and investment. The argument is that these processes will naturally lead, through things such as enhanced division of labour, rising productivity, and extension of the scope of market relations, to the condition of sustained intensive growth that is at the centre of modernity. This lends itself to the argument, set out later, that the appearance of modernity is a tipping point phenomenon where a process goes on for a very long time before reaching a critical point of inflexion where 'takeoff' happens. The problem here is not so much one of chronology (because the nature of the argument allows for that) but geography. The processes in question were found not only for a long time but also over most of the world and, crucially, to a greater degree in other parts of the world such as China than in the parts of Europe where modernity first appeared. That means that arguments of this kind cannot be a full explanation because they do not explain why the breakthrough first happened in Europe. So they have to be combined with other kinds of explanation. It is difficult to combine this with institutional arguments however because the point of those kinds of thesis is precisely that the favoured institution led to higher levels of exchange, capital accumulation etc and so brought about intensive growth.

Cultural Change

The third popular class of arguments focus upon intellectual and cultural change or breakthrough. Here ideas and cultural norms are made the driving force behind change, usually on the grounds that they lead acting human beings to behave and act in ways that they had not done before. Idealist explanations of this kind are not popular with those who favour materialist or incentive based arguments (so most economists) or those who believe that the human mindset has not changed that much over time but they are apparently stronger than the first two kinds of argument. The reason is that it is easier to fit this kind of explanation with the chronology. The geographical challenge is more difficult but can be met – typically ideas that are supposed to be specific to one part of the world turn out not to be but this can be rescued by arguments about the predominance of the ideas or cultural norms in one time and place rather than others.

Again there are many candidates for this kind of argument. Religion is a very popular one, with Weber's thesis about the crucial role of Calvinism the best known example. His friend and contemporary Werner Sombart made a similar case but with Judaism the key factor. There have been a number of scholars such as Rodney Stark who put the emphasis on Christianity in general but others mention Islam or the combination of Christianity and Classical Greek thought. Most of these face the same problem of chronology as the institutional arguments described earlier however. The most persuasive intellectual or cultural explanations are of two kinds. The first is the argument, made by several authors, that connects modernity to the scientific revolution of the middle to later seventeenth century. This is the case made for example by Joel Mokyr, who argues that this led for the first time in history to a real connection between the two principal kinds of human knowledge (for this see below, chapter Six) and that this in turn brought about the appearance of a culture of innovation that produced the modern transformation. Another is the argument made most extensively and forcefully by Deirdre McCloskey, that the seventeenth century saw the appearance for the first time of a positive view of business activity and above all entrepreneurship. For her this happened initially in the Dutch Republic before being taken up in Britain, and also happened independently but slightly later in early eighteenth century Tokugawa Japan.

These arguments do have the strength of locating the crucial change in a specific and appropriate time and place. However they do have two main problems. The first is that, as with intensive growth, episodes of this kind happened many times before in human history in various places but did not last. The question that has to be answered therefore is that of why they 'took' and had an impact in seventeenth century Europe but not elsewhere or before. That requires an appeal to some other factor. The other is the more fundamental difficulty with all idealist explanations of historical change, which is that it is hard to demonstrate the mechanism by which a change in attitudes and beliefs led to a change in concrete behaviour and output, particularly given that on many occasions in history major shifts in the beliefs of society did not lead to any dramatic change in material existence. Again it seems that intellectual explanations are insufficient by themselves, there has to be another agent that accounts for the impact of the ideas.

Demography

The fourth broad class of explanations make conscious human volition or the actions of particular people much less significant. These are ones that use demographic or population based explanations. Here modernity is explained by demographic factors such as family structure, birthrate, population levels and density or changes or variations in the genetic and behavioural structure of human populations. For many years a popular argument was that North-Western Europe had a distinctive marriage pattern and household structure, which emerged during the early Middle Ages (roughly the tenth to twelfth centuries). This combined a relatively late age of marriage with a system of nuclear households. The argument was that this kind of family structure exercised the kinds of voluntary restraints that Malthus thought might be a way out of the trap posed by his thought experiment (because people did not marry until they could set up a household of their own they tended to marry at a later age – particularly when times were bad – and this restrained the birthrate and meant there was more of a surplus, which accumulated over time). It also supposedly encouraged individualism and hence experimentation and innovation.

This theory falls foul of the two difficulties that bedevil others. It is argued that the family type described is not peculiar to Europe and, even if it were, there remains the difficulty of explaining why it took such a long time from its first appearance for it to have such a dramatic effect. This is not a problem with another theory, the one advocated by the late Julian Simon. His view was that the key factor was simply the number of people alive at any point, combined with a sufficient density of population in a sufficiently large part of the world. His reasoning was that the 'ultimate resource' as he put it was people, or rather their ingenuity, inventiveness and capacity for productive work. The more people there are and the closer they live together (so making communication easier) the more production. In this view the simple reason for modernity appearing when it did was that the later eighteenth century was the point where the population of the world reached a critical level. That is a strong argument but fails to answer the other question, of why this happened in Europe rather than elsewhere.

Another explanation, which suffers from both difficulties, is that put forward by Gregory Clark. He argues that a prolonged experience of settled and stable government led to a reproductive selection for people who were cooperative rather than predatory and eventually there were enough people like that in the population to make take off possible. Why though, given that the Chinese experience of settled governance was much longer than the European, did it not happen there first? In addition how do we know that the critical change in the makeup of the population had occurred by the later eighteenth century? The answer, that we know because that was when the take off happened, makes the whole argument circular and thus a 'just so' story rather than a proper explanation. Finally there are arguments to the effect that Europeans had a different and superior genetic endowment to the rest of the world. This thesis was once popular but has fallen from the limelight since 1945, for obvious reasons. However it still has advocates, such as Ricardo Duchesne (who combines it with cultural explanations) and Richard Lynn and Tatu Vanhanen. The problem once again is that of how to explain, if this is the critical factor (and assuming the underlying thesis is true), that it had little or no impact before the later eighteenth century.

Weather, Geography, and Energy

The final two kinds of explanation both posit a kind of automatic response to an outside shock or stimulus. Some scholars argue that the key factor in explaining most of human history is the natural world, and above all changes and fluctuations in the planet's climate. Obviously this is beyond human control, so the question is that of how and why people in different places and times respond to these climactic and other shifts. Two expatriate British academics, Bruce Fagan and Geoffrey Parker, have both argued that the 'Little Ice Age' of the later Middle Ages and (particularly) the seventeenth century played a central part in the development of the modern world and the course of modern history. This is certainly true and any account of the advent of modernity has to take it into account but it is hard to see climate as the only cause. Another argument, made by authors such as Jared Diamond (but also by David Landes among others) is that Europe was favoured by geography and that the physical structure and natural endowments of that part of the world (such as a highly indented coastline, many navigable waterways, and many species of domesticated animals) made economic growth and dynamism easier than in places such as Africa or the New World that lacked these. The problem here again is that this does not explain why these endowments took so long to have an effect and so have to be combined with other arguments plus the points made about Europe can be made with equal force for China or the lands around the Indian ocean, so Europe's primacy remains a puzzle. (Diamond's account does explain why settled civilisation and agriculture first appeared when and where they did in early antiquity but that is a different question).

The last class of explanations focus on human access to energy, and the way this was transformed by access to fossil fuels. Ian Morris (another British expat!) argues convincingly that the ability to capture and use energy is the crucial limiting factor in the complexity and dynamism of human civilisation, and that modern civilisation does this at a much higher level than that found in any previous period of world history. E. A. Wrigley put the case in a series of papers and books that it was only increased access to energy in the shape of fossil fuels that enabled the massive movement of labour out of agriculture that was the basis for economic modernisation. This makes modernity a consequence of human beings suddenly exploiting a windfall in the shape of reserves of coal and oil. Again though the question is that of why this did not happen sooner, given that the technology required for the initial stage of this process is not particularly complex. Even more problematic is the reality that coal only became really widely used in production and transport from the 1840s, about a hundred years after the widely accepted date for the start of modernity. This argument does however make a lot of sense as the explanation for the sudden acceleration of modernity after the middle of the nineteenth century and that does have interesting implications for the way we view our current situation and its sustainability.

Why the Later Eighteenth Century?

All this makes it clear that there are two big questions that any explanatory account of modernity has to address and try to answer. The first is chronology. Why did the elements of modernity start to occur in the later eighteenth and early nineteenth century and not before? One obvious argument is that the critical factor, whatever it might be, appeared just before the takeoff and so led to it directly – this might be the cultural and intellectual changes posited by Mokyr and McCloskey for example. There are however other candidates for that role. Many authors however reject this and argue that the breakthrough after 1750 had deeper roots, going back into previous history.

This is a challenging argument to make at first sight, given that what we have to explain is not a change produced by a continuous process but rather one where there is a sudden change of gear or state that took place in a relatively short pace of time by historical standards. One way is to argue that what we have is a slow, cumulative process that at a particular point in time reached a tipping point where there was a sudden shift to a different level and kind of change. An analogy would be a pot of water on a stove. The temperature of the water will rise slowly but the change from water to water to steam will happen in a matter of minutes once boiling point arrives.

An even closer analogy is that of a primitive atomic pile: as more and more blocks of fuel are added to the pile nothing much happens at first apart from a gradual rise in heat until suddenly there is a critical mass of fuel, i.e. enough material in sufficiently close proximity to sustain a continuous chain reaction. This means that the breakthrough to modernity could not happen anywhere until the various preconditions were in place (either locally or globally) and that this came about as the result of a gradual build-up. Therefore, for example, Julian Simon argues that the key factor was simply the number of people and that the population levels needed for all of the other changes were not reached until the later eighteenth century and could not have been sustained earlier because of the inability to mechanise agriculture in any significant way.

The other approach is to argue that the breakthrough to modernity could have happened earlier and may even have started to happen, but was stopped. Eric Jones for example argues strongly for this approach. He points out that the central phenomena of intensive growth and innovation are, or should be, the natural result of economic exchange. Moreover we do indeed see them arising at various points in history before the eighteenth century. The biggest example (for which see the next chapter) was China under the Song dynasty and indeed at some other points in its history but there are other instances, such as the central Middle East under the early Abbasids in the eighth and ninth centuries, or the classical Mediterranean civilisation during both the second century AD and the Hellenic era after the death of Alexander. In addition there are also episodes throughout history of what we may call 'ages of reason', which see the development and articulation of materialist and sceptical thought – these can be found in the history of China, the Islamic world, India, and classical civilisation. (Their extent is often underestimated because frequently little has survived of their written work because of later reactions).

The point here is that we have earlier episodes of many of the central features of the modern revolution, such as intensive growth, technological innovation, and the ideas of critical rationalism but that these 'eflorescences' (as Jack Goldstone calls them) were not sustained. Instead, something choked them off. This is of course compatible with the first approach – the fact that these episodes were not sustained would on that view show that there was, by analogy, not enough fuel in the reactor to keep the chain reaction going. The alternative is, to continue the analogy, that there was already enough 'fuel' in the 'reactor' long before the reaction finally sustained itself in the later eighteenth century but that before then there was a control mechanism (analogous to the absorbent control rods in an actual reactor) that suppressed the process and stopped it from continuing when it could have.

This explanation in turn can take two different forms. One is that the 'controls' that prevented such earlier episodes from sustaining themselves were features of the social, political, and economic order of traditional societies that could have been changed but were not, for various reasons. The strongest candidate is the set of institutions described in the previous chapter, which arose as a response to the Malthusian constraints facing traditional agricultural societies, along with the need to have between eighty and ninety per cent of the population engaged in agriculture. These social practices and institutions seem to have proved very resilient and they had the effect, above all, of preventing sustained innovation. The other way of explaining the termination of 'eflorescences' is to emphasise, in addition to wider social obstacles, deliberate policy by rulers or rather the way that the interests of certain social groups and above all ruling classes led them to follow a course that had the effect of terminating such episodes and making them less likely to start in the first place. This is the view of a number of scholars such as Goldstone himself, Eric Jones, and Mark Elvin. The key historical episode for those who take this view is that of China under the Song and it is the failure of that particular 'efflorescence' to sustain itself that has attracted the most attention.

Why North-West Europe?

This still leaves the question of why the breakthrough first happened (or rather first kept going) in North-West Europe. One view would have it that there was something distinctive about Europe and European society that eventually led to its becoming the place where the modern transformation took root and became established. There is some disagreement about when Europe became distinct in this way but the predominant view is that it happened during the Middle Ages, or even earlier.

The reason for making this argument is simple – it is that given modernity first appeared in Europe, that fact must reflect some distinctive and long standing feature of the society and culture of that part of the world. The underlying position is that modernity is a European or Western phenomenon, which begins in Europe (actually Western Europe) and then spreads to the rest of the world. For many years this was the dominant position and so most debate concentrated on what the distinctive features of European society were and how and when they came about. Recently however this view has come under strong attack, which in turn has produced a series of rejoinders reasserting the 'Eurocentric' position. David Landes puts the one view forcefully:

> "Until very recently, over the thousand and more years of this process that most people look upon as progress, the key factor – the driving force – has been Western civilization and its dissemination: the knowledge, the techniques, the political and social ideologies, for better or worse." (Landes, 1998, 513)

In this perspective European civilisation had some quality or set of qualities almost from its inception in the aftermath of the collapse of the Roman Empire that set it apart from the other great civilisations of the Old World and gave it a dynamism that they lacked. As we have seen there are many suggestions as to what those features were, with candidates ranging from geographical endowment through cultural factors, to social and economic institutions, but there is agreement as to the exceptional nature of the European experience and its product. This meant for its advocates that European or 'Western' civilisation was able to escape from the limits that confined human experience in other parts of the world, primarily through a process of innovation and discovery, which led to the appearance of modernity in Europe, whence it spread to the rest of the world (to a greater or lesser extent) via the processes of conquest, trade and emulation. This means that the two categories of 'modern' and Western' are seen as being the same or at the least as inextricably interlinked. It can also mean that the future is seen as one in which all of humanity will come to inhabit a single civilisation, one that is broadly Western. Most often (as with Landes and Eric Jones) the process is seen as ultimately benign. For some however (Immanuel Wallerstein is a good example) the exceptional features of the European system are seen in darker colours and its spread to the rest of the world as a disaster.

The alternative position is that there was nothing unusual or distinctive about Europe and that the fact of the great transformation starting there was purely a matter of good fortune or chance. This view has gained increasing support because of the accumulating evidence produced by economic historians such as Kenneth Pomeranz that Europe was indeed an economic and intellectual backwater when compared to other parts of the world for most of its history. There are many other examples of this globalist or 'anti-Eurocentric' approach, with the works of Mark Blaut and Andre Gunder Frank perhaps the best known. They simply reject the argument of European exceptionalism, whether in climate, geography, culture or economic and social institutions. They also argue that empirical research reveals that until very recently Europe was not particularly innovative or advanced technologically and economically compared to other parts of the world. The argument is that in fact Europe is a peripheral part of a worldwide system of trade and exchange until at least the later eighteenth century.

This however produces a new problem, that of how in that case to explain the undoubted predominant position of Europe and its North American offshoots since at least 1800 (some would say 1700 or even 1600) and the big question of why a major breakthrough happened in a part of the world that was not especially distinctive. One solution is to argue that something happened either outside Europe or in the relations between Europe and the rest of the world that led to a sudden acceleration of innovation and growth within parts of Europe. One example is the argument made by people such as Blaut, that Europe gained a windfall benefit from the resources of the Americas after 1492, which enabled it to increase its productivity to a point where it overtook other parts of the world. This view typically sees the good fortune as involving oppression or exploitation of other parts of the world, something that for some casts doubt on the moral standing of the modern world in general. The more radical position is taken by Frank, who argues for an explanation that ultimately denies any kind of discontinuity between modern and premodern and makes European dominance in the nineteenth and twentieth centuries a purely contingent and adventitious phenomenon brought about not by a European upsurge but a decline in Asia. This surely an unsustainable position given the extent of the predominance of Europe at that time and the degree to which world society and economy was transformed.

The problem with the now very fashionable view that Europe's sudden acceleration came from exploiting the rest of the world and windfall gains from things such as the conquest of the New World, the profits of the slave trade and plantation agriculture is that the empirical evidence simply does not support it. As Frank points out, the Atlantic trade (including the slave trade) is much less valuable and economically significant than the trade with and within the Indian Ocean. European empire in the New World did have a significant effect on the world trade system as a whole but this came from injecting large quantities of silver into the world monetary system, the bulk of which ended up circulating in Asia, above all China. Colonial trade and agriculture and the slave trade were indeed very profitable but they only contributed a small part of European and British capital formation as compared to domestic profits from agriculture. (O'Brien, 1982) Above all, arguments of this kind do not explain why all kinds of innovation suddenly took off after the early to mid eighteenth century in Europe. In fact this is a particularly problematic thesis given that the evidence from other periods is that large rents from imperial exploitation actually discourage innovation and economic dynamism.

The other position is to accept that there was nothing distinctive about Europe for most of the world's history (and so reject the case made by people like Jones, Landes and many others) but to argue that something happened within Europe not too long before the transformation's commencement. This would be something that *then* made Europe different from other civilisations in a way that it had not been before, and in doing so took the brakes off innovation by removing or weakening the factors that had held back innovation in Europe until then, in common with other civilisations, where they remained. This is the case made by the so-called 'California school' of historians, of whom Goldstone is the most prominent. This is indeed the argument made in the later chapters of this book. It is important to realise that this position implies a high degree of contingency or accident to the entire process and makes the breakthrough something that had sources or roots going back only a relatively short time and not the product of a long process. The question of course is what that sudden something was.

Inevitable or Contingent?

This does not exhaust the arguments, to put it mildly. We should notice two other, major debates. The first concerns the extent to which the various features of modernity described earlier are all equally inevitable. In other words, is it the case for example, that a modern society that has persistent economic growth, rapid innovation and critical rationalism must also see the absence of slavery and a particular kind of change in the status of women? Alternatively is it perfectly possible to have a society that is modern by most definitions but in which slavery is a major social and economic institution and women remain in their historically typical position as social, legal, and economic dependents?

For some this simply impossible, at least in the long run because the various other aspects of modernity will together make it incredibly difficult to sustain traditional social institutions of this kind. Others argue that *au contraire* it is perfectly possible. In that case, some features of the modern world are not a natural and inevitable by-product of its core features but are rather the contingent result of political argument and conflict, even if general conditions encourage a particular outcome. The social and political role of religion is the one most often regarded in this way, along with the other two mentioned above.

A Good Thing or a Bad Thing?

The other debate is equally important. Quite simply it is that of how we should evaluate the entire modern revolution. Is it, as some would say, something beneficent, which has brought about a huge increase in human well being and flourishing? Alternatively, should we view it in darker colours, as a disaster or as something deeply impious and hubristic or somehow contrary to the essential nature of human beings? Both views have their champions and the second in particular has had and continues to have many articulate and persuasive advocates. As we shall see, there is a persistent set of criticisms of modernity that have been articulated by a wide range of thinkers and observers, ever since the first faint intimations of the transformative shift getting under way. Indeed much of the cultural, social and political history of the last two hundred and fifty years consists of a set of reactions against that modern transformation, which seek either to resist it, to reverse it or (more commonly) to alter it in ways that will make it more compatible with traditional institutions and mores. Three persistent themes are that the modern world is impossible to sustain and will end in a crisis or systemic collapse, that it is impious and corruptive of true value, and that it is in some sense antithetical to what it is to be truly human.

This does raise the question of whether the changes described are indeed irreversible, as the earlier Neolithic revolution that created agriculture proved to be. Maybe the modern era will prove to be just another episode in human history and not a radical shift in human experience after all. Alternatively, it could be possible to reverse so that many of the changes described are undone and humanity reverts to an earlier state of affairs. Here the debate over why previous episodes did not develop into a self-sustaining process of change becomes highly relevant. If they were indeed checked by actual policy or action (whether intentionally or not) then this presumably would still be possible. This is very important both for those who think the modern world a catastrophe in the making if not already and for those, such as myself, who regard it as an enormous liberation for human beings and as generally beneficent.

Does Modernisation = Westernisation?

The question of causes and of whether there is historically something distinctive about European civilisation (whether long standing and structural or recent and accidental) leads to the further question of how to view the breakthrough to modernity from a global perspective. Because it first began in Europe there is a persistent tendency among both supporters and critics to see it as having a clearly 'Western' quality, as necessarily involving the adoption of what are seen as Western ways and institutions. In this way of thinking 'modernisation' is much the same as 'Westernisation'. A contrary view has it that this is not the case and that there are different 'roads to modernity' so that modernity can take a number of distinctively different forms. Although my own position is closer to the second than the first, it is still different from both.

Broadly, this work argues firstly that while obviously there will be local variations caused by particular circumstances and traditions, modernity is indeed essentially uniform in its main features – these are inescapable and unavoidable aspects of what it is to be modern. The second part of the argument is that these are not historically or in any other meaningful sense Western or associated with historical Western civilisation. Modern civilisation is not the current phase of historic Western civilisation. Rather modernity is a new civilisation, which has replaced or supplanted traditional Western civilisation. That actually no longer exists, except as an inherited memory or tradition. As the modern transformation moves on to other parts of the world so the other traditional world civilisations are in the process of being transformed or absorbed into what is a new and (for the moment) global civilisation.

In general there is a strongly polemical subtext to many of the arguments put by the globalists. Their intention is, as Landes puts it, to delegitimise modern civilisation, which is identified as Western, and to attack the values and institutions that are seen as being historically associated with "the West". To this end, Western achievements are belittled and denied while, to the extent that the historical pre-eminence of Western civilisation is admitted, it is ascribed to force and exploitation (that is it has been achieved by improper means and at someone else's expense). The arguments put by authors such as Jones and Landes are also partly polemical, intended to rebut the criticisms of Western civilisation made by the globalists and to sustain a positive view of its part in world history.

For their part writers such as Wallerstein and Samir Amin share the critical view of 'globalists' like Frank and Blaut but continue to stress the unique role of Europe and its offshoots in the creation of the modern world. If anything their view of Western civilisation is darker than that of the pure globalists since for them the West is primarily to blame for the emergence of a world society and economy that they see as exploitative and corrupt. Thus ideological divisions among scholars largely drive the argument over 'eurocentrism', above all by the view they take of the present day world economy and society. This should not surprise us as many of the divisions of opinion and interpretation among historians actually reflect their differing views regarding the times in which they live, so that competing interpretations and accounts of the past are a part of debates about the present. This has always been the case. It is this that explains the way answers to certain questions tend to be lumped together, even when there is no logical necessity for this.

There is also a cluster of debates that derive from differing assessments of the nature and impact of market relations (often put into the increasingly baggy portmanteau of 'capitalism'). On one side are those who see trade, exchange and market relations as both of critical importance for human development and modernity and as being ultimately creative and beneficial in their effects. On the other are those who rather emphasise the negative results of such relations and the part played historically by exploitative and involuntary relations, notably slavery and other kinds of unfree labour. (This often involves an assessment of market relations as essentially unfree or exploitative).

This typically involves contrasting human relations based upon trade with ones founded upon sharing or other kinds of exchange such as gifts. One view, originally articulated by Karl Polanyi, would have it that market and trade relations are normally subordinate to or 'embedded in' other kinds of human social relations, and that the extent of market connections in the modern world is both unprecedented and in some sense unsustainable. The radical form of this argument has been seriously undermined by research showing just how widespread exchange relations have been historically, and just how extensive, persistent, and long lasting the trade connections between different parts of the world actually are. However, the more moderate version, which emphasises the degree to which exchange connections were historically constrained and limited by other kinds of social relations (particularly those of the household and kin) is much more robust.

The realisation has grown among scholars over the last forty years that what is now commonly called 'globalisation', i.e. a process of economic integration and specialisation involving an ever larger part of the world's population and total economic output, is in fact not recent but historically long standing. For some, such as Eric Jones, Douglass North and Paul Seabright this is a generally benign process, leading to the emergence of an extended or 'great' society marked by an expansion of human potential and flourishing. Others see the entire process as either dominated by or leading to, exploitative, power based relations. This is particularly true for those scholars who espouse so-called "world-systems theory". In this view, put particularly by Wallerstein and Samir Amin (and in his earlier writings by Frank), the trade relations between different parts of the world lead to a structurally unequal kind of relationship between an advanced 'core' and a 'periphery' that is exploited and 'underdeveloped', i.e. prevented from realising its full economic potential by the exploitative economic relations with the 'core'. Other historians, such as Janet Abu-Lughod, employ the 'world system' model but do not emphasise the exploitative element.

A recurring feature of popular analysis has been to conflate this rather blurred division between those who see market relations as benign and those who rather see them as exploitative with the much clearer one between 'Eurocentric' and 'globalist' approaches to the origin of modernity that was described earlier. Because that debate largely grows out of divisions over the state and nature of the contemporary world and because the view taken of the role and moral standing of market relations is central to those divisions, this is not surprising. The assumption is that eurocentrism goes with a benevolent view of market relations and globalism with a more critical one. This is often true and many scholars do fall into one or other of the two combinations just set out.

However there is nothing inevitable or necessary about these associations, and the most recent research is leading to conclusions that do not fit either of them. There are clearly four possible ways of combining the positions taken on the two debates. As well as the two already described there are two others. It is possible to take a critical view of an economy based upon markets and exchange and regret the part they have played in the history of the world (however essential) while seeing this as an essentially European phenomenon. (As Frank says, this is the position of a succession of scholars from Marx onwards, including such figures as Karl Polanyi and, more recently, Immanuel Wallerstein and Robert Brenner). It is also perfectly possible to see the role of market exchange as broadly beneficent and as a critical force in historical development while rejecting the idea of European exceptionalism – Pomeranz generally takes this position for example as does Goldstone. Much of the empirical work that is now being done leads to this last position and a broad consensus may well form around such a view.

What About Capitalism?

Finally, there is a set of complicated arguments over the notion of 'capitalism', centring on such questions as when and where it appeared and what its central institutions are. The difficulty here is that the term 'capitalism' is used in two ways that are ultimately incompatible. Sometimes it is used in a wide sense, to mean any economic system that is based upon private property and private ownership of productive assets, together with free exchange and trade between economic actors. In this view the central features of capitalism are private property, markets, and money, together with related phenomena such as wage labour, and a geographical and functional division of labour. However 'capitalism' is also used in a more restricted way, to mean the economic system of modernity, as analysed by a number of well known authors, most notably Marx but also Max Weber, J. A. Schumpeter, and Werner Sombart. (Although the term is associated with Marx it was in fact Sombart who was the first to use it systematically). The problem with this is easy to see. If capitalism is the economic essence of modernity, then it cannot exist any earlier. To put it another way, the appearance of capitalist institutions and relations must, by definition, mark the appearance of modernity. However, capitalism in the first, wider, sense has been around for a very long time. Indeed markets, division of labour, money, trade, and most of the other institutions and practices associated with the notion of capitalism are found as far back as the ancient world.

This has a number of consequences, which have blighted academic scholarship and led to a truly remarkable waste of time and effort by many scholars. One is the debate already alluded to, over when to locate the advent of modernity (seen in this case as the emergence of capitalism). Marx himself was uncertain about this and in different places in his works located it in the fourteenth, seventeenth and eighteenth centuries. Consequently, a huge amount of ink has been spent on trying to define and measure the 'transition' to capitalism, a transition that for some authors took up to four hundred years. Another result has been the attempt to define various kinds of 'proto' capitalism, or to draw elaborate distinctions between 'agrarian', 'mercantile', 'industrial', and 'finance' capitalism. Again if capitalism, or at least its constituent elements, can be found in many historical periods, so too, presumably, can capitalists, leading to long and ultimately futile arguments over such questions as how to categorise aristocrats who engaged in trade or classes such as the ante-bellum Southern planters.

The basic dilemma is this: if capitalism is intrinsically associated with modernity and is defined in the wider sense given above then either modernity has to be redefined to effectively mean most of human history, which makes the concept meaningless, or what is distinctive about the modern world is not the advent of capitalism. The second option might seem the easy way out, were it not for the fact that it is economic conditions, and above all sustained economic growth and its effects, which are at the heart of the distinction between modern and non-modern. This has led some, such as Frank, to argue that we should scrap the whole notion of capitalism (and associated ideas such as 'mode of production'), along with the notion of modernity. Instead, we should simply talk about exchange relations and the unfolding or elaboration of a 'world system' based upon those relations over the last five thousand years.

A different solution, which is followed in this book, is to distinguish between the often-conflated notions of market economies and capitalism. In this way of thinking, the institutions commonly grouped under the heading of 'capitalism' are in fact the main elements of a wider category of 'market economies' and are found, to a greater or lesser degree, in most human societies since at least the advent of agriculture. Capitalism is a particular kind of market economy, with certain distinctive institutions not found in other types, and in which several of the institutions found in most market economies are intensified or more widespread. As such it can be given a distinct genesis, both temporally and spatially, and it does make sense to connect it to the advent of modernity. This means though that we should not use the term 'capitalism' when discussing market relations in earlier periods. Moreover, Frank is surely right to reject the stadial idea of a series of successive 'modes of production' with the associated implication that there is a time when conditions are ripe for a move from one to another. As we shall see, capitalism, defined in the way just set out, could have appeared in several places before it actually did clearly come about, in the later eighteenth and early nineteenth century in Western Europe and North America.

The other historiographical tradition regarding the phenomenon of 'capitalism' is the one associated with a number of German scholars, above all Max Weber and Werner Sombart, and also Joseph Schumpeter. This approach regards capitalism not so much as an economic system as a set of social relations, associated with a distinctive kind of psychology and set of cultural institutions and attitudes. The emphasis is on the 'spirit' (*geist*) or culture of capitalism, rather than its economic nature. The key figure in this is the bourgeois or entrepreneur, whose psychology and values are contrasted to those of both the aristocrat and the peasant. Ideas such as 'consumerism' and 'conspicuous consumption' also play a central role. Just as in the economic analysis of 'capitalism', this approach has led to wriggling over difficult cases such as entrepreneurial and profit seeking aristocrats or groups such as the New World plantation class. The solution followed here is, once again, to make clarifying distinctions. Following Michael Lind, the category of 'bourgeois' is best understood as a legal and cultural one that is commonly associated with the economic category of capitalist or entrepreneur but not in an exhaustive or exclusive way. (Lind, 2002) Most bourgeois are capitalists but there are historically capitalists and entrepreneurs who are not bourgeois, that is while they are profit seeking traders and investors in a market economy they do not espouse the values, culture or social relations of the 'bourgeois'. If cultural shifts are important as part of the emergence of modernity then it is the spread and changed valuation of this bourgeois spirit and value system that matters.

What all this means is that the concept of 'capitalism' is a useful one if employed in a well defined and historically specific way. It makes sense as a label or category for certain forms and institutions of market and exchange based economic life, which appear in widespread form in modernity. One big issue, which continues to be the basis of much political division, is that of whether it is possible to have a non-capitalist form of modernity. (In other words, is capitalism understood in this way one of the essential features of modernity or a politically contingent one). This use of the term 'capitalism' has a number of implications for the way we view the transition to, or emergence of, modernity. It means that we should reject the idea of a 'mode of production' and the often connected stadial view of history in which economic, social, and political organisation progress through a series of stages, each of which is higher or more developed than its predecessor. It also means that one cannot reduce the wealth explosion or advent of modernity to the appearance of capitalism, or see those particular economic relations as the cause of everything else. Rather it is one of the features of modernity (whether essential or contingent) that is produced or made possible by the factors or events that brought about the transformation of the human world after about 1750.

The Thesis of This Book

So there are a wide variety of theories put forward to explain the appearance of modernity in North-Western Europe in the second half of the eighteenth century. Where though does the argument of this book fit into these debates? The position it takes can be summarised in the following way. Obviously its starting point is that there is something distinctively and profoundly different about the modern world and that the move to modernity (by now throughout the planet) represents a decisive rupture or discontinuity in human life. There are a number of ways in which the modern world is different from previous human societies since the advent of agriculture. The most obvious or prominent is the explosive growth in wealth and output, due to sustained intensive growth. This leads to the transformation of everyday physical experience. However it is an error to think of this as something that produces all of the other differences, seeing these as simply consequences or epiphenomena of material economic change.

Alongside sustained intensive growth are at least two other crucial phenomena, innovation and critical rationalism as a way of thinking about knowledge and human understanding. These three things mutually reinforce each other and each may be seen as both cause and effect of the others. Innovation is intrinsically connected to the free exchange of goods and services between people, and the phenomenon of entrepreneurship while it is intellectual pluralism and free debate and development of ideas and arguments that are entwined with the phenomenon of critical rationalism. One visible aspect of the interaction of these three elements is capitalism, defined as being a particular way of organising a market economy that appears in the very late eighteenth and early nineteenth century before fully emerging after 1850. Others are modern science and modern political thought, particularly liberalism and egalitarianism but also including some kinds of conservatism.

This interrelated set of phenomena and their results start to appear in the middle to later part of the eighteenth century, in parts of North-Western Europe (particularly, but not exclusively, the British Isles). The two big questions this leads to are why then and why in that place. The key thesis is that this was because of events that had taken place in Europe about one hundred to a hundred and fifty years earlier, or more specifically the way that global processes had taken a particular and distinctive form in Europe at that time.

The argument is that for most of its history Europe is not exceptional or fundamentally different from other parts of the world and is no more dynamic or inventive than other places and civilisations. It is not the centre or dominant part of the world economy and trade system until around 1800 (although its military superiority over other Old World civilisations begins slightly earlier at the end of the seventeenth century). The divergence of Europe from the rest of the world happens because of a nearly global process that arose for contingent reasons (it was the consequence of natural and adventitious phenomena and not inevitable or predestined) in the populous and politically settled parts of the Old World between about 1450 and 1650. This is the series of changes commonly called the 'military revolution'. For purely contingent and accidental reasons it had a different outcome in Europe compared to what it led to elsewhere. This went alongside and interacted with a simultaneous set of intellectual and cultural developments.

This was enormously important, and critical for understanding why modernity first erupted when and where it did. There had been episodes of intensive growth and the other elements of modernity before, in other civilisations. In particular there had been a major one in China, under the Song. However none of these had lasted in the way that the one that began in Europe did. Instead there had always been a reversion to the norm of traditional societies, which included a set of institutions and practices that had evolved as a way of dealing with the Malthusian constraints faced by humanity but which checked and blocked innovation, free thought, and economic entrepreneurialism.

On this occasion the upsurge was not checked and reversed. Instead it burst through the social and political limits in an economic, social, and political explosion – the wealth explosion of the title. One explanation offered by Deirdre McLoskey is that this was due to a cultural change. However the argument made here is that it had to do with actions by the social group that for most of history has had the greatest agency or capacity for action, the ruling classes. These are groups that gain income and resources in the final analysis from their control of the means of organised violence, which they use to extract rents from the productive elements of society. Such groups have an ambivalent relation to innovation and growth but in general throughout history they ultimately act to suppress it or (which amounts to the same thing) allow established institutions and practices to do this. In the context of Europe and the wider world after about 1700 the way that the military revolution had worked out in Europe meant that European ruling classes faced a radically different set of incentives, which led some of them to act in a novel way. Simultaneously, the intellectual developments of the earlier period also suddenly accelerated, with a crucial interaction between that and the economic innovation. Again, the incentives facing European ruling classes meant that some of them were slow to react to this, or did so in half-hearted ways.

What followed was a series of political struggles and conflicts. The outcome was that the explosion of modernity was not contained or confined but allowed to continue and intensify. One result was the appearance of three related but distinct ways of thinking that have dominated public political and social argument ever since. The political conflicts had an insurgent aspect but should not be thought of as being simply an upsurge of formerly subordinate or subaltern groups. That is because, as explained, the traditional ruling classes were themselves innovators in many cases and participated in the explosion – their project (not always successful) was to find a way of exploiting it and guiding it.

The advent of modernity led to problems as well as benefits and has been evaluated in radically different ways by those who have experienced and observed it. Some welcome it (even if with reservations) but there is a consistent tradition of hostile analysis and description that sees it as inhumane and ultimately unsustainable. There was a crisis of modernity in the early part of the twentieth century but this was overcome. Some argue this will prove to be temporary and that ultimately modernity will prove to be only the most dramatic episode of its kind rather than a conclusive break with previous human history. The jury is still out on this.

Given this outline account of the argument of the book and its location in the debates described earlier, it should be clear that while concerned with explaining why modernity happens first in Europe, the history of other parts of the world is of equal importance. In particular the history of China in general and of one period of Chinese history in particular is central.

Further Reading and Bibliographical Essay

The study of global transformations can only be done properly if the world as a whole is made the object of study, rather than a particular part of it, no matter how important or active. This is the subject of the genre of world history. At one time this was a common approach, as with the 'speculative history' of the eighteenth century but it fell from favour with the rise of professional historiography and the focus upon document led research in national archives. The result was the domination of professional historiography by national histories with world history becoming the domain of amateurs or vagrants from other disciplines. Recently however the whole subject has seen a major revival and now forms a recognised part of university curricula and has its own professional journals. So the starting point for any examination of the big questions explored here has to be reading global surveys and the large scale narratives they spell out (metanarratives in the fashionable jargon). A good and short introduction to the field is Pamela Kyle Crossley, *What Is Global History?* (Polity, 2008). Paul Costello, *World Historians and Their Goals: Twentieth-Century Answers to Modernism* (Northern Illinois University Press, 1994) looks at the work of the major exponents of world history before its academic resurgence and sets out their theories and concerns. The revival is described and analysed in Patrick Manning, *Navigating World History: Historians Create a Global Past* (Palgrave Macmillan, 2003).

There are now several extensive survey histories of the world that are used mainly on degree level courses in the United States. Among the best are Richard Bulliet et al, *The Earth and its Peoples: A Global History: Volume I to 1550; Volume II Since 1500* (Wadsworth, 2014), Jerry H. Bentley & Herbert Ziegler, *Traditions and Encounters A Global Perspective on the Past: Vol. I From the Beginning to 1500, Vol. II From 1500 to the Present* (McGraw-Hill, 2014), Robert Tignor et al, *Worlds Together, Worlds Apart: Volume I From the Beginnings to 1500; Volume II 1500 to the Present* (Norton, 2017), Bonnie G. Smith, *Crossroads and Cultures: A History of the World's Peoples: Volume I to 1450; Volume II Since 1300* (St Martins Press, 2012). These can be supplemented by dedicated collections of primary sources such as Alfred J. Andrea, *The Human Record: Sources of Global History* (2 vols.) (Wadsworth, 2011), and Elizabeth Pollard, *Worlds Together, Worlds Apart: A Companion Reader* (2 vols.) (Norton, 2016).

The various arguments among world historians about the origin of Modernity are surveyed in Jonathan Daly, *Historians Debate the Rise of the West* (Routledge, 2015). As that title suggests many world histories take the form of accounts of the 'rise of the West', reflecting the views that it is the West (meaning typically Western Europe and its offshoots) that is the dynamic actor in world history and the source of modernity. A classic and well written example is J. M. Roberts, *The Triumph of the West: The Origin, Rise and Legacy of Western Civilisation* (Phoenix Press, 2001 1st ed. 1985). Another classic example is W. H. McNeill, *The Rise of the West: A History of the Human Community* (Chicago 1992 1st ed. 1963). A contemporary example is Lynn Hunt et al, *The Making of the West: People and Cultures* (2 vols.) (Bedford/St.Martins, 2015). McNeill's views evolved, as he explains in the essays and reviews collected in *Mythistory and Other Essays* (Chicago, 1986) and he has gone on to produce a series of world historical accounts. Some are thematic but several present a view of world history that emphasises interconnections and interactions between various parts of the world, and ecological factors and constraints. These are also major themes in the works by Bentley and Bulliet listed above. Examples of McNeill's more recent work are *The Global Condition: Conquerors, Catastrophes and Community* (Princeton University Press, 1993), *The Human Condition: An Ecological and Historical View* (Princeton University Press, 1980), Robert McNeill & W. H. McNeill, *The Human Web: A Birds-Eye View of World History* (Norton, 2003). An early work that began the process of challenging the 'Eurocentric' view of world history was Marshall G. S. Hodgson, *Rethinking World History: Essays on Europe, Islam, and World History* (Cambridge University Press, 1993). Johan Goudsblom, Eric L. Jones & Stephen Mennell, *The Course of Human History: Economic Growth, Social*

Process and Civilization (M. E. Sharpe, 1996) provides an antidote to ideas of linear progress. A materialistic account of the whole of human history that looks at the same issues as this one is Graeme Donald Snooks, *The Dynamic Society: Exploring the Sources of Global Change* (Routledge, 1996).

Andre Gunder Frank forcefully expresses the sceptical view of the notion that the modern is clearly different from the past in the introduction to *ReOrient: Global Economy in the Asian Age* (University of California Press, 1998). In that chapter he gives a fascinating account of the evolution of his thinking and of how he came to abandon his previous idea that the contemporary world was the product of a 'European World System' that had begun around 1450. His later thesis, that the present day world is merely the latest version of a world system that has been around for five thousand years at least, is expounded in some of the essays in Andre Gunder Frank & B. K. Gills (eds.), *The World System: Five Hundred Years or Five Thousand?* (Routledge, 1993). For Jonathan Clark's sceptical view and the argument that there is no escaping the past, which still determines us in various ways, see J. C. D. Clark, *Our Shadowed Present: Modernism, PostModernism, and History* (Atlantic Books, 2003). For the specific argument that technological innovation and dynamism is not distinctively modern (or at least found in modernity to a greater degree than in other times) see Lynn White, *Medieval Technology and Social Change* (Oxford University Press, 1966), and Frances & Joseph Gies, *Cathedral, Forge, and Waterwheel: Technology and Invention in the Middle Ages* (Harper Perennial, 1995).

The most thought out and theoretical definitions of modernity have come from sociologists and in some sense the very discipline emerged as a way of understanding the new world that became apparent by the middle of the nineteenth century. One classic early example is Ferdinand Toennies *Community and Society* (Dover, 2011; 1st published 1887) while another, contemporary example is Anthony Giddens, *The Consequences of Modernity* (Polity, 2013). For the currently influential notion of 'liquid' or 'late' modernity, see Zygmunt Bauman, *Liquid Modernity* (Polity, 2000).

The institutional approach to explaining the origins of modernity can be found in works such as Douglass C. North & Robert Paul Thomas, *The Rise of the Western World: A New Economic History* (Cambridge University Press, 1973), John A. Hall, *Powers and Liberties: Causes and Consequences of the Rise of the West* (Penguin, 1985), Jean Baechler, *The Origins of Capitalism* (Blackwell, 1976), Nathan Rosenberg & L. E. Birdzell, *How the West Grew Rich: The Economic Transformation of the Industrial World* (Basic Books, 1986), Eric L. Jones, *The European Miracle: Environments, Economies, and Geopolitics in the History of Europe and Asia* (Cambridge University Press, 1981), David Landes, *The Wealth and Poverty of Nations: Why Some Are So Rich and Some So Poor* (Norton, 1999), Harold Berman, *Law and Revolution: The Formation of the Western Legal Tradition* (Harvard University Press, 1983). The role of the company in particular is the subject of John Mickelthwait & Adrian Wooldridge, *The Company: A Short History of A Revolutionary Idea* (Modern Library, 2003).

The argument that explicitly links institutions to innovation is made in Avner Greif, *Institutions and the Path to the Modern Economy: Lessons from Medieval Trade* (Cambridge University Press, 2006) and Avner Greif, Lynne Kiesling & John Nye (eds.), *Institutions, Innovations, and Industrialisation: Essays in Economic History and Development* (Princeton University Press, 2015) and is the central theme of Douglass C. North, *Institutions, Institutional Change, and Economic Performance* (Cambridge University Press, 1990). One particular institution, property rights, takes centre stage in Tom Bethell, *The Noblest Triumph: Property and Prosperity Through the Ages* (St Martins Press, 1998). A book that makes the case of institutions retarding growth in the Islamic world is Timur Kuran, *The Long Divergence: How Islamic Law Held Back the Middle East* (Princeton University Press, 2012). One argument is that even if institutions do not explain why modern growth suddenly appeared they were a necessary condition for that growth, and it is the relative strength or weakness of key institutions that explains the different kinds of fortune enjoyed by different parts of the world in the general context of modernity. This case is powerfully made in Daron Acemoglu & James Robinson, *Why Nations Fail: The Origins of Power, Prosperity and Poverty* (Currency, 2012) and in Timur Kuran & Misahiko Aoki (eds.), *Institutions and Comparative Economic Development* (Palgrave Macmillan, 2012).

The argument that trade and the gains it brings (not always on a mutually beneficial basis to put it mildly) is the motor behind industrialisation and modern growth is the argument of Joseph Inikori, *Africa and the Industrial Revolution in England: A Study in International Trade and Economic Development* (Cambridge University Press, 2002). A classic work is Jacob Viner, *International Trade and Economic Development* (Free Press, 1952). A more recent example is William J. Bernstein, *A Splendid Exchange: How Trade Shaped the World* (Grove Press, 2009) and the same author's *The Birth of Plenty: How the Prosperity of the Modern World Was Created* (McGraw-Hill, 2010). A collection of short pieces that explores the role of trade and argues for its centrality in economic history is Kenneth Pomeranz & Stephen Topik, *The World That Trade Created: Society, Culture, and the World Economy, 1400 to the Present* (Routledge, 2012). As with institutions, the strong evidence that trade and the extent of the market correlates strongly with growth and modernity in the modern world does not mean that this phenomenon therefore caused the modern world to emerge. The problem is how to explain widespread trade and consequent economic effects such as the division of labour for hundreds of years with no discernable effect on growth. For the classic study of how extensive world wide long distance trade was almost eight hundred years ago, see Janet Abu-Lughod, *Before European Hegemony: The World System Ad 1250 to 1350.* (Oxford University Press, 1989).

Many authors have argued for the central role of ideas in the origins of modern growth and modernity. Classic examples are Max Weber & Stephen Kalberg, (translator) *The Protestant Ethic and the Spirit of Capitalism With Other Writings on the Rise of the West* (oxford University Press, 2008), Werner Sombart, *Economic Life in the Modern Age* (Routledge, 2018), and *The Jews and Modern Capitalism* (Transaction, 1982; 1st published 1913). A contemporary case that emphasises the role of Christianity is Rodney Stark, *The Victory of Reason: How Christianity Led to Freedom, Capitalism, and Western Success* (Random House, 2007), and *How the West Won: The Neglected Story of the Triumph of Modernity* (Intercollegiate Studies Institute, 2014). One work that makes the case by explicitly contrasting the West with the Islamic case is Jared Rubin, *Rulers, Religion and Riches: Why the West Got Rich and the Middle East Did Not* (Cambridge University Press, 2017). The precisely contrary case, which locates the origins of capitalism in Islam, is made in Benedikt Koehler, *Early Islam and the Birth of Capitalism* (Lexington, 2015). The most impressive case for a cultural and ideas based explanation for modernity has been advanced recently by Deirdre McCloskey in the series of works *The Bourgeois Virtues: Ethics for an Age of Commerce* (Chicago University Press, 2007), *Bourgeois Dignity: Why Economics Can't Explain the Modern World* (Chicago University Press, 2010), and *Bourgeois Equality: How Ideas, Not Capital or Institutions Enriched the Modern World* (Chicago University Press, 2017). Another impressive example of this approach is Joel Mokyr, *A Culture of Growth: The Origins of the Modern Economy* (Princeton University Press, 2016).

The demographic explanation for European exceptionalism in terms of family structure was put forward in D. V. Glass & D. C. E. Eversley (eds.), *Population in History: Essays in Historical Demography* (Arnold, 1965). The argument that a distinctive kind of marital pattern and household formation was established in the very early part of the Middle Ages as part of a wider set of changes is put in Robert I. Moore, *The First European Revolution, c. 970 to 1215* (Blackwell, 2000). The argument of Julian Simon is found in several of his books but is most clearly put in the posthumous publication *The Great Breakthrough and Its Cause* edited by Timur Kuran (Michigan University press, 2001). Gregory Clark's argument is made in *A Farewell to Alms: A Brief Economic History of the World* (Princeton University Press, 2009). The racial and hereditarian thesis is found in Ricardo Duchesne, *The Uniqueness of Western Civilisation* (Brill Academic, 2012).

The role of climate in history is told in a series of books by Brian Fagan, including *The Little Ice Age: How Climate Made History 1300 to 1850* (Basic Books, 2007), *The Long Summer: How Climate Changed Civilisation* (Basic Books, 2004), *The Great Warming: Climate Change and the Rise and Fall of Civilisations* (Bloomsbury, 2009). J. R. McNeill views the history of the last hundred years through this prism in *Something New Under the Sun: An Environmental History of the Twentieth Century World* (Norton, 2001). The best account of the origins of modernity that gives climate a central place is Robert B. Marks, *The Origins of the Modern World: A Global and Environmental Narrative From the Fifteenth to the Twenty-First Century* (Rowman and Littlefield, 2015). The part played by weather in a key time is the subject of Geoffrey Parker, *Global Crisis: War, Climate Change and Catastrophe in the Seventeenth Century* (Yale University Press, 2013). A well known work that explains both the emergence of settled civilisation in a particular place (the Fertile Crescent) and the advent of modernity in Europe, through geographical and biological factors is Jared Diamond, *Guns, Germs and Steel: The Fates of Human Societies* (Norton, 2005). The role of disease is covered in W. H. Mcneill, *Plagues and Peoples* (Anchor, 1976). It is also still worth reading the classic work of Hans Zinsser, *Rats, Lice and History* (Prelude, 2017; 1ˢᵗ published 1935).

The central place of energy in the history of the world and the modern world in particular is the subject of the outstanding and systematic work of Vaclav Smil, *Energy and Civilisation: A History* (MIT Press, 2017). Ian Morris puts energy capture at the centre of the story in *Why the West Rules-For Now: The Patterns of History and What They Reveal About the Future* (Farrar, Strauss, and Giroux, 2010). This should be read in conjunction with the same author's *The Measure of Civilisation: How Social Development Decides the fate of Nations* (Princeton University Press 2013) which sets out an elaborate index of development with the level of energy capture and use the central ingredient, and *War! What Is It Good For? Conflict and the Progress of Civilisation From Primates to Robots* (Farrar, Strauss, and Giroux, 2014). The latter adds an emphasis on the role of large scale empires as essential to development to the thesis set out in the earlier works. E. A. Wrigley, *Energy and the English Industrial Revolution* (Cambridge University Press, 2010) and *The Path to Sustained Growth: England's Transition from an Organic Economy to an Industrial Revolution* (Cambridge University Press, 2016) are masterful summaries of the argument that it is the release of fossil fuel that has made sustained intensive growth, and with it the rest of modernity, possible.

The question of why Europe was the location for the change rather than other parts of the world is a theme in many of the works cited above, particularly those that emphasise either ideas or institutions. A work that sets this up as a challenge and then tries to respond is Eric Jones, *Growth Recurring: Economic Change in World History* (Clarendon Press, 1988). The argument that Europe was not distinctive in a way that can explain its being the location is made by Frank in *ReOrient* (although this does leave one wondering how the European hegemony of the 1850 to 1950 period actually happened). The idea of periodic eflorescences or bursts of intensive growth that were not sustained is put forward by Jack Goldstone in *Why Europe? The Rise of the West in World History 1500 to 1850: Global Change in a Global Context, 1500 – 1900 AD* (McGraw-Hill, 2008) and "Efflorescences and Economic Growth in World History: Rethinking the 'Rise of the West' and the Industrial Revolution" *Journal of World History*, 13

2002, pp. 323 – 389. He explains the way the efflorescence in Western Europe led to industrialisation and sustained technological innovation through a series of contingent social changes in Britain, in an argument very similar to that made by Joel Mokyr in the work cited above and also *The Enlightened Economy: An Economic History of Britain 1700 to 1850* (Yale University Press, 2012). The other side of this particular story is accounts of exactly what stopped other parts of the world from achieving the same results or continuing their own progress. The works by Rubin and Kuran cited earlier do this for the Islamic world, while Mark Elvin, *The Pattern of the Chinese Past* (Stanford University Press, 1973) is an attempt to do so for China.

The question of the sudden divergence between Europe and other parts of the world that were superior in terms of output and importance to the world economy as late as 1750 or even 1800 (above all China) is the subject of Kenneth Pomeranz, *The Great Divergence: China, Europe and the Making of the Modern World* (Princeton University Press, 2001), Bin Wong, *China Transformed: Historical Change and the Limits of European Experience* (Cornell University Press, 2000), Peer Vries, *State, Economy, and the Great Divergence: Great Britain and China, 1680s to 1850s* (Bloomsbury, 2015), and Prasannan Parthasarathi, *Why Europe Grew Rich and Asia Did Not: Global Economic Divergence 1600 to 1850* (Cambridge University Press, 2011). Angus Maddison makes the case that while China and India were larger than Europe in absolute terms and as a proportion of the world economy until a late date, Europe had overtaken them in output per capita from a much earlier date, maybe even as early as the fourteenth century. This can be found in *Growth and Interaction in the World Economy: The Roots of Modernity* (AEI Press, 2005).

The view that modernity began in Europe but that this happened because while Europe was exceptional the exception came about by virtue of an exploitative relation with the rest of the world is the subject of many works. These typically focus on two things, the nature of the world trade system and the structural relations of dependency and underdevelopment that is supposedly created, and the nature of early European colonialism, above all plantation slavery and the exploitation of the new world. One central example of the latter is J. M. Blaut, *The Colonisers Model of the World: Geographic Diffusionism and Eurocentric History* (Guildford Press, 1993). Blaut attacks the positive accounts of European exceptionalism in *Eight Eurocentric Historians* (Guildford, 2000). It is also worth looking at his article "Where Was Capitalism Born?" in R. Peet (ed.), *Radical Geography,* pp. 95 – 110 (Maasoufa Press, 1977). A more recent and interestingly different version of this thesis is Peter Gran, *The Rise of the Rich: A New View of Modern World History* (Syracuse University Press, 2009)

The idea of an exploitative 'world system' that originated in Europe in the later Middle Ages is most associated with Immanuel Wallerstein and his massive four part work *The Modern World System Volume I: Capitalist Agriculture and the Origins of the European World Economy in the Sixteenth*

Century (University of California Press, 1974; 1ˢᵗ published 1974), *The Modern World System Volume II: Mercantilism and the Consolidation of the European World Economy, 1600 – 1750* (University of California Press, 2011; 1ˢᵗ published 1980), *The Modern World System Volume III: The Second Era of Great Expansion of the Capitalist World Economy 1730s to 1840s* (University of California Press, 2011; 1ˢᵗ published 1989), *The Modern World System Volume IV: Centrist Liberalism Triumphant, 1789 – 1914* (University of California Press, 2011). It is also worth reading Theda Skocpol, "Wallerstein's World Capitalist System: A Theoretical and Historical Critique" *American Journal of Sociology* 82 (1977), pp. 1075 – 1090. The argument against colonial exploitation and the slave trade being central to economic development in Europe is made in Patrick O'Brien, "European Economic Development: the Contribution by the Periphery" *Economic History Review* (second series) 35, 1982, pp. 1 – 18.

The Marxist view of modernity is of course that what we call modernity is the capitalist mode of production that grew out of feudalism. The theory is in practice Eurocentric and Marx and Engels developed the idea of an 'Asiatic' mode of production that applied in the world outside Europe to explain its supposed stagnation. Therefore the distinctive feature of Europe was that capitalism first appeared there. Interestingly, imperial exploitation does not play a major part in this and in fact Marx saw European imperialism as a broadly progressive force, if also a brutal one. The best contemporary example of a classic Marxist approach to explaining the advent of modernity in Europe are the articles by Robert Brenner which can be found with responses in *The Brenner Debate: Agrarian Class Structure and Economic Development in Pre-Industrial Europe* (Cambridge University Press, 1987). An approach that combines Marxism (and indeed classical economics such as that of Smith) with a world systems analysis is the works of Giovanni Arrighi, *The Long Twentieth Century: Money, Power, and the Origins of Our Times* (Verso, 2010) and *Adam Smith in Beijing: Lineages of the Twenty First Century* (Verso, 2009).

The concept of capitalism and the questions of how to define it and how the idea is connected to modernity have become very confused in recent years, with arguments that cut across many other divisions. Broadly, orthodox Marxists and the economists who emphasise the role of institutions tend to make capitalism the central feature of modernity and to locate its origins in the later Middle Ages or Renaissance. (They disagree about its future and how to evaluate it of course). A part of this is the idea that true market relations are a relatively recent development. The classic text for this, from a perspective that regrets this emergence, is Karl Polanyi, *The Great Transformation: The Political and Economic Origins of Our Time* (Beacon Press, 2001; 1ˢᵗ published 1944). The problem is that the point at which these capitalist institutions and forms appear keeps on being pushed further back in time and they keep on turning up outside Europe and the Mediterranean. Markets and exchange appear to be a natural and beneficial feature of human life, for this see Paul Seabright, *The Company of Strangers: A Natural History of Economic Life* (Princeton University Press, 2010). For more examples see John McMillan *Reinventing the Bazaar: A Natural History of Markets* (Norton, 2002), Peter Temin, *The Roman Market Economy* (Princeton University Press, 2010), Christianne Eisenberg, *The Rise of Market Society in England, 1066 – 1800* (Bergahn Books, 2013), and particularly the works of Karl Moore and David Lewis, *The Origins of Globalisation* (Routledge, 2009), *Foundations of Corporate Empire: Is History Repeating Itself?* (Prentice Hall, 2000), and Karl Moore, *Birth of the Multinational: 2000 Years of Ancient Business History – From Asshur to Augustus* (Copenhagen Business School Press, 1999).

Faced with this Andre Gunder Frank argued towards the end of his life that the whole notion of 'capitalism' should be abandoned (along with the counter idea of 'socialism') and that we should in particular give up the idea of a series of stadial 'modes of production'. For this see Andre Gunder Frank "Transitional Ideological Modes: Feudalism, Capitalism, Socialism" *Critique of Anthropology* 11 (1991), pp. 171 – 188 reprinted in Stephen Nugent (ed.), *Critical Anthropology: Foundational Works* (Routledge, 2012). The best book by far on this whole topic is Jack Goody, *Capitalism and Modernity: The Great Debate* (Polity, 2004) which argues that market institutions are widely found in all parts of the world for most of history and that Europe is not particularly unusual or dominant in this respect but in addition that something quite new, which we may call capitalism appears with the industrial revolution (modernity in other words) and for the first time in Europe. Crucially this has short term causes.

The main features of the new kind of economic organisation, which becomes established after 1850 are those defined by Alfred D. Chandler most notably in his trilogy of works *The Visible Hand: The Managerial Revolution in American Business* (Belknap Press, 1977), *Scale and Scope: The Dynamics of Industrial Capitalism* (Belknap Press, 1990), *Strategy and Structure: Chapters in the History of the American Industrial Enterprise* (MIT Press, 1990; 1st published 1962). Another feature is modern finance and for this see Carlota Perez, *Technological Revolutions and Financial Capital: The Dynamics of Bubbles and Golden Ages* (Edward Elgar, 2002) which looks at both theory and history, and William N. Goetzmann & K. Geert Rouwenhorst (eds.), *The Origins of Value: The Innovations That Created Modern Capital Markets* (Oxford University Press, 2005). Even here though it is continuity that is more impressive – see also William N. Goetzmann. *Money Changes Everything: How Finance Made Civilisation Possible* (Princeton University Press, 2016).

The cultural way of thinking about capitalism is of course the subject of the works by Weber, Sombart, and McCloskey cited earlier (although their evaluations are very different). Another of Sombart's works was *The Quintessence of Capitalism: A Study of the History and Psychology of the Modern Business Man* (Dutton, 1915 reprinted 2013). One author who has developed this kind of argument extensively is Alan Macfarlane – see *The Invention of the Modern World* (Odd Volumes, 2014), *The Liberty of the Modern World: Of Liberty, Wealth, and Equality* (Palgrave Macmillan, 2000), *The Making of the Modern World: Visions from East and West* (Palgrave Macmillan, 2002), and *The Culture of Capitalism* (Blackwell, 1987).

The best way of dividing the various authors who have participated in these debates is by using two issues. The first is European exceptionalism versus globalism – the first side think that Europe is the dynamic force in history for most of world history and had some quality that set it apart from other civilisations for a long time while the globalists deny that and say that any change is comparatively recent. The second is that of how to evaluate markets and capitalism – one group see it as a beneficial force that has brought the benefits of modernity while the second see market relations as exploitative, and their spread as either a disaster or at best a transitional phase to something better. Combining these produces four groups. The first are people who support markets and believe in European exceptionalism: this includes people such as Jones, Landes, Macfarlane, Stark, North, and Gregory Clark. The second are those who regard Europe as having been exceptional for a considerable time but are sceptical of markets: this includes people such as Wallerstein, Arrighi, Marx, and Brenner. Thirdly are authors who combine scepticism about markets with a globalist approach and denial of European exceptionalism, at least before around 1800. These include Frank, Blaut, and Goody. The final group are those who are globalists in the same way but have a broadly positive take on markets and regard them as the source of most of the benefits of modernity: this list includes McCloskey, Goldstone, Pomeranz, and myself.

CHAPTER III

Song China and the Ming Restoration

AS we have already seen China and its history are of particular interest when thinking about the issues described in the previous chapter. That is because if we look at the appearance of the modern from a global or world history perspective rather than simply looking at the history and development of Europe and its offshoots, it is China that poses the greatest puzzle. The work of contemporary economic historians such as Angus Madison, Kenneth Pomeranz and others clearly shows that China was the most economically developed part of the world and the hub or centre of the global trade system for most of recorded history, at least until the later eighteenth century or even later (according to Pomeranz). Even more significantly, the work of Joseph Needham and his students demonstrates that China was more technologically advanced than other parts of the world until the seventeenth century and on an equal footing in that regard until the later eighteenth century. This reflected an even more significant reality. Although systematic innovation was limited and hampered in all pre-modern societies and civilisations, this was less true in China than elsewhere for a very long time. The list of major innovations and inventions that were first made in China is a very long one and includes such things as paper, porcelain, gunpowder, the blast furnace, the wheelbarrow, and a civil service recruited on something like merit. China's lead in this respect lasted until the fourteenth century but it then ceased.

The Song Dynasty and its Policy

The thing that most clearly distinguishes China from the other great civilisations is that for most of its history it has been united into a single empire. There have been periods when it seemed as though it would break up but the centripetal forces have always eventually triumphed. In the later years of the Tang dynasty in the eighth century, power passed increasingly to provincial military governors.

Following the end of the dynasty in 907, the empire broke up into fifteen separate states, ten of which were under Chinese rule. (The other five were under the rule of non-Han Chinese populations). At this point it looked as though China was going the same way as Europe, India and the Middle East at the same time, in the direction of political division and fragmentation, particularly as the so-called 'ten kingdoms' were natural geographical and demographic units. However, after 960 the Song Taizu (960 – 976) and Song Taizong (976 – 997) emperors reunited China and established the Song dynasty, which ruled all of China until 1127 and the more populous southern part until 1279. Taizu and Taizong established a series of policies which were broadly followed throughout the Song period and which were very different from those pursued under both previous and later dynasties. Whether those policies were the result of intellectual conviction or expediency is impossible to say but there is no doubt about the result.

The main elements of Song policy and governance were these. First and foremost they established constitutional, rule bound government and moved away from the absolute and often arbitrary imperial rule that had been the practice under the Tang and the Han. The organisation of the government was significantly changed with the creation of a council of ministers, which acted as both a deliberative policy making, and administrative body and was headed by a Prime Minister. The whole system of administration was reformed and in particular the bureaucracy was made much more meritocratic. There was a major reform of the law of land ownership, which gave peasant farmers full ownership rights to their lands including the crucial one of alienation. In marked contrast to earlier practice there was deliberate encouragement of trade and commerce, as the government came to be increasingly dependent upon taxes on trade rather than agriculture. One important aspect of this was the effective abolition of the distinction between 'tribute' and 'private' trade, of which more later. Another was a shift from taxes in kind, in the form of labour services, to ones paid in money. Internal controls on the Chinese population were relaxed, particularly with respect to movement.

The Economic Revolution of Song China

The outcome was a dramatic episode of modern style intensive growth and social transformation, the most significant such 'efflorescence' before the one that was finally sustained in eighteenth and nineteenth century Europe. The more we learn about the economy of Song China, the more impressive it appears. By the twelfth century it was clearly monetised to a degree that had no equivalent anywhere else at the time. The main circulating medium was copper coins or 'cash', which were conventionally counted in thousands or 'strings'. In just one, typical, year (1085) the state minted no fewer than six million strings of cash, amounting to six billion actual coins. In contrast in 997 the total number of coins minted had been eight hundred million so the quantity of coins minted per year had gone up more than sevenfold in eighty-eight years. (Also, this huge increase in circulating medium was not accompanied by inflation so it must have been matched by an increase in production). (Jones, 1988) By the later years of the dynasty the annual output of copper cash was twenty times its maximum level under the Tang. Another sign of the thorough monetisation of the economy was the shift in the nature of taxation. Under the later Tang about forty per cent of taxes were paid in money whereas by the twelfth century ninety-five per cent of all taxes were paid this way. In 1120 alone no less than eighteen million ounces of silver were collected in taxes. Paper money, which had been introduced under the Tang as an administrative device, became widely used following the reign of Song Renzong (1022-1063) and by the end of the dynasty the total value of the paper money printed every year was equivalent to seventy million strings of cash. The paper money was produced in four government owned factories, the largest of which (in Hangzhou) employed over a thousand people.

The monetisation of the economy was part of a general move away from a subsistence economy to one based on markets and exchange. Production of most goods became 'commodified' as we would now say. Moreover, one aspect of the general line of policy under the Song was for a movement away from government control and in the direction of a more market driven economy and society. At least initially, this was not driven by any kind of analysis but was rather a response to reality, in particular the way that the actual development of economic life and relations in China at this time undermined power and control. The interesting thing is that the response of the Song elite was to go along with this process rather than to resist it or try to reverse it. The result of this policy of ad hoc and pragmatic adjustment was a kind of mixed economy, predominantly market based but with a significant role for government. One part of this, which seems strange to the modern observer, was to have the same industry run as a state monopoly in some provinces, as a private enterprise but under a government license in others, and as a private enterprise with free entry in the rest. At one point a number of sectors, particularly wine, tea, and salt were taken out of the private sector and made into government monopolies throughout China. This was very controversial however and was reversed after a while. Along with the move towards money and markets, at every level and in every part of Chinese society, was a dramatic increase in output and economic activity of all kinds.

The most significant part of this was the transformation of agriculture. Here output more than doubled over the period from 960 to 1260. At the same time, there was an increase in the variety of crops being cultivated, and of the kinds of livestock being kept. The many surviving restaurant menus from this period show this, with a varied cuisine, including items that were not widely available before the Song. The increase in output was partly due to the introduction of new crop varieties, especially new kinds of rice imported from Annam, which allowed for two crops a year as opposed to just one. It also derived from improvements in technique such as the wider use of terracing and the adoption of wet cultivation as well as more use of rotation.

A critical element in addition was a gradual change in the organisation of this vital sector. The reforms to land tenure introduced by Taizu and Taizong had given peasants full property rights in their land, including the right of sale. As time passed many took advantage of this and the consequence was that peasant smallholdings were increasingly consolidated into large commercial farms and estates, which were much more productively efficient and innovative. Along with greater commercialism in agriculture went specialisation as regions and localities came to specialise in producing cash crops such as sugar cane, thanks to the economic integration produced by expanded trade. Many of the peasants who sold their land became landless labourers but many others went into the rapidly growing manufacturing sector. Here they produced goods such as paper, charcoal, silk, textiles, machinery, and a wide range of domestic products such as nails, pans, needles, and a whole range of metal products for everyday use.

It is the growth and scale of manufacturing in Song China that is most impressive to the modern observer. Much of this was dispersed around the countryside in small to medium sized workshops, often attached to households that had partly or totally moved out of agriculture. (This pattern of manufacturing, sometimes referred to as 'protoindustrialism', was to be found in many parts of the world in subsequent centuries, not least in Europe.) So for example, as early as 1078 China produced on average no less than one hundred and twenty-seven thousand tonnes of iron per year, a level that would not be reached anywhere else in the world until later eighteenth century Britain. This industry alone consumed the equivalent of seventy per cent of the total amount of coal used by all metal industry in eighteenth century Britain. At that time in just one district of the Xuzhou province there were thirty-six iron foundries, run by families and each employing several hundred people. (Hartwell, 1966 & Wagner, 2001) Originally iron was produced using charcoal but in the eleventh century there was a move to coal. Coal was mined on a large scale and used in a number of industries in addition to iron and steel. The figures for other manufacturing industries such as porcelain and textiles are just as striking.

There was also a huge growth in trade, both internal and external. Internally the Song government greatly expanded the system of internal navigation via rivers and canals, especially the 'Grand Canal' (actually a network of canals) that linked the Yellow River and the Yangtze. This, along with the lifting of controls on movement, created an integrated market, the largest in the world at that time both geographically and in terms of its population. The canal system was made much more efficient by the tenth century invention of the pound lock. Interestingly the polymath and scientist Shen Kuo (1031 – 1095) discussed this and calculated that its introduction at just one point on the system in the later eleventh century had saved one and quarter million strings of cash annually through removing the need for five hundred labourers. These figures give some idea of both the volume and value of the internal trade and the level of wages. He also said that at the time he was writing (about the 1080s) government owned boats could carry cargoes of up to forty-nine and a half tons while private ones could carry up to one hundred and thirteen tons. Given the thousands of boats plying the rivers and canals at any one moment, this again gives some idea of the volume of trade.

This internal trade therefore brought about a much greater level of economic integration within China, massively expanding the size and extent of the market and leading to a sharp rise in specialisation and consequently in output. Above all, it integrated the interior provinces and the coastal ones. The latter also saw a remarkable growth of external trade in the shape of both imports and exports. Traditionally the Chinese state had sought to limit and regulate trade between its subjects and outsiders through the system of 'tribute trade' in which trade with foreigners was conducted under government license and was portrayed not as an exchange but as the payment of tribute to the emperor by foreign powers. In practice, there was a great deal of private trade but this always had a semi-illegal status. This was swept away under the Song and Chinese merchants became actively involved in direct import and export trade.

The greater part of this trade was maritime. One of Song China's most remarkable achievements was its fleets, both mercantile and naval. These were of a size and sophistication well beyond anything found anywhere else in the world for several hundred years. Under the Song Chinese merchants built thousands of sea-going junks, the overwhelming majority privately owned. We know from both archaeological evidence and contemporaneous accounts that these made use of several innovations in maritime technology such as stern rudders, the compass, and watertight bulkheads to divide the hull. The thirteenth century Muslim traveller Ibn Battuta stated that these ships could have a crew of up to a thousand men and be well over a hundred feet in length. Chinese merchants travelled all over the Indian Ocean, trading with India, East Africa, and the Middle East. We can tell from the evidence of urban life that they imported a wide range of goods including foodstuffs, livestock and textiles while exporting a whole range of Chinese products, above all silk and porcelain and metalware.

Was Song China Close to Being a 'Modern Economy'?

Faced with this kind of evidence, a number of historians have argued that Song China was in fact the world's first 'modern' economy and society and that had it continued we would now be speaking of the transition to modernity in the fourteenth century rather than the nineteenth. Certainly, by a number of measures Song China was as developed as mid eighteenth century Europe. Not only that but it displayed several of the distinctive features of modernity outlined in the first chapter, and the direction of development seemed to be for these 'modern' features to become more marked rather than less. What though were the modern aspects of China under the Song that have so caught the imagination of subsequent authors?

In the first place, Song China had rapid, even 'explosive' population growth. World population as a whole grew throughout the medieval warm period but the growth in China was much more rapid than that found elsewhere. By 1190, China's population had reached at least seventy three million: seventy years later it had arrived at the hundred million mark. China's population more than doubled between 960 and 1100. (It had remained stable at roughly fifty million for the previous six hundred years.) As a contrast, world population grew from about two hundred and fifty million to three hundred and thirty million between 960 and the later thirteenth century, an increase of thirty-two per cent. As in the contemporary modern world this process of population growth, which took place throughout the Song dynasty, accelerated as time went on and the rate of increase seems to have been at its most rapid during the last years of the dynasty, in the thirteenth century.

Moreover, this rise in population was exceeded by the rise in output of both agriculture and manufacture, both of which showed again a rising rate of productivity increase as the years went by. So for example, the level of iron output in 1078 mentioned earlier represented a six-fold increase from 806, in the last years of the Tang. In Shanxi in the 1040s annual production of iron amounted to some sixty tonnes per annum but by the 1110s this had risen to three hundred and sixty tonnes per year. This means that what we have in Song China, from at least the eleventh century, is modern style intensive growth, in contrast to the pattern of broadly extensive growth found elsewhere.

This went along with a 'commercial revolution' every bit as dramatic as that of eighteenth and nineteenth century Europe. By 1200, all of the institutions of the kind of market economy found in Europe in 1800 were already present in China. These included large firms and partnerships with tradable stock and a whole range of sophisticated financial and banking institutions and instruments. The Song economy had a wide range of forms and varieties of business venture from large government monopolies to major private firms, often organised into confederations, and an enormous range of small private businesses engaged in all kinds of productive activity, including an expanding range of services for the urban population of the empire. Much of the production was decentralised and performed in households or small workshops with the goods being sold to professional middlemen or brokers who in turn sold the products to merchants who distributed and sold them using the dense internal trade network or exported them in exchange for foreign products.

Perhaps most significantly, the changes in agriculture made possible by the legal reforms of Song Taizu meant that there was a clear movement of population from the countryside to the cities and of labour from agriculture to manufacturing. Our best estimate is that by the later twelfth century, between six and seven and a half per cent of the population of Song China lived in cities with a population of over one hundred thousand with a similar proportion living in smaller urban centres, which would make it clearly the most urbanised society on the planet at that time. The capital before 1127, Kaifeng, had a population of over a million, as did Hangzhou, which became the capital after that year. What is really striking is the <u>rate</u> of urbanisation. Kaifeng grew from half a million in 1021 to over a million by 1100. Hangzhou went from four hundred thousand inhabitants in late twelfth century to over a million by 1270. Moreover, urbanisation on this scale was not just a feature of the capital. Guangzhou, China's major seaport at this time reached a population of half a million by 1120 and the inland city of Jiankang had a population of two hundred thousand at the same time.

In contrast to the cities of Tang China, which had been mainly centres of administration, these were primarily commercial centres, even if they also housed the imperial court. In contrast to the Tang period when there were a limited number of strictly regulated markets, Song cities had markets and retail establishments on all of their main streets as well as huge commercial markets, which were only lightly regulated. There were also large covered entertainment complexes known as pleasure grounds where games and entertainments would be available until the early hours of the morning. One prominent feature of urban life under the Song was clubs and associations of all kinds. Patricia Ebrey for example cites a document of 1235 that mentions the West Lake Poetry Club, the Buddhist Tea Society, the Physical Fitness Club, the Anglers' Club, the Occult Club, the Plants and Fruits Club, the Antique Collectors' Club, the Horse-Lovers' Club, and the Refined Music Society – all of these in Hangzhou.

Song China also saw the most rapid and sustained technological innovation anywhere in the world before the later eighteenth century. As well as the innovations already mentioned in maritime technology the period saw the invention of the dry dock for repairing ships and of paddle powered vessels for use as tugs or in warfare. Block printing was invented in the eleventh century and movable type printing in the thirteenth – in this case borrowed from the Koreans. There were important refinements and inventions in the area of mechanical devices, particularly the use of belt drives and complex toothed gears. One important element of technological progress in China at this time, in marked contrast to other periods, was openness to and adoption of innovations made elsewhere. As well as the examples of movable type, and the superior varieties of rice imported from Annam, the most dramatic case was that of the windmill, invented in the Middle East and then adopted by the Chinese in the early thirteenth century. Notably, the Chinese did not simply take up the Middle Eastern technology but adapted and improved it.

Perhaps most striking was the increasing use of complex machinery in textile manufacturing. As early as the twelfth century devices were invented for the mechanical spinning of silk, which could be powered by men, animals or waterwheels. The text describing this machine stated that with its thirty-two spindles it could spin about sixty kilos of thread per day. It was very similar in design to the water frame of Richard Arkwright, which plays such a prominent part in most accounts of the Industrial Revolution. The missing ingredient was rollers to draw out the thread as it was being spun but this kind of device was known to the Chinese at the time in the form of the cotton gin, for removing seeds from raw cotton. So far as we know cotton spinning was never mechanised in this way, but its use as a fabric only became common at the end of the Song period.

Alongside technological innovation were intimations of scientific investigation. The key figures here were polymaths, similar to Renaissance figures such as Leonardo, who combined empirical experimentation and investigation with scientific speculation, typically in a wide range of fields and areas of knowledge. The most famous was Shen Kuo (1031-1095) who published much of his ideas and findings in a collection of essays known as the *Dream Pool Jottings*, covering topics as diverse as mathematics, geology, economics, medicine, and engineering. As this shows, Song China saw investigation and discovery in a range of areas of knowledge, the most notable being mathematics, astronomy, metallurgy, medicine (including forensic medicine), and optics (where there seems to have been borrowing from the Arabs).

This was linked to important developments in philosophy and abstract thought. The key here was the ideas of Neo-Confucian philosophers, above all Chu-Hsi (1130 – 1200). He argued that an essential part of the process of self-perfection (a key idea in Confucianism) was the investigation of 'material things', that is empirical enquiry. What we can see here are early intimations of the idea of scientific method, which were as well developed in thirteenth century China as they would be in seventeenth century Europe. As in Europe some four to five hundred years later, there was a mixture of philosophical speculation, magic, empirical investigation, and practical (often commercial) endeavour all mixed together into a single intellectual and physical exercise.

There were also distinctively 'modern' developments in the structure of government and in social structure and hierarchy. The change here was a very clear movement from a hereditary elite to a more meritocratic one. Reforms to the examination system by which government officials were recruited made the process much more open and significantly increased the size of the pool of applicants. By the later years of the dynasty in the early thirteenth century, the number of candidates taking the exams was eleven times what it had been in the early eleventh century and the number who passed was five times what it had been under the Tang. However, the number of government posts hardly increased at all. The result was the appearance of a class of degree holders who formed the local elite, but were not actual holders of government office. Their Confucian training led them to see themselves as moral leaders of society through the force of example as much as administration. The reforms to the system also meant that it was now rare for the status of being a degree holder to persist in the one family for more than three generations. Despite the way in which educated Confucians tended to look down on soldiers and merchants both commerce and the military also provided routes for upward social mobility. The result of all this was to make society much more socially mobile and to make status increasingly non-heritable, as well as increasing income (as opposed to status) inequality.

The government of Song China was, like that of earlier dynasties, organised on a departmental basis. The main innovation, already mentioned, was the creation of a council of ministers with a deliberative as well as an administrative role and a Prime Minister (the actual title was First Privy Councillor) who headed the administration. The most famous holder of this office was Wang An Shih (1021-1086) who began a major series of reforms between 1069 and 1074. These reforms proved very divisive and led to the appearance of two factions, one known as the New Policies Group that supported them and another, led by another scholar-politician Sima Guang (1019-`1086) that opposed them. This division persisted throughout the remainder of the dynasty's history and so a form of elite party politics came into being, based on this division between reformers and conservatives, which reflected intellectual debates within Confucianism. Song government had a distinctly modern flavour, as it was not household or clan based and operated through a professional bureaucracy. Among its particularly modern elements were several agencies to monitor and assess public opinion, each one using a different method of doing this.

Why Did the Song 'Modernisation' Not Continue?

Given all this, Song China poses a huge problem for historians. Quite simply the question is that of why this modernisation, if that is what it was, did not continue. Why did the world have to wait another seven hundred years before a successful breakthrough into modernity and 'sudden modern progress'? The point is that in the key areas of economy, government, social structure, and intellectual life and scientific investigation Song China was as close to modernity as eighteenth century Europe. However, it fell short in critical ways or the process that had produced these did not continue so they did not develop further in the way that they were to some five hundred years later. There are a number of possible answers to this conundrum, several of which are not mutually exclusive, that is they may all be at least partly correct.

The most straightforward is to deny that Song China was in fact moving towards modernity in any meaningful way. In this view, China at this time was only the most striking example of pre-modern style extensive growth and what historians have done is to overemphasise the apparently 'modern' aspects of Chinese society at this time while downplaying the persistence of the traditional. The problem with this view is simply that the evidence for Song China's moving towards the kind of modernisation later found in eighteenth and nineteenth century Europe is so strong. Things such as the degree of urbanisation, the movement of labour out of agriculture, the monetisation of the economy and the level of technological innovation were central features of Song society and economy. In addition the evidence suggests that in some areas at least the trends were for the modern aspects of Song society to become more marked, that is for the rate of change in that direction to accelerate.

One possible explanation is that in some way the 'time was not ripe', that is that some kinds of necessary preconditions for a breakthrough to modernity did not exist at that time. In that case the near modernity of Song China was something that could not be sustained and was bound to peter out, it was simply not possible to have a breakthrough to modernity at that time. It may be that something about the world economy as a whole was not ready to support a breakthrough in one part of it. For example, it may be that the global economy and trade system were not sufficiently developed or that population levels both inside and outside China had not yet reached a level that would sustain a 'modern' economy. Alternatively it could be that China had itself not reached a level of development that would sustain the kind of growth and change seen under the Song over a longer time. The first makes sense only if we think that one of the various features of modernity identified in the first chapter, such as population or the level of economic integration, is exogenous, that is independent of the others and the one that ultimately makes the others possible. The other is weaker, because China by the 1260s had most of the features found in Europe in the 1760s, including the ones that historians identify as being crucial for the subsequent rapid transformation. So, if Europe continued to develop at that time, then why did China not continue to after the thirteenth century?

The other kinds of explanation all start by asserting that there was no inherent reason why modernisation could not have continued in China at this time. This means that some factor or combination of factors stopped it. This does not necessarily mean that a continuation of the process of development found in Song China to full blown modernisation was the natural or default course of events (in which case we would be talking about some factor that diverted an otherwise inevitable process). It is much more likely that a continuation of the process was one possibility among several but for some reason it was not the possibility that was realised.

At this point it is important to spell out the implications of this argument. It means that there was also nothing inevitable or automatic about the breakthrough to modern progress that did actually take place after 1750 since it must also have been only one among several possible trajectories. It also implies that there could have been other moments when a breakthrough of this kind was possible but was not realised. If this is true then the question becomes that of why one possible outcome, that of modern progress, did not happen at least once and maybe more often, but did certainly happen on one occasion. What were the kinds of factors that led to other historical trajectories being followed on these earlier occasions, and why did this not apply in Europe after 1760?

There are a whole variety of explanations of this kind on offer to explain the case of China after the thirteenth century. These can be grouped together however under four main heads. One set of arguments highlights the role of ideology and beliefs, in this case the ideas of Confucianism, and argues that these inhibited certain developments in areas such as government, economic and social organisation, and technological or scientific innovation. Another set emphasises contingent factors, above all that of access to energy. The main argument here is that difficulties in obtaining access to fuels of various kinds meant that it was not possible to mechanise agriculture, which was a necessary condition for the kinds of developments seen in Song China to continue. One very influential thesis is the one first put by Mark Elvin, that China developed what he terms a 'high equilibrium trap', that is it arrived at a form of social and economic organisation, above all in agriculture, where there was no need or strong incentive for further innovation. Yet others, such as Janet Abu-Lughod, stress the impact of events outside of China itself, in particular the worldwide slump in trade and economic activity from the mid-fourteenth century onwards.

All of these kinds of explanation have attractions. However, the argument with the greatest traction is another one that emphasises the part played by the conscious decisions of political actors, in this case the Chinese ruling elite, and the way these derived from a profound structural conflict within all human societies since the appearance of agriculture between what we may call the economic and social relations on the one side and the power based relations on the other. As argued in the first chapter, there is a fundamental division in all traditional societies (and indeed in modern ones) between groups who gain resources through production or trade, and others who get resources through predation of various kinds. At the same time there is a division in everyday life and social interaction between relations that are consensual and those that involve power and its correlates, domination and submission. Moreover, there is a tension between actions that are innovative or encourage innovation, and other actions and institutions that inhibit innovation and uphold the settled way of doing things. This is found both at the level of social interaction in general, and also in relations between the productive and exploitative classes. From this perspective, what happened in China at the end of the Middle Ages was the classic example of how this kind of tension worked itself out in a way that foreclosed the possibility of continued intellectual, social and economic development. This was partly a matter of conscious policy on the part of the political elites and partly a more widespread social reaction against the dynamism and increasing social change and complexity of the late Song period. How and why did this happen?

Invasions and Conquest

As mentioned before, the scope and size of the Song state did not expand in line with the growth in China's population and economy and the reaction of the elite to social and economic change was to go along with it rather than to resist it. We may say therefore that the state was relatively weaker under the Song than under earlier dynasties. What though of the primary function of all governments before the late nineteenth century, i.e. organised violence or, in a word, war? In Song China, as in most pre-modern societies, military spending consumed about ninety percent of the budget. Despite this, the traditional Chinese view of the Song emphasises their military weakness. One undoubted problem they faced was a lack of horses due to the loss of Northwestern pasturelands after the fall of the Tang, which were never recovered. The response to the lack of cavalry was to rely upon a large infantry force, which may have numbered as many as a million men by the early twelfth century.

There was also a clear shift away from the military system of the Tang dynasty, the so-called fubing system. In this, the bulk of the military consisted of part-time soldier farmers who were grouped into regional commands and called up when needed, while being supplemented by a central body of professionals. Under the Song, this system gradually stopped working and the number of professionals grew ever larger. This meant that Song army consisted primarily of paid professionals, recruited from the lower classes of society for the most part. The need to pay large numbers of soldiers money wages, as well as their requirements for housing and supply of necessities and equipment explains why this military was so expensive and also the pressing need of the Song government for cash revenue. The Song also relied increasingly on equipment such as heavy armour, crossbows and early gunpowder weapons to counter the cavalry threats from the states beyond the Great Wall. Interestingly, they also made great use of drill and coordination in a way that foreshadowed later innovations in seventeenth century Europe.

Despite the size of this military and its cost most think it was ineffective. The main evidence for this is the Song state's policy of buying off threats from the states to their North or using diplomacy to play one off against another, rather than engaging in open warfare. However, this may simply have reflected pragmatism and cost-benefit analysis rather than military weakness. What is not in doubt though is that in 1125 – 1126 there was a major military disaster. In those years a sudden incursion by the Jurchen, a people who controlled present day Manchuria, led to the capture of Kaifeng and the loss of the Northern half of China – and this came after the Jurchen had been encouraged and paid by the Song to attack another of the states bordering China to the North, the Liao. The Jurchen went on to rule North China, together with their homeland in Manchuria, as the Jin dynasty.

Meanwhile the Song state was rescued and stabilised by one of the dynasty's most remarkable rulers, Song Gaozong (1127-1162), who established the new capital at Hangzhou. Under the Southern Song, the pro-commerce policy of the dynasty was if anything intensified. There was also a major innovation in military policy. While continuing with a professional infantry based army, the Song state came to rely increasingly on naval power and for the first time in its history China came to have a permanent and very large naval establishment. The fleet was intended to protect against invasion from the North by holding the line of the Yangtze and to control the waters of the East and South China Seas in order to protect and support the trading enterprises of the empire's subjects, as well as projecting Chinese power in the lands around these waters.

In 1161, despite being outnumbered by a factor of almost five to one, they were able to defeat an attempted invasion by the Jin at the battles of Tangdao and Caishi. One of the reasons for the success of the Song fleet was its use of technological innovations, especially the use of paddlewheel powered ships for attack in river and coastal waters, and the employment of ship-mounted catapults to hurl gunpowder and incendiary bombs. By the 1230s the fleet had grown in size and now had up to fifty-two thousand marines as well as sailors. Song China was thus one of the most important examples of a recurring phenomenon, that of a predominantly mercantile and commercial power that depends primarily upon naval power rather than a land army.

However, the Song and indeed the other settled civilisations of Eurasia were about to be confronted with one of their greatest challenges. Throughout the history of Eurasia there had been constant challenges to the settled civilisations from the nomads of the Central Asian steppes. Formidable warriors and masters of horse warfare they were typically more than a match for the sedentary populations of the old world. However the nomads were also fragmented, with a clan based society, and only rarely united in large numbers under a single leader. However at some point around 1162 the greatest of those leaders was born, a man who had as much of an impact on history as anyone. His name was Temujin but he is best known by the title he took in 1206, Ghengis Khan. Born into difficult circumstances he united all of the Mongol tribes into a single confederation by a combination of military genius and charismatic leadership. More importantly he created a system of military and political organisation that meant his achievements outlived him while his agenda, of creating a universal empire, was carried on by his sons and grandsons.

Once Genghis Khan had unified the Mongols by 1206, his next move was to attack the Jin Empire – an enterprise in which he received assistance from the Song. The Jin Empire was shattered by a series of campaigns between 1205 and 1211. Following this, the Mongols went on to conquer the Khwarezmian Empire and with it a huge part of the Islamic world. By the time Ghengis Khan died in 1227 he ruled an empire that stretched from the Arctic Circle to the Indian Ocean, and from Eastern Europe to Korea. His sons carried on his mission and in 1236 – 41 conquered Russia and were poised to sweep into Western Europe. At that point Ghengis Khan's successor, Ogedai died and the Mongol armies went back to Karakorum to elect a new Great Khan. They never came back.

Instead the Mongols turned their attention to the Middle East, with Hulagu Khan storming and sacking Baghdad in 1258. The great prize however was China and the Mongols made repeated attempts to conquer Song China, particularly after the accession of the third of the Great Khans, Mongke. (1251 – 1259) However, the Song navy was able to hold the line of the Yangtze and the army was able to resist repeated invasions from both the North, and the Southwest via Szechuan and Yunnan. For a while after Mongke's death in 1259 and the ensuing succession dispute, they were able to take the offensive and push the Mongols back. By 1265 however, the Mongol power was firmly under the control of the last of the Great Khans, Khubilai (1260 – 1294). He also had one of the great generals of history in Bayan (1236 – 1295) who took command of the assault on China, and in a series of brilliant campaigns did what nobody had been able to do before and conquered Song China. After a series of victories on the Yangtze, including the defeat of the fleet at Nanjing, he defeated the main Chinese army in 1275. The following year Hangzhou surrendered and three years later in 1279, the last Song forces were defeated off the Southern coast in the battle of Yamen.

The Impact of the Mongol Conquest

The Mongol conquest was one of the greatest disasters in Chinese history. We might say from our perspective that initially the effects of the conquest were not too severe, at least in material terms. Kublai Khan was not interested in laying waste to his new domain but rather to draw revenue from it. Hangzhou and the other major cities were spared the horrors of the sack and the policies of the Song were continued. One aspect of this was the continued use of naval power, used for unsuccessful attempts to invade Japan in 1274 and 1281 and to attack Java in 1284. When Marco Polo and Ibn Battuta visited Hangzhou, both of them saw a city every bit as prosperous as it had been under the Song.

In Northern China however, things were not so comfortable. Here the Mongols depopulated large areas and displayed a persistent animus against settled civilisation. Moreover, after about 1320 things fell apart. In 1323, a terrible epidemic broke out in Hubei province before spreading to at least eight other provinces of China. According to some later estimates, it may have killed as much as ninety percent of the population in Hubei and up to forty per cent of the population elsewhere. Almost certainly this was the first major episode of the disease that would go on to ravage Europe in 1348-1353 under the name of the Black Death. A second wave of the epidemic swept through China in the 1350s and by the end of that decade China's population had fallen back to pre-Song levels.

Khubilai Khan's successors proved incompetent and after a civil war over the succession in the 1320s, the central authority progressively disintegrated. Banditry and warlordism became rife. Furthermore, the economy went into a slump, brought on partly by the increasing rapacity of the Mongol rulers but also by a worldwide economic decline that took place in those years – for the disasters that befell China were part of a worldwide catastrophe. Meanwhile, misuse of the institution of paper money led to inflation in the middle of economic slowdown – an early case of 'stagflation'. Even so, these physical disasters and the increasingly predatory and incompetent Mongol rule had less significance in the long term than the psychological impact of the Mongol conquest. This was an enormous psychological blow, as it was the first time in their history that the Chinese had been conquered by and subject to foreign 'barbarians'. The result was to discredit the Song and their policies, which became associated thereafter with weakness, humiliation and defeat, and also in the minds of many commentators with social disorder and corruption.

In the final years of the Mongol or Yuan dynasty China was fought over by several factions including the remnants of the Mongol regime itself. Several of the actors in these struggles were peasant movements led and organised by secret societies or tongs. One of these, the Red Turbans, attracted a young man of humble origins called Zhu Zhuanchang. (1328 – 1398) After joining them in 1352, he soon became the movement's leader and proved to be a very capable general. In 1356, he captured Nanjing, which then became the base for a series of campaigns that extended his control over South China. In 1363, he defeated his major Han Chinese rivals at the battle of Lake Poyang. He went on to defeat the Mongols and in 1368 he proclaimed himself emperor, taking the regnal name of Ming Hongwu and so founding the Ming dynasty, which would rule China until 1644.

The Policy of the Early Ming Emperors

The Hongwu emperor, who ruled from 1368 to 1398, faced enormous challenges, made worse in some ways by his own character. He was public spirited and devoted to his role as emperor yet also fearful and suspicious, completely untrusting and often savagely vindictive and vengeful. Above all, he was profoundly conservative and deeply opposed to the commercialised and open society that had grown up under the Song and which survived, albeit severely damaged, after the near hundred years of Mongol rule. He inherited a realm where public order either was under severe strain or had broken down, where the population as recorded in the official census had collapsed dramatically from where it had been under the Song, and where economic activity was entering a prolonged period of decline, and which still faced considerable military challenges. In some ways, this was similar to the situation that had faced Song Taizu in 960 but the Hongwu emperor's response was very different.

The policy of the early Ming emperors can be described simply as restorationist. However, they did not seek to simply restore or bring back into working order the government and society of the Song period. Rather, they sought to reverse the changes and innovations of that period and return to those of the Tang, now seen as a golden age. This took all kinds of forms, including even attempts to revive Tang styles of dress – the contemporary equivalent would be to revive the styles and clothing of the thirteenth or fourteenth centuries. They were not of course able to do this and the outcome of their policy was the creation of something new but still significantly different from the state of affairs under the Song. The reactive ideal though was important, because it helped to drive and shape the policies that were followed. The central reality was a systematic attempt to reverse or significantly alter the main features of the social and economic developments that had taken place under the Song. Much of this was set out in the law code drawn up at the start of the Hongwu emperor's reign, which acted as a legal code, a constitution, and a manifesto for the principles that were supposed to guide administration.

At the heart of the Ming program was a transformation (or as they saw it, reformation) of government. The core notion was that of a paternalistic government that ruled in the general interest but was free of any institutional checks, as opposed to the internalised public spiritedness of the officials and rulers. This meant in philosophical and political terms a move away from the hands-off policy of the Song, where the government had largely gone along with the spontaneous social changes produced by free human interaction and a much greater emphasis on the need for control and direction and the use of power.

The government, which moved from Nanjing to Beijing under the third of the Ming Emperors, the Yongle emperor (1403-1424), became much more centralised than it had been under the Song or indeed the Tang and the Han. It came to depend much more than had been the case before on the person and ability of the emperor as he was the ultimate decision maker and the alternative sources of policy that had begun to come into existence were removed. This meant that the government functioned effectively when the emperor was active and competent, but when he was idle and disengaged, as several of the later Ming emperors were, it could become paralyzed and lack direction. Perhaps the most important change that led to this concentration of power was the abolition of the office of Prime Minister and the deliberative Council of Ministers. (The office of Prime Minister was replaced by that of 'Senior Grand Secretary' but although individual holders of this post might have great influence they did so purely because of their closeness to the emperor and not as a function of the office itself).

As well as becoming more centralised, the administration acquired a much more arbitrary quality, subject only to the personal qualities of the emperor and senior officials. One aspect of this was a series of savage purges of the bureaucracy which tended to take place at the start of each reign, often leading to the execution of thousands of officials and the exiling of many more to remote positions in the provinces. Alongside this was the reintroduction of strict censorship and control of the press and the creation of a network of spies and intelligence agents. The Hongwu emperor, whose paranoia and fear grew greater with age, was particularly fond of this and created the feared secret police known as the Jinye Wei but this was in fact only one of a number of intelligence services – a common practice of governments and not unknown even today. Controls on the internal movements of ordinary people were also reintroduced.

Even more significant than this transformation of the state were the policies that this new regime pursued. Perhaps the most significant was the abolition of the land reforms of the Song and a deliberate policy of recreating a class of peasant smallholders as the economic and social base of society. Among other measures, this involved the removal of the right of individuals to freely alienate land and the breaking up of the large commercial farms that had appeared under the Song and their replacement by peasant smallholdings.

Along with this went an ideological hostility to trade, which was seen as morally corrupting and as socially disruptive and dangerous because of the way it weakened both public spiritedness and control by the paternal government. This hostility found expression in many pronouncements by the early Ming emperors and in a series of specific measures designed to discourage trade in general and long distance trade in particular. All trade by sea was banned after the mid fifteenth century and internal long distance trade was restricted by a series of laws from even earlier. The aim was to promote what we would now call 'localisation', a diminution in the scope of trade and economic integration and the enforcement of a more local society and economy in which economic and social relations were made simpler and more local. At the same time the government run postal and courier system was improved and made much swifter so that (in theory), while the governance became more integrated over a wider area the other kinds of social relations became more constrained.

Alongside these policies were a number of others that were also designed to restore a traditional society and limit the disruptive effects of voluntary economic and social interactions. In taxation, there was a move away from taxes on commerce and money taxes in general and a reversion to the use of payment in kind, particularly by forced labour. The monetary policy of the

Ming state was confused and driven as much by events as any conscious design but the kinds of decisions taken all tended to have effects that reinforced those of other policies. Initially they continued the use of paper money as one of several kinds of circulating medium but eventually this was abandoned, in the late fifteenth century. Meanwhile, the number of copper coins in circulation had diminished considerably and the result was a move to a silver-based currency, with much higher effective denominations. Initially, due to the shortage of silver this had a deflationary effect, although this would change later, because of events outside China. It also initially reduced the amount of money based trade exchange because of the difficulty of making change, although again this would change later.

Since not all long distance trade within the empire could be stopped the early Ming sought to control it through the creation of a series of regionally based merchant cartels, which were given monopoly rights in a number of important products in return for payments to the public treasury. The most dramatic policy however was the reintroduction of the idea of tribute trade and a deliberate policy of trying to prevent private trade between Chinese merchants and foreigners. This was part of a self-conscious and deliberate policy of seeking to withdraw from contact with the rest of the world, at least to the extent that it had grown to under the Song. One striking aspect of this was the scrapping of the great navy that the Ming had inherited and initially expanded, something that would have enormous geopolitical consequences.

In social relations there was also a clear move, in this case an attempt to undo the more fluid and meritocratic kind of society that had appeared under the Song and to enforce a much more formally hierarchically ordered society. This involved, inter alia, sumptuary laws intended to control people's dress and overt consumption, a social classification that was reflected not only in dress but also in prescription of the kinds of occupation one could follow and a series of laws designed to control what we would now call 'conspicuous consumption'. There were also many laws enforcing morality and attempts to regulate behaviour by enforcing moral obligations such as filial piety. Although the bureaucracy was still recruited by competitive examination, these became more formal and restricted in their scope than before and were increasingly the preserve of an elite class (although still less so than under the Tang).

An Anti-Modern Revolution?

What though did this amount to? The important thing to grasp is that while much of this was, as is always the case with government policy, an ad hoc response to particular circumstances, a great deal of it was a carefully thought out attempt to pursue a particular vision by able and intelligent rulers and administrators. Because there was a distinct philosophy behind it, even the ad hoc measures tended to follow a particular pattern and aimed to achieve ends of a particular kind. The point is firstly that this was an attempt by a ruling elite to bring the personal relations that had become much richer, more complex and more varied with the commercialisation and urbanisation of society under the Song under greater control, to regularise them and make them conform to a particular vision of social good and harmonious living. This was done even though it had a cost in terms of foregone wealth – far from being seen as a problem or even as a price worth paying, this was one of the goals. Secondly, this was a deliberate attempt to strengthen both governing power and control and social cohesion, what we may call the informal controls and discipline of society, and the non-state forms of authority such as the authority and influence of parents, relatives, elders and neighbours. If Song China was an early intimation of modernity or what we may call a proto-modern society and state, then this was effectively an anti-modern revolution, a deliberate attempt to roll back the modernisation that had started under the Song and to 'restore' a more stable society.

How far though were the Ming emperors and their administrators successful? From one perspective the answer is, not very much. Much of the legislation proved impossible to enforce and ordinary Chinese proved extraordinarily adept at finding ways to evade the controls. Moreover, the whole policy depended for its effectiveness upon having competent and hard working leadership. In addition, much of it was also in some sense a response to or taking advantage of the slump that the Chinese economy went into from the early fourteenth century onwards, which was partly a product of global conditions and which lasted for almost two hundred years.

Eventually both of these two factors changed. From the early sixteenth century onwards, the Chinese economy revived, in part because of an inflow of silver from the New World and Japan and because of a revival of trade, which began to involve China, despite the efforts of the imperial government. These were increasingly feeble in any case, and this became particularly true during the long reign of the Wan Li emperor (1573-1620). While able and talented he was also incorrigibly idle and uninterested in government business, driving his mandarins to transports of rage and despair as government papers were allowed to pile up for years while he devoted himself to personal pleasures. In the Chinese countryside, the reforms of the Hongwu emperor, when coupled with the effects of newly imported New World crops and the more efficient road system, produced an agricultural surplus and a market for cash crops and rural products at a local and increasingly a national level, which the increasingly feeble government was unable to control.

The result was that in the period from the mid to late sixteenth century onwards, Chinese society once again became highly commercialised, with another upsurge of conspicuous consumption, affluence and urban growth, and in addition a significant rise in population from the 1520s onwards. During this period the Chinese government was also plagued by Japanese 'pirates' known as the wokou, who became a major problem in all of the coastal provinces, particularly those from the Yangtze delta southwards. Although often described as pirates they were actually more like armed smugglers and often worked in co-operation with the locals, which was a sign of popular evasion or flouting of the rules laid down by government.

Despite this very heavy qualification, we would have to say that the counter-revolution of the Ming was essentially successful. In the first place its core elements, the creation of a centralised paternalistic government and the recreation of China as a society and economy based upon a class of peasant smallholders, remained in place even in the face of the renewed commercialisation of the period after 1550 and persisted after the breakdown of the dynasty in the 1640s and its replacement by the Manchu Qing dynasty. However, even more important was the way it had clearly brought about, or played a central part in bringing about, a fundamental alteration in Chinese society.

Although China was once again a highly commercialised society after the early to mid sixteenth century, it never regained the innovative dynamism that had been such a feature of the Song period (or indeed certain earlier episodes). From being the most technologically innovative society on the planet by a considerable margin, it fell well behind the ever more inventive Europeans from the later seventeenth century onwards. In economic terms, while China remained a highly commercial, enterprising, and by the standards of the time, wealthy culture, it did not recover the kind of intensive growth that had been such a feature of society under both the Northern and Southern Song. The nature of urban life and government also seems to have changed and Chinese cities, while still large and wealthy did not have the central economic and social role they had enjoyed under the Song (or were to have later in Japan).

Intellectually the kind of flourishing and wide ranging inquiry that had been such a feature of the earlier period, gradually faded away. The idea that became common in later eighteenth century Europe, that China was a civilised but 'stationary' society, is clearly not true when one looks at the entire course of Chinese history or even when one compares Qing China with most of its contemporaries. However, one reason why this idea gained such a hold was that European observers from the mid-eighteenth century onwards were struck by the intellectual and social conservatism that they perceived in China. Most importantly, as we shall see, when the in many ways still comparable societies of eighteenth century Europe and China confronted similar challenges, the responses were critically different.

How much of this though is down to the policy of the early Ming emperors and their administrators or to put it another way, the reaction of the traditional Chinese elite? Clearly, a great deal must be put down to this cause and we should not underestimate the ability of political power to have significant and long lasting social effects. Social engineering may be difficult, have unexpected consequences, and be undesirable but that does not make it impossible. In addition though there was clearly an intellectual and social reaction in China, which went along with the policies of the elite in broadly the same direction. Many argue that the crucial element was a revival and then triumph of Confucianism. This in itself is much too simplistic. Under the Song Neo-Confucianism had been varied in its ideas and prescriptions and much of the thinking put under this rubric was very important for the flourishing intellectual and scientific enquiry of that time. Moreover, there was a revival of these kinds of Confucian thought under the later Ming, with radical individualist and rationalist ideas making an appearance. In fact though, this was in the nature of a 'last flowering' of that tendency in Confucian thought. What happened then and to some extent earlier was the victory not of Confucianism per se but of a particular variety of that philosophy, one that emphasised the dangers of wealth and commerce and the need for paternalistic government. Another important part of this story was the triumph of a sophisticated and sceptical epistemology, which undermined the early moves towards scientific investigation.

Socially, a critical role seems to have been played by the great mass of Chinese society, the peasantry, who while maybe chafing under particular aspects of policy supported the main thrust of much of it or at least did not oppose it. It is here though that the role of power was critical. The kinds of activity and innovation that were allowed under the Song were now criminalised in many cases. Even when this was ineffective, social processes and innovations were not able to flourish and develop in the way they had before and they always had a provisional character. Several scholars such as Philip Huang and Mark Elvin have argued that this course of social evolution would probably have happened anyway because of the way rural society developed a kind of stable technological and economic equilibrium that left no incentive for further innovation. However, if the policy of the Song had continued, then the minority who did not wish to persist in the traditional way of doing things would have been able to innovate freely and the effects of that would have undoubtedly eventually transformed or undermined any stable equilibrium, particularly when it was confronted by severe demographic and environmental challenges.

What Was the Outcome?

What though was created? Clearly, the Ming did not realise the Hongwu emperor's ideal of a society of largely self-contained and self-sufficient rural communities. Nor are we looking at a reversion to an earlier pattern of social relations, even if that was the idea that was aimed at. Rather, we may say that a combination of factors, including crucially an active policy by the ruling elite, meant that China after the shock of the Mongol conquest and its aftermath followed a different kind of development to the one that would happen later in eighteenth and nineteenth century Europe. This was one in which the disruptive effects of free exchange and commerce were contained and directed and traditional society was able to reassert itself. The result was a form of development in which a broadly traditional agricultural society becomes increasingly commercialised and experiences considerable extensive growth, but still remains predominantly rural and agricultural, does not experience intensive growth, remains stable and closed intellectually and does not have rapid and systematic technological innovation. As a result, the social system and form of government also remain broadly stable. What also occurred under this kind of development was continuing population growth and it was this that would eventually undo it, in China and elsewhere.

So the case of China and its reaction to the Mongol incursions and wider events thereafter has a number of important implications. In particular, if we do understand Song China to have been a proto-modern society and Ming China a turn away from a kind of development that could have continued, then this shows that a modern breakthrough can be cut short and even reversed, in the face of a widespread reaction against some of its features and a response by the power elite in particular. It also raises another question. Why did something like this not happen in the eighteenth and nineteenth centuries in Europe? The answers to both of these questions are found in a set of changes that happened after the end of the medieval period of world history on a global basis but which produced very different outcomes in Europe to those that they led to elsewhere. The rise of the Ming and their policy was in fact just one part of a wider crisis, one that affected the entire world from about the 1320s onwards if not before.

Further Reading

Chinese history can seem daunting as a topic to those unfamiliar with it but fortunately there are several outstanding introductions. One of the best is Patricia Buckley Ebrey, *The Cambridge Illustrated History of China* (Cambridge University Press, 1996) and the same author's *East Asia: A Cultural, Social and Political History: China* (Houghton-Mifflin, 2006). Another very helpful starting point is Caroline Blunden & Mark Elvin, *Cultural Atlas of China* (Facts on File, 1988). Ainslie T. Embree & Carol Gluck (eds.), *Asia in Western and World History: A Guide for Teaching* (Columbia University Press, 1997) is a comprehensive bibliographical aid. F. W. Mote, *Imperial China 900 – 1800* (Harvard University Press, 2003) is one of the best one volume histories of imperial China while Morris Rossabi, *China Among Equals: The Middle Kingdom and its Neighbours, Tenth to Eighteenth Centuries* (University of California Press, 1983) places Chinese civilisation in a wider geographical context.

The creativity and inventiveness of Chinese civilisation is the subject of the monumental work of Joseph Needham and his collaborators, *Science and*

Civilisation in China, which amounts in total to twenty-five volumes. There is a five volume shorter edition Colin A. Ronan, *The Shorter Science and Civilisation in China* (Cambridge University Press, 1984 – 2007). For those who find that still too daunting there is Robert Temple, *The Genius of China: 3,000 Years of Science, Discovery, and Invention* (Inner Traditions, 2007), and Joseph Needham, *Science in Traditional China* (Harvard University Press, 1981). For China's historical place in the world economy see Angus Maddison *Chinese Economic Performance in the Long Run: 960 – 2030 AD* (OECD, 2007) and Richard von Glahn, *The Economic History of China: From Antiquity to the Nineteenth Century* (Cambridge University Press, 2016).

A very good account of Song China and the level of social and economic development reached by the end of the Song period is Jacques Gernet, *Daily Life In China on the Eve of the Mongol Invasion 1250 – 1276* (Stanford University Press, 1962). Another useful study is Shiba Yoshinobu, *Commerce and Society in Sung China* (University of Michigan Centre for Chinese Studies, 1970). The best recent general survey of Song China is Dieter Kuhn, *The Age of Confucian Rule: the Song Transformation of China* (Belknap Press, 2011).

The work of Shen Kuo is now available in a complete English translation Shen Kuo Wang Hong (trans.), Zhao Zheng (trans.), *Brush Talks From Dream Brook* (Paths International, 2011). Maddison's work contains detailed accounts of China's general economic performance. For further reading the best source is Robert Hymes "Song China, 960 – 1279" in Ainslie T. Embree & Carol Gluck (eds.), *Asia in Western and World History: A Guide For Teaching* (M. E. Sharpe, 1997), pp. 336 – 351.

The reforms of politics and governance under the Song, and the controversies these led to are covered in John Chaffee, *The Thorny Gates of Learning in Sung China: A Social History of Examinations* (Cambridge University Press, 1985), James T. C. Liu, *Reform in Sung China: Wang An Shih and His New Policies* (Harvard University Press, 1957) and Xiao Bin-Ji, *Politics and Conservatism in Northern Song China: The Career and Thought of Sima Guang (1019 – 1086)* (Chinese University Press, 2000). Craig Clunas, *Superfluous Things: Material Culture and Social Status in Early Modern China* (University of Hawaii Press, 2004) looks at the complicated relationship between the mercantile economy and traditional Chinese mores throughout this period.

The career of Ghengis Khan and the role of the Mongol Empire in world history is the subject of J. J. Saunders, *The History of the Mongol Conquests* (University of Pennsylvania Press, 2001), Morris Rossabi (ed.), *The Mongols and Global History* (Norton, 2010) (a collection of primary texts), and Jack Weatherford, *Ghengis Khan and the Making of the Modern World* (Broadway Books, 2005). Khublai Khan and his achievement is described in Morris Rossabi, *Khubilai Khan: His Life and Times* (University of California Press, 1989).

The debate about exactly how and why Chinese society became less innovative after the Ming came to power, and what exactly had been going on under the

Song (and even for some the Yuan or Mongol dynasty) has produced a range of interesting works in recent years. One of the most important is R. Bin Wong, *China Transformed: Historical Change and the Limits of European Experience* (Cornell University Press, 2000). Mark Elvin, *The Pattern of the Chinese Past* (Stanford University Press, 1973) gives one of the most influential interpretations. Gang Deng, *The Pre-Modern Chinese Economy: Structural Equilibrium and Capitalist Sterility* (Routledge, 2007) makes a similar structuralist case and should be read with the same author's more specialised *Development Versus Stagnation: Technological Continuity and Agricultural Progress in Pre-Modern China* (Greenwood Press, 1993).

The various answers to the question "Why not China?" are ably summarised in the chapter of that title in Jonathan Daly, *Historians Debate the Rise of the West* (Routledge, 2015).

Early Ming history is explored in Edward L. Dreyer, *Early Ming China: A Political History, 1355 – 1433* (Stanford University Press, 1982), and John Dardess, *Confucianism and Autocracy: Professional Elites in the Founding of the Ming Dynasty* (University of California Press, 1983). The history of both the Ming and the Yuan is covered in Timothy Brook, *The Troubled Empire: China in the Yuan and Ming Dynasties* (Belknap, 2013). The ideology of the early Ming emperors is examined in Jiang Yonglin, *The Mandate of Heaven and the Great Ming Code* (University of Washington Press, 2013) while the key text is translated by the same author, *The Great Ming Code/Ya Ming Lu* (University of Washington Press, 2014).

The aggressive maritime strategy of the Yong Le Emperor and the voyages of Zheng He are described in Gang Deng, *The Maritime Sector, Institutions and Sea-Power of Pre-Modern China* (Greenwood Press, 1999), Louise Levathes, *When China Ruled the Seas: The Treasure Fleet of the Dragon Throne 1405 – 1433* (Oxford University Press, 1997), and Edward L. Dreyer, *Zheng He: China and the Oceans in the Early Ming Dynasty 1405 – 1433* (Longmans, 2006). The state of technology under the Ming is the subject of Francesca Bray, *Technology and Society in Ming China* (American Historical Association, 2000).

The revival of a mercantile culture in Ming China under the Wan Li Emperor and his successors is deftly handled in Timothy Brook, *The Confusions of Pleasure: Commerce and Culture in Ming China* (University of California Press, 1999). William Theodore de Bary (ed.), *Self and Society in Ming Thought* (Columbia University Press, 1970), and Yang Ye (ed.), *Vignettes From the Late Ming: A Hsiao-P'in Anthology* (University of Washington Press, 1999) look at particular aspects of late Ming society. Ray Huang *1587, A Year of No Significance: The Ming Dynasty in Decline* (Yale University Press, 1982) is a superb social history that gives a clear idea of life in China at that time. The policy of the early Qing emperors is treated in William T. Rowe, *China's Last Empire: The Great Qing* (Belknap, 2012).

CHAPTER IV

The Military Revolution and the World it Made

SHOULD time travel ever become possible there are some periods of the past you should avoid visiting. The fourteenth century of the Christian era ranks very high on that list. It was a truly dark time in human history, marked by a huge and lasting decline in population, the breakdown of stable political orders right across the Old World, wars and rebellions, and a global economic slump. No wonder many thought at the time that the end of the world was at hand and they were experiencing the end times. This was a crisis of civilisation and one that was truly global in scope, affecting every part of the world to some degree (including the Americas), a period of disaster on an enormous scale and marked by widespread suffering and disorder. Yet the major civilisations did not collapse or succumb as their ancient predecessors had done some eight hundred years earlier. However, they emerged from the great crisis of those years changed in various ways and the way that change worked out in some parts of the world was to make possible the sudden explosive transformation that would happen four to five hundred years later.

A Malthusian Crunch

The background to the great crisis had several elements. The first was a growing problem of population relative to production that became apparent by the end of the thirteenth century. The slow but persistent growth of trade and economic activity during the medieval period had sustained and gone along with a steady rise in total world population – our best estimate is that this increased from two hundred and fifty million to three hundred and fifty million between the early eleventh century and 1300. Initially this was accompanied by growth in output, particularly agricultural. However, the productivity increases did not continue, with the exception of Song China. The result of this was that living standards began not just to stagnate but also to actually decline. In particular, there were increasing problems in the agricultural sector.

In fact, by about 1300 the Old World was overpopulated and facing a Malthusian crisis – that is population was starting to significantly exceed the food producing capacity of the settled areas of the planet. The thing to grasp is that overpopulation is not a matter of absolute numbers or of density of population. It is rather a function of the capacity of the way in which production is organised and of the technology and techniques used in that system of production. This is true above all in agriculture. A world population of several billion can be supported by the kind of economy and agriculture that we now have, so the world is not overpopulated today. However, the productive systems found throughout the medieval world were increasingly unable to support the much lower population of 1300, so we can say there was overpopulation then. By the end of the long medieval upswing these productive systems had reached their limits and production of all kinds but above all of food was no longer keeping pace with rising population. How though do we know this? The answer is that we can discern a series of phenomena that we can now retrospectively see as flashing warning signs, evidence of an increasing 'tightness' in the system as population pushed up against structural limits.

In the first place, evidence suggests a rise in various prices and a decline in real wages in those parts of the economy where wage labour was found. More serious is the evidence of increasing malnutrition, shown by the skeletal remains of people from the later thirteenth and early fourteenth century. The most important evidence though comes from agricultural yields and land use. All the evidence suggests that by 1300 there was severe 'land hunger' in most parts of Eurasia with rising rents and land prices one of the most visible signs. Above all, ever more marginal land was being brought into cultivation and the consequence of this was a decline in the average agricultural yield of a number of staple crops. Thus, the yield for wheat in Europe declined steadily after 1280.

This reveals a crucial difference between an economy marked by predominantly extensive growth (such as that of the Medieval world) and one dominated by intensive growth. In the latter case pressure of population on finite resources such as land leads to improvements in productivity through various kinds of innovation so that more is produced using the same area. In the other the response is to extend the area being cultivated without any increase in productivity. As this involves moving into ever less productive land, there is a problem of diminishing marginal return – every extra acre of land brings less return in the shape of actual food until eventually the average return per acre actually declines. This does not mean necessarily that the world in 1300 was about to face an inevitable collapse in population, the more likely prospect at that time was for a condition of chronic problems. The world's population would have stagnated rather than growing so the outcome would be a stable population facing a chronic problem of subsistence. In fact, this did not happen and world population did indeed decline sharply but this was due to the impact of the other two background factors upon the primary one, of a productive system that was reaching its limit.

The Little Ice Age

The second part of the backdrop to the crisis, which made the first one even more acute, was a progressive worsening of the planet's climate. The long period from roughly the eighth century onwards had been marked by what historians term the 'medieval warm period' (or more controversially 'the medieval climate optimum'). At this time, the planet's average temperature had been just below where it is today. This had a number of results, such as viticulture being practised much further north in Europe than at other times. More important was the way it made warm summers more frequent and longer. The result was to increase the length of the growing season and to make poor harvests less likely. At some point the Earth began to cool down and eventually entered into a period of much colder weather, generally known as the 'little ice age', which did not finally end until the mid nineteenth century.

The exact starting point is uncertain as the various indicators point to different dates, reflecting the way that the cooling affected different parts of the planet to varying degrees and at different times within a long time span. Thus the extent of Arctic pack ice started to grow as early as 1250 but a worldwide expansion of glaciers did not really get under way until as late as 1550. Other indicators such as tree rings and recorded patterns of summer and winter weather suggest the turn for Europe and Northern Asia began at the end of the thirteenth century. From that time long and warm summers became increasingly rare and unpredictable, and cold wet ones more frequent while winter came sooner and was increasingly severe. The result was to significantly increase the likelihood of a harvest failure to the point where there was a one in five chance of a failure in any one year. The change in the weather also reduced yields even in years when there was not an outright failure and tended to push them down towards the lower end of the range of between 2:1 and 7:1 commonly found in medieval Eurasia. (By contrast present day yields are on the order of 200:1 or higher).

This had disastrous results when it was combined with the growing pressure of population on resources and productive organisations. In Europe, the impact first became clear with the Great Famine of 1315 to 1317. Three years of torrential rain brought total harvest failure and massive famine to almost all of northern Europe and the food supply did not fully recover until 1325. It was not only Europe that suffered however, as there were major famines in China and India in the 1320s. Frequent and widespread famines and harvest failures did not end with the 1320s; rather they became a regular feature of the life of ordinary people throughout the subsequent centuries. Even when the harvest did not fail, the reduced yields made chronic malnutrition much more widespread.

The Black Death and Its Impact

The effects of widespread food shortage and malnutrition and frequent outright starvation played their part in what was the third and most dramatic part of the background to the crisis, the huge mortality brought about by a massive epidemic that affected most of the Old World. This is usually known by the name later European historians gave it, the Black Death. Traditionally the disease is identified as a particularly virulent form of the bubonic plague and this is still the most widely held view, although certain features of the epidemic have led to doubts on that score. Whatever it was, its effects were devastating and long lasting. They were also widely spread. Recent historical research has placed Europe's experience of the Black Death into a wider context and we now have a better understanding of the full history, extent and impact of the epidemic. What is also now clear is how the Mongol empire and its unification of such a large part of Eurasia played a central part in the spread of the disease.

It seems to have first appeared either on the edges of the Himalayas, or else in central Asia, in both cases among Mongol soldiers who then transmitted it to China. The first major outbreak occurred in Hubei province in South-West China in 1323 and in the next seven years it swept right across China, affecting almost every part of the country. The disease then moved across the vast expanse of the Mongol empire, carried by Mongol armies and by traders. The connection between trade routes and the spread of the epidemic is clear, as is the direction of the transmission from East to West as we can see from the dates of major outbreaks. The disease arrived at the port of Caffa in the Crimea in 1347, brought by the Mongol soldiers besieging the city. Genoese merchants then took it to the Sicilian port of Messina, where it then broke out in 1348. It then spread northwards across Europe, until the first wave of the epidemic ended in 1353. Meanwhile the plague had also arrived in Alexandria, via the Red Sea route, in 1347 and from there it spread northwards into the Middle East, arriving at Antioch in 1348, westwards into Africa, reaching Morocco by 1351. A second outbreak then took place in China in 1353 to 1354 followed by another wave of outbreaks right across Eurasia and Africa.

Wherever it struck, the Black Death had a massive impact. The initial outbreak in Hubei may have killed as much as ninety per cent of the population in that province and as much as forty per cent of the population of China during its spread in the following years. The second outbreak in China, during the 1350s, seems to have had an even greater effect, perhaps because it was even more widespread geographically and by some estimates accounted for as much as sixty percent of the Chinese population. In the case of Europe and the Middle East the best estimate until recently was that the epidemic carried off between a quarter and a third of the population in both areas. A more recent work however argues that the death toll in Europe during the initial outbreak of 1348 to 1353 was as high as forty-five to fifty per cent in Europe as a whole and as high as seventy to seventy-five per cent in the Mediterranean region. As yet, not much use has been made of the Indian source material but indications are that the death rate there was comparable to those found in Europe and the Middle East. The Black Death spread so rapidly and widely because of a combination of two things, the increased trade and movement brought about by the Pax Mongolica and its apparently very long incubation period of up to thirty days (this is one reason why contemporary scholars increasingly doubt that the Black Death was in fact bubonic plague).

As the figures given above indicate, the impact of the Black Death on population levels was huge. It reduced China's population from around a hundred and twenty million to around eighty million at most. The Middle East and Europe both suffered a drop of between thirty to forty per cent. This is a massive decline by any standards and consequently world population was nearly halved. Even more remarkable however was how long the decline persisted. In Europe, the population continued to decline until about 1420 and did not start to recover until the 1470s. Many areas did not reach the level of population they had had in 1340 until well into the sixteenth century or even later. This is surprising and poses a continuing puzzle to historians. Generally, human populations are highly resilient and show a remarkable capacity to recover from a large mortality in a relatively short time, whether that mortality is due to disease, war or political mass killing. The failure to recover from the Black Death is therefore a puzzle and suggests that some other factor was at work. One must have been the recurrent outbreaks of the plague that affected many areas of Eurasia after the initial epidemic and which continued to cull the human population. The main explanation however must have been something that seriously depressed human fertility for a long period. Possible candidates include a widespread increase in the age of marriage, and the effects of continuing malnutrition. Another could be that the original outbreak somehow reduced the fertility of the survivors but this is speculation.

Another feature of the Black Death was the unevenness of its impact. The figures given are averages and conceal considerable local variation. Generally speaking, towns and urban settlements of all kinds suffered much more severely than more rural areas, partly because they were more densely populated and also because the disease was spread by trade and traders who were predominantly urban. Geographically some areas suffered very severely while others got off comparatively lightly. Although the wealthy had more opportunity to escape than the poor, one characteristic of the epidemic was that it struck down people from all social classes and carried off many members of the elite including even royalty. All this meant that the great epidemic had a number of effects apart from obvious ones such as population loss. It weakened trade links and caused a sharp decline in urban life and economic activity. The deaths of members of the elite and the capricious way in which some areas escaped while others did not meant that it destabilised politics by altering the balance of power and undermining dynasties. All of this fed into the political and social turmoil that made up the great crisis of the fourteenth century.

The World Crisis 1310 – 1450

The combination of a devastating pandemic, a worsening of the planet's climate, and a structural failure of the economy to keep pace with population growth – at least until the Black Death intervened – produced a pattern of political, economic and intellectual crisis found in all of the major civilisations. This combined a number of related but distinct phenomena. One was a renewed series of nomadic incursions, which were in many ways more devastating than those of the thirteenth century that had created the Mongol empire. The most damaging were those launched by the last of the great nomad conquerors, Timur the Lame, better known as Tamerlane (1336 – 1405). From his base in Samarqand, he launched a series of attacks, ranging as far as Russia, Northern India, and Anatolia. However, Iran bore the brunt of his ferocity as he invaded it eleven times over the course of seventeen years. A cruel and ruthless leader, he was entirely destructive in his impact. Unlike Genghis Khan he did not create an institutional state that would survive his death for any significant time and he brought death and destruction rather than anything constructive. Although himself a Muslim, he inflicted enormous damage on the Islamic world, particularly Iran, and completed the destructive impact of the earlier Mongol invasions and the Black Death upon the classical political order of the Islamic Middle East.

A central part of the crisis was a decline in trade and the breakdown of the eight or eleven circuit world trade system that had grown up during the Middle Ages. (Abu-Lughod, 1989) while the nascent unified world trade system of the Mongols was cut short. Long distance trade declined sharply, as can be seen from the rise in the cost of goods that were traded over long distances such as silk, spices, and porcelain. Cities that had been important entrepots went into decline. The kinds of links and diplomatic contacts between geographically separated parts of the Old World that had been a feature of the thirteenth century were disrupted. Many areas saw a decline in urban populations with people fleeing to the countryside and not returning. Nevertheless, rural areas could also suffer depopulation, as the phenomenon of the 'deserted medieval village' attests.

Moreover, it was not only long-distance trade that declined. The volume and importance of trade in general declined, including at the regional and local level. There was a general trend towards less economic integration and more self-sufficiency. All of the information we have indicates a severe economic slowdown or slump. Thus, there was a decline in most prices, a general deflation in fact. While this brought about a rise in real wages for those still getting them, it also both reflected and drove the decline in activity. Another indicator was the debasement and decay of currencies, again both reflecting and encouraging a decline in the use of money and movement away from exchange and complex economic relations.

The decline in trade and wealth creating activity, combined with the fall in population, put ruling classes everywhere under increasing pressure. As their revenue base (trade generated income flows and tax paying peasant households) shrank so they were forced to all kinds of expedients in order to survive. One was a vain attempt to control and regulate prices and wages and the responses to the crisis of economic actors such as landlords, peasants and merchants. The other was to seek out new sources of revenue or to try to squeeze even more out of existing tax bases. The result of course was violent protest from productive classes already feeling the squeeze from the economic slump and natural disasters. This typically took the form of peasant and urban rebellions, often on a massive scale. In Europe, examples included the English Peasants' Revolt of 1381, the Jacquerie in France in 1358 and the rebellion of the 'Ciompi' in Florence in 1378. There were huge revolts also in China, India, the Middle East and Russia.

Alongside the popular revolts were wars, driven by the efforts of ruling elites to corner as much of the declining revenue as possible in competition with other elites. Some were struggles between different ruling groups and the territories or political entities they controlled. One such was the Hundred Years War, which in many ways marked the start of the crisis in Europe. Often seen as a two-way fight between England and France or more realistically Plantagenet and Valois, it was actually a more complicated struggle, involving at least three distinct factions.

In fact, most of the conflicts were rather civil wars within ruling groups and as such were both cause and product of a process of political deliquescence and the breakdown of complex political order. This was most noticeable in the Middle East but examples of it occurred everywhere. In China, the later years of the Mongol Yuan dynasty after the 1320s were marked by civil war and the effective collapse of imperial authority. In Japan the Kamakura shogunate collapsed in 1333, after ruling Japan since its foundation by Minamoto Yoritomo in 1185. Although a new shogunate arose, the Ashikaga, it was much weaker and in 1467, it effectively broke down, thereafter continuing in name only. Japan then fragmented into many small states ruled by feudal lords (daimyo) who engaged in an endless series of conflicts. In India, the Delhi Sultanate, which had come to control most of the subcontinent by 1230, was severely weakened by the Black Death and then shattered by the invasion of Timur in 1398, which culminated in the sack of Delhi. Following this, the Sultanate fell to pieces and

India reverted to its earlier state of piecemeal division and internal conflict.

The Balkan territories of the Byzantine Empire, which had never recovered from the sack of Constantinople by the Fourth Crusade in 1204, were now divided among many smaller states while Anatolia, Syria, Iraq and Iran after the death of Timur were all fragmented among competing groups and clans. Europe saw war and conflict within the monarchies of England, France and the Holy Roman Empire, to name just three. This disintegration was different from the process of fragmentation that had marked the Middle Ages. The former had taken place within broadly stable political orders, so while there had been a process of political devolution and the breaking up of large political units into smaller subunits, this had not been associated with general political disorder. After the early fourteenth century the entire political order was in flux in many parts of Eurasia and this meant that the fragmentation was not a process that took place within a stable framework but rather a product of the breakdown of that framework.

The turmoil of the times was not confined to politics and economics. Unsurprisingly, the combination of unprecedented and inexplicable natural disaster with political and economic upheaval led to a crisis of thought and faith, as people tried to make sense of the world they found themselves in. One response was to reject the teachings and beliefs of the orthodox and established religions and philosophies. This reaction took two quite different forms. For some it led to scepticism and nihilism, a rejection of belief and an emphasis upon earthly pleasures and living for the moment – not a surprising response to the likelihood of a sudden and capricious death that no amount of prayer or devotion seemed to be able to avert. For others it led to an increased piety and a focus on introspection and personal religiosity.

The religious enthusiasm and fervour this often produced was frequently inspired by apocalyptic and millenarian notions – again hardly surprising. Examples of this were the flagellants of Europe and other movements such as the Brethren of the Free Spirit while China saw the appearance of similar movements or tongs, often inspired by millenarian varieties of Buddhism. Such millenarian ideas often fed into or inspired popular revolts or civil conflicts. Examples include the Hussite wars in the Holy Roman Empire, the series of uprisings in China in the 1350s, culminating in the Red Turban uprising that finally overthrew the Mongol Yuan dynasty, and several uprisings led by members of the 'Pure Land' Buddhist sect in Japan.

In response to this the orthodox position was asserted with greater force and subtlety but often with the paradoxical effect of producing new heresies and threats to the established spiritual and intellectual order. A frequent phenomenon was thinkers who sought to defend the established view by purifying it of accretions and ended up by implicitly or explicitly criticising it as corrupt and full of improper notions. Examples of this tendency include Jan Huss (1369 – 1415) and John Wycliffe (1320 – 1384) in Europe, and Ibn

Taymiyyah (1263 – 1328) in the Islamic world. Later on, when the worst of the crisis had passed there was a more successful reassertion of the orthodox position in all of the civilisations and also a tendency towards eclecticism with an attempt to unite divergent strands of thought and belief.

So a general feature of the Old World between roughly the 1320s and the 1450s was that of a general breakdown of the systems that had come into being during the Middle Ages, whether economic, political or religious and intellectual. Clearly, as said before, this put enormous pressure upon institutions and ruling classes everywhere. However the order that had grown up during the long Medieval upswing proved to be more robust than the civilisations of antiquity and there was no general systemic collapse of the kind experienced by the lands of the Roman and Sassanian Empires – although this was a close run thing in some areas. Moreover, one of the truest statements that can be made about both politics and trade is that when looked at in the right way every problem is also an opportunity. The disorder and decline of the years provided astute and ruthless political entrepreneurs with opportunities to expand their power in various ways and it also opened up opportunities for innovation elsewhere.

Response to Crisis – The Military Revolution

In fact, the pressure brought to bear by the crisis on both political and economic actors led to innovations in both areas of life. This was because of an intensification of competition between both economic actors (businessmen, traders, producers of all kinds) and ruling classes. In the second case the competition was both between distinct ruling groups controlling particular parts of the planet and within those ruling groups. This increase in ruling class competition meant the downfall of some groups but rapid rise for others, just as in the world of commerce it meant bankruptcy or takeover for some established firms and individuals and the rapid rise to prominence of able and ambitious upstarts.

Among ruling groups, the increased competition and the pressures they faced led to innovation in two areas. One was in the structure and practice of actual government and administration. Here we can see the appearance of new ways of exercising political power, as in the so-called 'new monarchies' of Renaissance Europe. In many ways however the changes in this area, at least initially were more a matter of improving and making more effective existing institutions rather than radical innovation. This was not the case however in the other principal arena of ruling class competition, that of warfare. Here there were truly profound changes, which led to a transformation of warfare, one that in turn brought about a great shift in the political organisation of most of the civilisations of the Old World.

So great were the changes in warfare that took place in response to the fourteenth century crisis that historians have come to refer to a 'military revolution' as taking place in what is commonly called the 'early modern' period. The term and the basic idea were both first formulated by the British historian Michael Roberts, in a lecture in 1955. He identified a transformation of warfare in early seventeenth century Europe and emphasised the role of the Swedes and to a lesser extent the Dutch. Subsequent authors, most notably Jeremy Black and Geoffrey Parker have amended and extended the thesis and there is now a considerable literature.

Most of this is focussed on Europe, for two reasons. One is that most of the individuals involved are experts in European history in one way or another. The other is the question that drives much of the research. One of the most striking results of the military revolution was a turnaround in the military position of Christian Europe compared to the other major world civilisations. In 1400, European powers were at most on an equal footing with Asian powers in terms of military power, and often not even that. By 1750 at the latest they were clearly more powerful and effective in this area and had come to dominate large parts of the planet as a result, something that would continue for at least the next hundred and fifty years.

However, the focus on Europe can lead to a loss of perspective. In particular, it means that there is not enough attention paid to what was perhaps the most important aspect of the military revolution, the way that it had different outcomes in various parts of the world. This in turn changed the relations between them and made possible the sudden breakthrough to modernity that took place in eighteenth and nineteenth century Europe. The key point, made by W. H. McNeill, is that there was a military revolution with common elements in *all* of the major world civilisations at some point between 1400 and 1715. This reflected the shared experience of the worldwide economic crisis between roughly 1300 and 1450, which caused similar problems for ruling classes throughout the world. Therefore, the intensified competition between them for resources also took place everywhere and that led in turn to military innovations in every part of the world. These then produced important changes in government and the political order, many of which in turn fed back into military organisation. The precise details of the military revolution and its consequences varied between different parts of the world. In particular, it had a quite different outcome in Europe to that which it had everywhere else. One result of that was that military innovation continued in Europe when it had stopped elsewhere. It was the changes made during that later period, which gave Europe military predominance over the rest of the world.

The Military Revolution – Content

Historians have retrospectively recognised various interconnected phenomena as constituting a revolution in the art of war at this time. The first was a gradual and patchy but definite increase in the importance of infantry relative to cavalry. Ever since nomads had introduced the use of the horse in warfare around about 700 BC cavalry had tended to dominate. The one very large and significant exception were the Roman legions and to a lesser extent the classical Greeks. For some authors a move towards giving infantry a more central role starts as early as the fourteenth century in Europe, with victories of infantry over cavalry at Courtrai in 1302, Bannockburn in 1314 and the rise of the Swiss pike men as a force in warfare at about the same time. As we have seen, Song China had moved to a predominantly infantry based army even earlier.

However, cavalry remained the principal arm in warfare for a long time and in many places. The armies of the Ottoman and Mughal empires had cavalry as their principal components and the same was true initially of Safavid Iran. This reflected the reality that for a long time heavily armed and armoured horsemen would still win most battles against infantry, unless the terrain or location hindered them significantly. It therefore made sense to keep it as the central component of an army, while supplementing it with other forces. On the other hand however, infantry in the shape of the famous Janissary corps was a crucial component of the Ottoman army in a way that had not been true of earlier Middle Eastern powers such as the Seljuks and the same point can be made about Iran and Mughal India. So, although still the subordinate force, infantry was much more significant than in previous historical periods. Moreover, in Europe the movement towards a predominantly infantry based military continued after 1600 and became one of the distinguishing features of the European way of war.

The second part of the revolution was of course the use of gunpowder, above all in heavy artillery. This was so significant and had such extensive consequences that for many authors it *was* the military revolution and they prefer to speak of a 'gunpowder revolution'. Like so much else gunpowder was first discovered by the Chinese, probably at some point in the ninth century. They soon became aware of its possibilities for use in warfare and the Song dynasty saw a number of innovations, above all the use of 'fire arrows' (primitive rockets), gunpowder bombs, and devices designed to fire projectiles and missiles at the enemy.

This technology was transmitted to other parts of Eurasia during the period of Mongol rule. The onset of increased pressure on ruling elites meant that it was widely adopted as the fourteenth century wore on – in all parts of the Old World. This meant that military competition led to a number of significant innovations. The most important, which first happened in Europe, was the ability to cast large metal guns without major flaws, which made them reliable and effective and more dangerous to the enemy than their users. Initially the relative brittleness of cast iron meant that most guns were made of brass but the discovery of purer sources of iron meant that by the mid to late fifteenth century most were made of this much cheaper metal.

New techniques of this kind spread rapidly from one part of the world to another, often with significant consequences. Thus, the Ottoman sultan Mehmet II imported European gunnery experts from Transylvania in 1453 and was able to reduce the hitherto impregnable walls of Constantinople. Both the Ottomans and Safavids then adopted the technology and developed it independently. Meanwhile similar techniques were developed independently in China and India. Early guns were large and heavy and were often actually cast at the place they were needed but with time they became lighter and more mobile, making them much more effective as a continuing threat rather than as a one-off response to a particular situation.

The invention and diffusion of heavy artillery had important consequences. The low cost fortifications of the medieval period, which were within the means of even small towns and wealthy private individuals or organisations, were now obsolete. Moreover, while the guns themselves became less costly with time this was not true of the skilled metalworkers needed to mine and produce the metal and cast the guns. They remained few in number and correspondingly expensive. In addition, once iron became the main metal used for cannon the location of high-grade iron ores gave a significant advantage to those who controlled or had access to it. Any ruling group that got a head start in the use of artillery had a huge advantage in warfare from the mid fifteenth century onwards, which was magnified even further if they were able to consolidate an effective monopoly of this technology. If this was the case then no rebellion or adversary that lacked the new artillery would be able to resist for very long or to take the offensive itself. For this reason a large artillery park under their sole control was the key to the power of most rulers from that time onwards and this is why historians often refer to the new states that emerged as 'gunpowder empires'.

In warfare however as soon as a breakthrough in technology gives an advantage to one side the response is to discover a countervailing technology that wipes out that advantage. The third part of the military revolution everywhere was the creation of new kinds of defence that could resist the new guns. The precise form varied but the common element everywhere was fortifications that were sufficiently massive and thick to absorb the kinetic energy of cannon shot. In Europe this took the form of the so-called 'trace italienne', which became widespread from the 1500s onwards. A similar kind of fortification had been developed much earlier in China, and in Japan there was the building of the massive castles such as the one at Osaka, which were a feature of the gunpowder dominated wars of the later Sengoku period from the 1520s until 1600.

The effect of the new kinds of defence was to nullify the advantage gained by artillery. A town defended in this way was virtually impregnable and could only be captured by betrayal or starvation, meaning a long siege that required a large force, kept in existence for a long time. This did not though mean a reversion to the situation that had existed before the introduction of artillery.

For one thing, the new kinds of fortification were far more expensive than their medieval predecessors were and so were beyond the means of many ruling groups, much less individuals however wealthy. In addition, in places where a ruling group had managed to establish a monopoly of power (thanks to their control of artillery) before the new fortifications became widely adopted, the new technology was moot. This is why we only find the new fortifications in areas where there was direct competition between different empires or states, such as the border between the Ottoman Empire and Iran or at various points in Europe.

The use of gunpowder meant more than heavy artillery, moreover. Its other aspect was the more general use of fire weapons in combat, something that became common from the early sixteenth century onwards and was crucial to the increasing importance of infantry. The category of fire weapons included not only personal firearms such as the musket and the harquebus but also light and mobile field artillery, used in set piece battles as well as sieges. The date of the introduction of this innovation is a matter of controversy among the scholars. Many argue that it happened after about 1580 and date the widespread adoption of such weapons to the period of roughly 1580 to 1630. However, both the Spanish and Ottoman armies had made use of them a considerable time before then. Indeed, the effectiveness of the Janissary corps was mainly due to its deployment of this kind of firepower from as early as the first decade of the sixteenth century, which partly accounts for the Ottomans' decisive victory over their main rivals in the Middle East, the Mameluke Sultanate of Egypt. It seems that infantry firearms were pioneered by these two powers and then adopted by their rivals, as well as being independently taken up elsewhere (as in Japan for example). Thus, Safavid Iran moved decisively in this direction under Shah Abbas the Great in the later sixteenth century. The period after 1580 did however see further development of personal firearms and major breakthroughs in the use of field artillery, which took place in Europe and were initially mainly associated with the Swedish army of Gustavus Adolphus (ruled 1611 – 1632).

Above all the use of fire weapons led to a significant change in battle tactics and consequently the organisation of troops, particularly infantry. It also meant that a key part of warfare from the mid-sixteenth century was the combination of the three distinct forces of cavalry, infantry and artillery into a single coordinated fighting force, something that required important innovations in military organisation. It meant that armies became much larger than had normally been the case in the Middle Ages, when they consisted of highly skilled professionals, as they now came to be made up of large numbers of trained but relatively unskilled soldiers. These new large armies and the battlefield tactics they employed, which required the coordination of the movements and actions of thousands of people, necessitated a clear, hierarchical chain of command, quite different from the more flexible, quasi-democratic kinds of organisation that had been common in many places during the Middle Ages.

The Military Revolution – Consequences

Changes in military organisation and methods, when combined with the effects of developments in fortification, meant that military establishments became permanent fixtures and much more elaborate. This is not to say that such a thing was novel. The empires of the ancient world had maintained large standing military establishments; indeed, it was their increasing cost that was the main cause of the collapse of ancient empires. China had also always had a standing military of sorts. The rest of the civilised world however had not seen this kind of institution during the Middle Ages. Generally, armies were raised and then disbanded on an ad hoc basis, as the occasion required. Most rulers would have a body of warriors attached to them but these were supplemented by peasant levies and hired mercenaries for actual wars. Above all, there was no permanent military support bureaucracy in place to deal with the housing, feeding, supplying and equipping of a military force that remained in existence with many people in active service for year after year. Gradually the demands of the new kinds of armies and warfare meant that this could not be avoided and so the states and their ruling groups that were the most successful in military competition were those that had a large and effective infrastructure in place.

This had far reaching implications for politics. It required a much larger and more efficient administration than most medieval states had at their command. Above all it required a much larger tax base and a more efficient means of raising funds through either taxes or loans. Because most of the costs of war were current rather than capital the important factor was to have a sustained cash flow – raising a large lump sum could not fund wars. Changes in military organisation and tactics therefore led directly to a strengthening of government and to an increase in the burdens it imposed in the shape of taxes and charges. At the same time, it was innovations in administration and taxation that made the recruitment and organisation of large permanent armies possible in the first place.

Rather than get into futile 'chicken and egg' arguments we must realise that the causal connections between these two related phenomena ran in both directions which each of them being simultaneously cause and effect of the other. In other words, a kind of positive feedback loop could arise in which reforms in military organisation led to changes in administration and government which in turn fed back into an increase in the size of the military, which in turn made a more professional government a necessity and so on. The main constraints were the limits of the productive capacity of the economic system and the resistance, often violent, of the taxpaying classes together with limits imposed by natural conditions and technology, above those due to distance and the inevitably slow and haphazard movement of information and commands in a world without the telegraph or telephone, much less radio.

European Exceptions: Organisation and Drill

All of these changes took place throughout Eurasia in one form or another. However, there were two other parts of the military revolution that only happened in a permanent fashion in Europe. This had profound consequences for relations between European powers and the rest of the world. The first was a specific change in the organisation and training of armies that as far as we can tell took place only in Europe. This was the introduction of regular, systematic drill, and the organisation of armies into permanent units of roughly fifteen hundred men, made up in turn of smaller permanent sub-units. Although the Spanish army had some early intimations of this, the real inventor of it was the Dutch commander Maurice of Nassau (1567 – 1625). His innovations in this area were then extended and elaborated by subsequent generals such as Gustavus Adolphus.

Again, this was not new. It was in fact a quite conscious revival of the military practice of the Roman legions and before them the Greeks. These may seem at first sight to be trivial innovations but they had a profound effect on the soldiers who experienced them. Indeed, they continue to do so to this day. The regular drilling of soldiers who also lived and fought together in units of a particular size created a very powerful bonding between them and produced the vital quality of *esprit de corps*. This made them far more effective as soldiers, not least because the loyalty they felt for each other made them far less likely to break in combat and also made for much closer and more effective cooperation in combat and in manoeuvres and fighting methods such as firing in unison to order. The combination of the unity created by drill and the organisation of platoons, companies, and battalions gave armies employing this method a uniquely effective combination of coordinated obedience to commands with initiative and independence further down the chain of command. It also created a more egalitarian form of warfare that depended far less on the bravery, skill and strength of individual warriors and far more on the way that undoubtedly brave and skilful individuals cooperated.

At the start of the seventeenth century when these innovations were getting under way in Europe, European powers were militarily at best on a par with the great empires of Asia, as the history of conflicts with the Ottomans showed. By the last two decades the balance had shifted decisively in favour of the Europeans, with Prince Eugene driving the Turks out of Hungary and the Russians expanding rapidly across the North and centre of Eurasia. The Chinese were able to defeat Dutch attempts to conquer Taiwan in 1662 and to inflict a severe defeat on the Russians in 1689 but by the mid-eighteenth century comparatively small numbers of European or European trained soldiers were able to completely defeat much larger traditional Asian armies, as for example at Plassey in 1757.

Naval Power in China and Europe

The other aspect of the military revolution that was not found almost everywhere was a breakthrough in naval warfare. Until then naval warfare remained much the same as it had been since the time of Salamis, dominated by ramming and boarding, with the galley the main kind of warship in many of the world's seas. The crucial development was the invention of large, heavy ships that could carry artillery, initially catapults, latterly cannon. The first breakthrough in this respect took place in China under the Song and, as we have seen, naval power became the main feature of Song strategy after the loss of Northern China in 1126. The Yuan continued the policy and it was initially maintained and even extended under the Ming.

This was particularly true under the third Ming emperor, Wu Di, who ruled as the Yongle emperor from 1403 to 1424. Under his rule, the Chinese navy was expanded and a whole series of naval expeditions were mounted under the command of the eunuch admiral Zheng He (1371 – 1433). Between 1405 and Zheng He's death in 1433 no fewer than seven of these expeditions were mounted. The fleets involved had up to three hundred ships in them, each with an average crew of over one thousand. The largest ships had nine masts and were up to four hundred feet in length, the largest ships built anywhere in the world before the nineteenth century. In his voyages he sailed to South-East Asia, India, Hormuz, the Red Sea, and as far down the African coast as what is now Northern Mozambique. In other words, Chinese fleets sailed all over and completely dominated, the Indian Ocean.

What though was the point of these impressive displays of naval power? Historians have pointed out that these were not directly profit motivated enterprises. Consequently, the voyages of the 'treasure ships' (as they were called) have been presented as mere display, a way of flaunting China's power and of acquiring exotic animals for the imperial zoo in Beijing and so not driven by the desire for trade and wealth. The problem with this view is that such a policy seems very unlikely for the tough minded Yongle emperor or the pragmatic Chinese elite. For one thing, the ships did indeed engage in trade and carried Chinese goods. The voyages, like many later ones by Europeans, actually had a combined political and economic purpose.

In fact, it seems likely that the purpose of the expeditions was to project power and to establish a Chinese hegemony over the trade and sea routes of the Indian Ocean, at that time and for a long time thereafter the true hub of the world trade system. This is one of the great advantages of naval power for rulers who have access to it. It enables the projection of power over much greater distances than can commonly be managed on land, because of the greater speed and lower cost of travel by water as compared to land for most of history, and also because intermediate powers and territories can be bypassed, which is not often the case with armies. Moreover, because of its lower transport costs, most of the world's trade has historically been maritime trade. Controlling the world's key sea routes enables the ruling class of the controlling power to gain income and to control trade to their own advantage. The Ming system of managed 'tribute' trade was perfectly complemented by the aggressive naval policy of Zheng He and the Yongle emperor.

However it was not continued. The enormous fleet did indeed impose a great burden on the resources even of the Ming Empire, given that it had to simultaneously rebuild the Great Wall and face down the continuing threat from the Mongols to the North. Moreover, the increasingly dominant faction in the court at Beijing opposed the forward naval strategy on ideological as well as pragmatic grounds, since it conflicted with their desire to reduce contact between China and the rest of the world. The common factor linking these two concerns was the decline in world trade that was such a prominent feature of the crisis of 1320 to 1450. Given this, it made less sense for China to pursue such a naval strategy as well as a defensive land based one.

After Zheng He's death, there were no further expeditions and eventually in 1451 the great fleet was scrapped. Following this, in 1476 the entire technology of ocean going ships was both abandoned and suppressed. This was a decision with enormous geopolitical consequences. Taken at the end of the long economic downturn that had started in the early fourteenth century, it meant that the Chinese withdrew from the seas as a naval power precisely at the point that the world trade system revived, but in a new form. Their withdrawal left a vacuum of naval power in the Indian Ocean and this was filled by the other part of the world to see a breakthrough in naval military power as a part of the military revolution, the Europeans.

Faced with the slump in trade and the effective closing of the overland routes to China and the Indian Ocean, West Europeans, particularly the Portuguese and the Genoese, sought to circumvent the control of the lucrative trade between the Mediterranean and the Indian Ocean by the Venetians and their Muslim allies. The outcome was a breakthrough in maritime technology in the second half of the fifteenth century, produced by combining Middle Eastern sails and rigging (which gave an ability to sail close to the wind) with North European techniques for the building of ships. The result was the caravel, a ship that was both manoeuvrable and able to sail long distances over the world's oceans. Further innovations were improvements in navigational aids, gained directly from Muslims although the Chinese originally invented the technologies in question (the compass and the astrolabe). Following initial innovations by the Portuguese there were later improvements made by North Europeans in the course of the sixteenth century, most notably by the Dutch.

The military implications of this were that the new kinds of ship could mount cannon on board and fire broadsides. Ship borne artillery of this kind made traditional warships completely ineffective, however large and impressive they might be. Given that the only other power with this kind of technology (i.e. Ming China) had abandoned its use, European powers, initially the Portuguese and the Spanish, latterly the Dutch and even later the French, English and Danes had a significant military monopoly, which had far reaching results. In the Mediterranean, galleys remained the main type of warship and the Ottomans a match for their Italian and Spanish opponents but the former never succeeded in producing an ocean going fleet with ship born artillery to challenge Portuguese and later Dutch power in the Indian Ocean. The new maritime technology also had important consequences for world trade. The great conundrum is that of why similar breakthroughs did not happen in the lands around the Indian Ocean, by the Ottomans, Indians and the inhabitants of South East Asia. This is yet to be satisfactorily explained but the reason seems to be that there was not a pressing need for an improvement in maritime technology in that part of the world as there was for the inhabitants of the Iberian Peninsula and later on the Low Countries.

The Rise of Gunpowder Empires

The military revolution was thus a complex phenomenon, found in varying forms in all parts of the Old World, and deriving from the universal increase in competition between ruling classes occasioned by the world crisis of the fourteenth century and the pressure for innovation that it brought about. It was essentially a combination of changes in technology, above all the adoption of gunpowder to warfare on both sea and land, in tactics and fighting methods, and in military organisation. Because organised violence is the basis of political power and war the ultimate test of a state or political system, this had profound effects for the nature of politics. Although universal, the military revolution was not uniform and had varying forms and outcomes in different parts of the world. Thus the revolution in naval warfare took place only in China (where it was abandoned) and in Europe. The emphasis upon infantry was more marked in Europe and China than in India or the Middle East. The process of innovation continued in Europe after it had effectively ceased elsewhere, with the result that Europe saw innovations in military training and organisation that did not happen elsewhere.

Above all though, the military revolution had different political and geopolitical outcomes in different parts of the world. In most places, the result was the emergence of large consolidated empires, which historians have dubbed 'gunpowder empires'. Another way of thinking of this is to use the models of international relations theory, in particular the notion of a hegemonic power. The military revolution began in and was the product of, a situation where the political order of the Middle Ages had been shattered or put under immense strain by the combination of the Mongol conquests, the Black Death, and the economic crisis occasioned by the pandemic when combined with an underlying subsistence crisis and the impact of the little ice age. In most places, the initial situation was one of political conflict and breakdown, with large numbers of competing powers and factions. The result in most cases was the emergence of a single hegemonic power that united all or a very large part of one of the medieval world's major civilisations. This was partly the outcome of the way the dynamics of competition played out, particularly once the military innovations had become established. Essentially one of the competing powers, which took early advantage of military innovation or was blessed by a combination of luck, outstanding leadership, and geographical advantage, was able to establish a clear lead over its rivals. This set up a self-reinforcing positive feedback, in which the dominant power became steadily more and more predominant in a part of the world until its growth was finally checked either by geographical constraints or by its coming into contact with another military power of equal force. The obvious analogy is with competition in commerce, where the initial situation of a large number of competing small firms gives way by a process of competition, merger and acquisition to one with a predominant firm or a stable small number of larger firms.

Ming China

One partial exception to this rule was Ming China. Here the creation of a large centralised empire took place earlier than anywhere else, in 1368. However, the situation was significantly different, inasmuch as we are not talking about the unification of a number of competing independent states by one of their number but rather the refurbishment and reform of an existing empire. The breakdown of government under the Yuan had indeed reduced China to a state of rampant banditry and warlordism but it had not seen the kind of clear fragmentation into distinct states that took place in India or Russia, much less the radical breakdown of political order that occurred in much of the Middle East. However the military aspect of the foundation of Ming China was important, and the kinds of government and policies followed by the early Ming regime, described in the previous chapter, had part of their basis in a reform of the military system of the Chinese empire, which contributed significantly to the change in its quality and nature.

At its foundation the success of the Hongwu emperor in driving out the Mongols and reuniting China had depended upon the use both of firearms and artillery and the new style of fortification that provided protection against them. By fortifying Nanjing and other strongholds in south and central China he was able to have a secure base that his rivals could not successfully assault, while his rapid success against both the remnants of the Yuan and his main Chinese rivals (due in part to his use of new technology, particularly in the crucial battle of Lake Poyang) meant that they had no chance to build fortifications of their own. Had they done so, China could well have split up permanently into several states, as it had threatened to do before. The military system of Ming China sought to revive the peasant levy system of the Tang and was thus closely connected to the revival of peasant agriculture that was such a prominent feature of Ming domestic policy. It led to the creation of a large but essentially static permanent yet predominantly part-time army. Initially this was supplemented by a large full time professional military, mainly infantry, and an aggressive policy was followed with a number of expeditions into central Asia. However, as the worldwide economic decline bit and following the disastrous expedition of 1449, which culminated in the capture of the emperor, this was abandoned and there was a reversion to a more defensive policy.

The Mughal Empire

In most of Eurasia, the military revolution led to the creation of large new empires, which united all or most of the area of each main civilisation. In India, the initially successful player in the competition for dominance that followed the breakdown of the Delhi Sultanate was a central Asian adventurer and politico-military entrepreneur called Babur (1483 – 1531). He was an outstanding cavalry commander and also made use of the new technology of gunpowder artillery. After becoming the ruler of Kabul and large parts of Sind in 1504, he went on to defeat the last of the Lodi rulers of Delhi in 1526 at the First battle of Panipat and captured Delhi, which became his 'base'. From there he expanded his control south and eastwards until his death in 1531. His son, Humayun (1508 – 1556), lacked his qualities and was driven into exile in 1540 by yet another political entrepreneur, an Afghan warlord called Sher Shah Suri (1486 – 1545). He effectively took over the dominion established by Babur but had no heir and in 1555 Humayun returned from exile and recaptured Delhi.

He died soon afterwards in an accident and was succeeded by his son Akbar (1542 – 1605) who ruled from 1556 to 1605. He was able to conquer most of the northern two thirds of India and unite it into an empire that lasted until it effectively broke up in the 1720s. This reflected the way in which, building on his inheritance from Babur and Sher Shah, he was able to use the new military techniques to rapidly expand the territory and resources he controlled to a point where there was no rival with the power to challenge him, at least in Northern India. At the same time, he created something new, compared to the simple 'extractive' empire of the Delhi sultanate and its predecessors by establishing an elaborate permanent system of administration and tax collection. This provided a stable framework of laws, public order and money (in the shape of the silver-based rupee) for production and commerce. At the same time, it also provided a machinery to extract wealth from these productive activities, mainly to support the military but also to fund the elaborate court of the Mughals, and to control and channel trade and exchange.

Russia

Following its conquest by the Mongols in 1238-40, Russia was ruled for some hundred and fifty years by the Golden Horde, one of the successor khanates of the empire of Genghis Khan. This rule was simply an extractive suzerainty in which the Mongols drew resources from the various princes and city-states. As elsewhere, the fourteenth century brought a breakdown of political order and in 1380 the Mongols were defeated at the battle of Kulikovo and although they remained a military threat, their political suzerainty was broken. As in India, the result was competition between the various rulers. In this case it was the Grand Dukes of Moscow who emerged as the winners. The decisive breakthrough came in the reign of Ivan III (1462-1505). Once again, the key factor was the use of artillery and a larger military with the Muscovites taking advantage of their geographical position which enabled them to use the great Russian rivers as transport routes to move their artillery park to attack the states that surrounded them. One state was absorbed after another with Muscovite predominance increasing with each victory. The tipping point came with Ivan's victory over the great trading city of Novgorod in 1478, followed seven years later by the annexation of Tver, the most likely rival candidate to unify the Russian lands.

Following his marriage to a Byzantine princess in 1472 Ivan took the title of Tsar (i.e. emperor). He and his successors Basil III (1505-1533) and Ivan IV (the Terrible) (1533-1584) created a system of rule and an empire that would last until at least 1917, and arguably until today. As with the Mughals, a crucial part of the process was creating stable conditions for trade within the bounds of the empire while trying to control that trade and also to strictly regulate contact with those outside the bounds of the empire – a key event in this was Ivan III's expulsion of German Hanseatic merchants from Novgorod in 1494. The empire continued to expand under Basil III and Ivan IV, with an important event the capture of Kazan and Astrakhan by Ivan in 1552-56, until the Livonian War of 1557-82 checked its expansion. Although the empire fell into a state of crisis after Ivan IV's death, it did not disintegrate as it might have done two hundred years earlier – the new states created by the military revolution had an institutional form and staying power that enabled them to survive political disorder and incompetent rulers that would have proved fatal to many medieval polities.

The Ottomans

In the Islamic world, the political slate was wiped clean by the Black Death and the incursions and rule of the Mongols and Timur. By the early sixteenth century, however it was more united than at any time since the early Abbasids some seven hundred years earlier. The people responsible were of course the Ottoman Turks who took advantage of the crisis and the military revolution to establish one of the most powerful gunpowder empires, which would survive until 1919. The Ottomans were initially just one Turkish tribe among many in Anatolia but they had the good fortune of being led by a succession of outstanding military leaders, who came out as winners in the intensified competition of the great crisis.

Their military power was initially a cavalry based army as with all of the other Turkish emirates but they made early use of gunpowder in the form of both artillery and firearms and early on established an effective infantry arm in the shape of the famous Janissary corps. The initial breakthrough came under Murad I (1361 – 1389), who adopted the crucial military innovations and was able to conquer large parts of the Balkans and Anatolia. In 1389 he inflicted a crushing defeat on the Serbs at the battle of Kossovo and although he lost his own life in the battle, this eliminated the Serb kingdom as a competitor in the Balkans. His successor Bayezid I (1389 – 1402) expanded the Ottomans' control in Anatolia and completely defeated a crusader army at Nicopolis in 1396. However he was then himself completely defeated and taken captive by Timur at the battle of Ankara in 1402. Following this the Ottoman supremacy was in serious danger of disintegrating but, as with the Mughals after the defeat of Humayun, the dynasty was able to make a comeback. This took place under Murad II (1421 – 1451) who conquered most of the Balkans. Advance up the Danube was checked by the Hungarians under the leadership of another of the politico-military entrepreneurs characteristic of the era, Janos Hunyadi (1387 – 1456). Murad's eventual successor Mehmet II (1451 – 1481) was of course the sultan who finally captured Constantinople in 1453. He was also the ruler who, like Akbar and Ivan III, finally turned a military supremacy into a permanent institutionalised empire.

The next major expansion of the area under Ottoman control came under Selim I (1512 – 1520). He began his reign with a war against Shah Ismail, the founder of the Safavid state of Iran but although he gained a victory at the battle of Chaldiran in 1514 he was unable to destroy the Safavid regime. His victory did however prevent the Shiite regime of Shah Ismail from expanding into areas of the Middle East with a largely Shiite population, most notably eastern Anatolia and Iraq. Moreover, just two years later in 1516 he inflicted a crushing defeat on the Mameluke sultanate of Egypt at the battle of Marjdabik near Aleppo and the following year he captured Cairo. This was an event of enormous importance because it meant that he had eliminated a major rival power in terms of the resources at its disposal. Had he not done so, the Middle East would have remained divided at least three ways but as it was, with Egypt now part of the Ottoman Empire and with the smaller states of the Mahgreb (Tripoli, Tunis and Algiers) accepting Ottoman suzerainty, the larger part of the Islamic world was now under a single ruler.

It is important to notice that one reason why he could do this was that he did not face a serious threat from outside – the Iranian state had not fully established itself and the threat from that direction was temporarily removed by the victory at Chaldiran while the Christian West was divided and unable to mount a serious challenge in the Balkans. Selim's successor Suleiman I (1520 – 1566) continued the expansion. In 1521 he captured the great fortress city of Belgrade. Then, in 1526 he defeated and killed the Hungarian ruler Louis at the battle of Mohacs, following which the Ottomans overran most of Hungary. However at this point the Ottomans had reached a limit to their expansion as they now faced powers sufficiently large and with a sufficiently modernised military to be able check them. In the west they confronted the newly formed Habsburg Empire of Charles V, with the failure to capture Vienna in 1529 a decisive check, while from 1534 onwards there were a series of indecisive wars with the Iranians on the eastern frontier.

The Ottomans, like the Russian Tsars and the Mughals, created a new kind of Islamic empire, which was long lasting and institutionalised, unlike the evanescent supremacies of the past that had been a feature of the Islamic world since the gradual decline of the Abbasids in the tenth century. There were clear parallels to the systems created in other gunpowder empires such as the Mughals but it also had distinctive features, the most important being the use of slave soldiers, acquired through the *devshirme* system in which certain Christian communities surrendered young children in lieu of the poll tax normally paid by non-Muslims. The children were then raised in a crèche to be loyal only to the sultan and became either soldiers or bureaucrats. The Ottoman sultans also created a system of administration that could incorporate conquered territories into a system of governance so that they became parts of a system of common rule and law rather than just part of a collection of territories that all paid tax to a common overlord.

Safavid Iran

The Ottomans' major rival within the Islamic world, and the last of the great land based gunpowder empires was Safavid Iran. Again, the Safavids were initially just one of many political competitors in the chaotic legacy of Timur's devastating invasions and the disorder of the eastern parts of the Islamic world. Originally they were a reformist cult based in Azerbaijan but under the founder of the regime, Ismail (1502 – 1524) they rapidly expanded from their base and were able to unite all of what is now Iran plus large parts of Baluchistan and Afghanistan under their rule. The regime survived the shock of defeat by the Ottomans in 1514 and went on to hold off Turkish attempts to extend their rule beyond Mesopotamia in the central part of the sixteenth century. As with the other successful empire building powers the key factor in their success was the adoption and use of new military technology and organisation. In this case Ismail inherited a powerful fighting force from his father in the shape of the Kizilbashes, the infantry of the order that the dynasty had founded back in the early fourteenth century, plus a more traditional cavalry force. Another element was sectarian Shiism, along with an emphasis on the Iranian nature of the regime.

The regime was finally consolidated and the military revolution completely adopted under the greatest of the Safavid rulers, Shah Abbas I (1587 – 1629). They were now able to take the offensive against the Ottomans but eventually this resulted in a stalemate and the establishment of a permanent frontier. Meanwhile the Safavids' ambition to expand into central Asia and so recreate the empire of Timur was blocked by the powerful Uzbek sultanate. However Iran remained a large and powerful imperial state. As with the other cases it followed a policy of supporting trade within the bounds of the territory it controlled while being linked to other parts of the world by trade through specific outlets, in this case the key port and trading hub of Hormuz. This was initially through the Portuguese and after 1616 via the English. As with Russia, there was a dynastic collapse, during the eighteenth century, but the state survived as a recognisable entity although it has been ruled by several dynasties since then.

Patterns in the World of Gunpowder Empires

So in all of these cases we can discern common patterns, with China a partial exception, mainly because it was already united under a single regime before the process began, however debilitated it might have become. In each case a process of intense competition among ruling groups and would be rulers together with military innovation led to the eventual triumph of a single group who went on to establish a large empire that controlled a significant portion of the world's resources and population. Chronologically, apart from China, the process happened in the later phase and aftermath of the fourteenth century crisis with the key period between 1450 and 1550.

Each victor can be though of as being the hegemonic or imperial power in a particular roughly defined zone of the Old World. These zones can essentially be defined as all or a very large part of one of the civilisations that had grown up in the medieval period, or as broadly geographical entities, or again as economic ones, each incorporating one or more of the trade circuits that had defined the medieval world trade order. However, what really defined the limits was military capacity, with each imperial power having a tendency to expand until it reached either a natural limit or was checked by an external military power that was sufficiently strong to do so, usually via a series of inconclusive conflicts.

Thus, each of them controlled a large part of the world's productive resources and some of the key trade routes and hubs. None however controlled the great majority in the way that the Mongols had done and several important trade systems ran across the limits of the various large empires. Moreover, all were plugged into a new world trade system that had emerged from the ruin of the medieval one, via long distance trade connections, particularly oceanic ones.

The pattern in all cases was to have free trade and exchange within the bounds of the empire but very tight control of what we may think of as external trade (because that was how the rulers saw it). In each case, the imperial rule effectively created a single large unified economic order through the provision of internal peace and security together with common institutions such as law, currency and markets. Initially there were considerable gains from this (not least when this was compared to the disorder of the period before the emergence of these empires) because it reduced predation and brought greater predictability and hence confidence about the future. In every case though, it became clear subsequently that there were also considerable costs. These arose from the way the ruling groups of the new empires sought to regulate and control the processes of exchange and the relations they created, partly for their own economic advantage but mainly in the interests of political control and stability for its own sake. The effect of this was to stifle innovation and check spontaneous development processes, with Ming China perhaps the most clear-cut case, at least initially.

There were also common features to the kind of government that the successful conquerors established. These proved to have great staying power, and the regimes or systems of rule that they established (as opposed to the particular groups that controlled them at any one time) lasted for centuries, in some cases arguably to the present day. The most significant common element was a military system that combined a permanent force with a larger military run on a quasi-feudal basis in which land was granted out on a strictly non-hereditary basis to military subcontractors who supplied a certain number of soldiers in return for a particular area of land. In the Chinese case the supplementary force was a part-time peasant soldiery. This meant that the ruling group had something much more like a monopoly of force than medieval rulers had, especially when it went with a central monopoly of artillery. The cost of this required large administrative machinery for tax collecting and economic regulation. Although these were much more professional than the kinds of administration (or more simply resource extraction) that had been found in the Middle Ages they were still not like a modern government, with great reliance upon such practices as the sale and inheritance of public office, tax farming, and systematic use of clientage to fill positions.

Exceptions to these Patterns

There were though some exceptions to the general pattern of the military revolution and its outcome. A possible one was Morocco but it was really just another, slightly smaller gunpowder empire, comparable perhaps to Safavid Iran. A more significant exception was Japan. Here the introduction of firearms by the Portuguese in 1542 rapidly destabilised the kind of competition between local lords that had been a feature of life there since the end of the Kamakura shogunate in 1336 and particularly since the effective demise of the Ashikaga shogunate in 1467. As elsewhere, political competition rapidly became a game of 'winner takes all' and the eventual outcome was the decisive battle of Sekigahara in 1600 and the unification of Japan under the rule of the Tokugawa, the first time that Japan had been effectively under one regime since the early fourteenth century. Again this was long lasting, with the Tokugawa ruling Japan until 1867. However, Japan took a different course after 1600 compared to the other states produced by the military revolution. One notable difference was that the Tokugawa shoguns were able to outlaw the use of firearms, the only case in history of a military technology that had been widely adopted being abolished without being replaced by a more advanced one. One reason for their being able to do this was the second unique feature of Japan's experience. Initially Japanese had participated enthusiastically in the newly emerging world trade system of the post-medieval world and this had continued in characteristic fashion via the system of licensed 'red seal' ships and merchants even after Sekigahara. However, in the mid-seventeenth century the Tokugawa acted to sever most trade links and to cut Japan off from the rest of the world, a major departure from the pattern found elsewhere. There was also no attempt to expand the boundaries of the Japanese state, after the failure of the attempt to conquer Korea under Toyotomi Hideyoshi in the 1590s.

However the really significant exception to the general rule was Europe. Here the outcome of the crisis and the military revolution was quite different to what it was elsewhere. Empires were indeed created but these were of a quite different kind and the sort of political order that finally settled down in Europe was quite different from the gunpowder empires that emerged elsewhere. This had huge effects and implications for Europe's subsequent development. Moreover, the form the military revolution took in Europe, together with other contingent factors meant that from being peripheral actors Europeans came to be much more central in the kind of world order that grew up to replace the old medieval one.

Further Reading and Bibliographical Essay

There are a number of general surveys of the 14th century and the state of crisis that most contemporaries noted, as well as later commentators. One popular and accessible account of European history in this period is Barbara Tuchman *A Distant Mirror: The Calamitous Fourteenth Century*. (Ballantine, 1987). The best introduction to the contemporary scholarship is the outstanding work of Bruce Campbell, which can be found in *The Great Transition: Climate, Disease, and Society in the Late Medieval World*. (Cambridge University Press, 2016). A classic account of European history in this period that explores the cultural and intellectual as well as the political aspects is Johan Huizinga *The Waning of the Middle Ages: A Study of the Forms of Life, Thought, and Art in France and the Netherlands in the XIVth and XVth Centuries*. (Normanby Press, 2016. 1st pub. 1924).

The best short introduction to the 'Little Ice Age' and its impact is Brian M. Fagan *The Little Ice Age: How Climate Made History 1300 – 1850*. (Basic Books, 2001). The best recent work on the Great Famine of 1314-16 is William Chester Jordan *The Great Famine: Northern Europe in the Early Fourteenth Century*. (Princeton University Press, 1997). The Black Death has, not surprisingly, had a great deal written about it and its impact over the years. An outstanding work in this respect, which also sets out the case for a Malthusian crunch becoming apparent by the later thirteenth century, is David Herlihy *The Black Death and the Transformation of the West* (Harvard University Press, 1997). Herlihy convincingly argues that had the epidemic not occurred the most likely outcome would have been a prolonged subsistence crisis or Malthusian stalemate, rather than the sudden drop in population that actually happened. Among the histories of the Black Death are Robert S. Gottfried *The Black Death*. (Free Press, 1983), John Kelly *The Great Mortality: An Intimate History of the Black death, the Most Devastating Plague of All Time*. (HarperCollins, 2005), Samuel K. Cohn *The Black Death Transformed: Disease and Culture in Early Renaissance Europe*. (Hodder Arnold, 2003), Michael W. Dols *The Black Death in the Middle East*. (Princeton University Press, 1977). Two works that look at the role of disease throughout history and so place the epidemic in a longer historical context are William H. McNeill *Plagues and Peoples*. (Anchor, 1977) and Sheldon Watts *Epidemics and History: Disease, Power, and Imperialism*. (Yale University Press, 1999).

The political history of the world in the fourteenth century can be traced using the various world history texts listed in the bibliography for the first chapter – doing this makes it clear how the process of political disintegration and intensified elite competition affected all of the Old World's major civilisations. The best recent survey of the career of Timur is Justin Marozzi *Tamerlane: Sword of Islam, Conqueror of the World*. (Da Capo, 2006).

For military history in general and to provide the best context for understanding the military revolution of the fifteenth to seventeenth centuries the starting points are William H. McNeill *The Pursuit of Power: Technology, Armed Force and Society Since AD 1000.* (University of Chicago Press, 1984), Robert L. O' Connell *Of Arms and Men: A History of War, Weapons and Aggression.* (Oxford University Press, 1990), and Geoffrey Parker *The Cambridge Illustrated History of Warfare.* (Cambridge University Press, 2000). It is still worth looking at the classic works on medieval and renaissance warfare by Sir Charles Oman *A History of the Art of War in the Middle Ages. Vol. I: 378 – 1278. Vol. II 1278 – 1485.* (Greenhill, 1998 1ˢᵗ pub. 1924) and *A History of the Art of War in the Sixteenth Century.* (Greenhill, 1999 1ˢᵗ pub. 1930). The main texts in the debates about the Military Revolution, including the original lecture by Michael Roberts, can be found in Clifford J. Rogers (ed.) *The Military Revolution Debate: Readings on the Military Transformation of Early Modern Europe.* (Westview Press, 1995). The two outstanding historians of this subject are Geoffrey Parker and Jeremy Black, the two main works in which their arguments are summarised are these: Geoffrey Parker *The Military Revolution: Military Innovation and the Rise of The West, 1500 – 1800.* (Cambridge University Press, 1996) and Jeremy Black *War and the World: Military Power and the Fate of Continents.* (Yale University Press, 1998). The specific topic of drill and its importance is covered in William H. McNeill *Keeping Together in Time: Dance and Drill in Human History.* (Harvard University Press, 1997). The new defences in Europe are covered in detail in Parker's work.

For an example from another part of the world of the way defence responded to the challenge of gunpowder weapons see Stephen Turnbull *Japanese Castles 1540 – 1640.* (Osprey, 2003). The history of firearms is covered in Kenneth Chase *Firearms: A Global History.* (Cambridge University Press, 2008). The military history of China in this period is covered by Peter Lorge *War, Politics and Society in Early Modern China 900 – 1795.* (Routledge, 2005), and David Andrew Graf & Robin Higham *A Military History of China.* (Westview Press, 2002). That China remained on a par with Europe for longer than previously thought and continued to innovate in military technology is the thesis of Tonio Andrade *The Gunpowder Age: China, Military Innovation, and the Rise of the West in World History* (Princeton University Press, 2016). Ottoman military history is explored in detail in Rhoads Murphy *Ottoman Warfare, 1500 – 1700.* (Routledge, 1998). In addition to the accounts by Parker and Black two good surveys of European military history at this time are John Rigby Hale *War and Society in Renaissance Europe 1450 – 1620.* (McGill-Queens University Press, 1998), and Geoff Mortimer *Early Modern Military History 1450 – 1815.* (Palgrave Macmillan, 2004).

There is increasing attention paid to the transformative effect of the Military Revolution on politics and governance. A really good survey is Brian Downing *The Military Revolution and Political Change* (Princeton University Press, 1992). One by now classic work is Martin Van Kreveld *The Rise and Decline of the State.* (Cambridge University Press, 1999). The other, classic study of the connection between organised violence and political rule, and the way these changed over time is Charles Tilly *Coercion, Capital, and European States 900 – 1992.* (Blackwell, 2007). An important account of an alternative kind of political order, which was common before the Military Revolution, can be found in Hendrik Spruyt *The Sovereign State and its Competitors.* (Princeton University Press, 1996).

The outstanding study of the global order that appeared as a result of the military transformations is John Darwin *After Tamerlane: the Global History of Empire Since 1405.* (Bloomsbury Press, 2008). This work is particularly valuable because of the way it looks at the non-European forms of aggressive imperialism after 1500 and not just the well known European examples. The other outstanding work of recent scholarship that looks at the range and pattern of relations between the various major civilisations during the age of 'gunpowder empires' is Charles H. Parker *Global Interactions in the Early Modern Age, 1400 – 1800.* (Cambridge University Press, 2010). One very useful work that compares three of the great empires that rose to prominence is Stephen F Dale *The Muslim Empires of the Ottomans, Safavids, and Mughals* (Cambridge University Press, 2009).

The individual empires that grew out of the Military Revolution have all been the subjects of libraries of detailed scholarship, both academic and popular. The wars that led to Muscovy's emergence as an imperial power are recounted in Carol Stevens *Russia's Wars of Emergence, 1460 – 1730* (Routledge, 2007). For the Ottoman Empire some worth reading are Lord Kinross *The Ottoman Centuries: The Rise and Fall of the Turkish Empire.* (HarperCollins, 2002. 1st pub. 1977), the classic work of Halil Inalcik *The Ottoman Empire: The Classical Age 1300 – 1600.* (Phoenix, 20001st pub. 1973), Heath W. Lowry*The Nature of the Early Ottoman State.* (SUNY Press, 2003) looks at the early period and establishment of Ottoman governance. A book that corrects notions about the military backwardness of the Ottomans before the eighteenth century is Gabor Agoston *Guns for the Sultan: Military Power and the Weapons Industry in the Ottoman Empire* (Cambridge University Press, 2005). Suraiya Faroqhi *The Ottoman Empire and the World Around It.* (I B Tauris, 2006) and *Subjects of the Sultan: Culture and Daily Life in the Ottoman Empire.* (I B Tauris, 2005) are two beautifully written surveys. Colin Imber *The Ottoman Empire, 1300 – 1650.* (Palgrave-McMillan, 2002) is one of the best recent studies while Halil Inalcik (ed.) *An Economic and Social History of the Ottoman Empire Vol. I* (Cambridge University Press, 1997) is a good introduction to Ottoman economic and social history during this period.

Mughal India has also had many historians. Some works are: Abraham Eraly *The Mughal Throne: The Saga of India's Great Emperors.* (Phoenix, 2004), Francis Robinson *The Mughal Emperors: and the Islamic Dynasties of India, Iran, and Central Asia.* (Thames & Hudson, 2007), John F. Richards *The Mughal Empire.* (Cambridge University Press, 1996), Catherine B. Asher & Cynthia Talbot

India Before Europe. (Cambridge University Press, 2006). Robinson is useful for locating Mughal India in a wider network of relations and connections.

For Safavid Iran the best recent work is Andrew J. Newman *Safavid Iran: Rebirth of a Persian Empire.* (I. B. Tauris, 2006) but see also the following works: David Morgan *Medieval Persia 1040 – 1797.* (Longman, 1988), Roger Savory *Iran Under the Safavids.* (Cambridge University Press, 2007), Charles Melville *Safavid Persia: The History and Politics of an Islamic Society.* (I. B. Tauris, 1996). One very valuable study, which locates the Iranian state in the international economy of its time and explains the crucial part played by silk, is Rudolph P. Matthee *The Politics of Trade in Safavid Iran: Silk for Silver 1600 – 1730.* (Cambridge University Press, 2006).

Two useful introductions to Japanese history during the later part of the Sengoku Period are George Sansom *A History of Japan 1334 – 1615.* (Stanford University Press, 1961) and George Ellison & Bardwell L. Smith (eds.) *Warlords, Artists and Commoners: Japan in the Sixteenth Century.* (University of Hawaii Press, 1981).

The concept of the 'seaborne empire' as the form taken by European imperialism in the aftermath of the Military Revolution and the breakthrough in maritime military power in North Western Europe has shaped much of the historiography since it was first formulated by Christopher Boxer. Two surveys that between them tell the story of the rise and growth of these new thalassocracies are the works by J. H. Parry *The Age of Reconnaissance: Discovery, Exploration and Settlement 1450 – 1650.* (Phoenix, 2000 1ˢᵗ pub. 1963), and *Trade and Dominion: The European Overseas Empires in the Eighteenth Century* (Phoenix, 2000 1ˢᵗ pub. 1971). Three works that recount the rise of the largest and most significant of these, the Spanish Empire, are: Henry Kamen *Empire: How Spain became a World Power 1492 – 1763.* (HarperCollins, 2003), Hugh Thomas *Rivers of Gold: The Rise of the Spanish Empire.* (Phoenix, 2004), and J. H. Parry *The Spanish Seaborne Empire.* (University of California Press, 1966). A recent study of Portugal's moment as a global maritime power and its lasting impact is J. R. Russell-Wood *The Portuguese Empire, 1415 – 1808: A World on the Move.* (Johns Hopkins University Press, 1998). It is still well worth reading Boxer's classic works on Portugal and the Dutch Empire, Christopher R. Boxer & J. H. Plumb *The Dutch Seaborne Empire 1600 – 1800.* (Penguin, 1991), Christopher R. Boxer *The Portuguese Seaborne Empire 1415 – 1825.* (Knopf, 1969). The late arriving British case is the subject of Jeremy Black *The British Seaborne Empire.* (Yale University Press, 2004).

CHAPTER V

The European Divergence

THE world that grew out of the great crisis and the military revolution was one of empires. Great imperial powers dominated the world and have done so for most of the four hundred and fifty plus years that have passed since they emerged. Economies and social orders were also changed by the events of those years between 1320 and 1550 and a new world system appeared that replaced the medieval one. This was still however one constrained by the same kinds of limits that had affected all societies since the discovery of agriculture. It was also one where Europeans came to play an increasingly prominent though not yet dominant role. This was despite, or rather because of, the way the military revolution had a different outcome there compared to the rest of the world. Instead of a hegemonic empire appearing, as happened in China, Russia, India and the Middle East, the result was a stable yet dynamic system that changed the incentives facing rulers. This happened within a world economic order that was changed in important ways by the doings of European powers, even though Europe as a whole remained economically marginal for a long time.

The Incorporation of the New World and the Creation of Oceanic Trade Routes

The most obvious way in which the human world of the sixteenth century and later differed from that of earlier periods was that it was one single world, something that had not been true before. Although the Vikings had made fleeting contact and there may have been knowledge of the existence of North America at a later date because of the demand for fish that drove European fishermen to venture ever further afield, the Old World and the Americas had remained separate and self-contained. This ended with the voyage of Columbus in 1492 and from then on we have a truly global system of trade and along with it an increasingly global human ecology.

The initial impact of Columbus and those who came after him on the inhabitants of the Americas was devastating. This was mainly because of the diseases they brought with them, to which the indigenous inhabitants had no resistance. This inadvertent biological warfare was unidirectional (apart from the significant exception of syphilis) because native Americans (and also aboriginal Australians) did not have the wide range of domestic animals found in the Old World, which provided a constant source of pathogens to which the inhabitants of the Old World had perforce become resistant. The result in the Americas was the greatest demographic disaster in recorded history, with as much as eighty to ninety percent of the population wiped out by epidemics of smallpox, measles, and influenza. Given this, it is not surprising that small numbers of Spanish conquistadors were able to conquer huge territories in the Americas and overthrow large complex empires such as those of the Aztecs and Incas. Whether they would have enjoyed such overwhelming and rapid military success had they not had this biological advantage is an open question, but it seems likely that they would still have done so because of other advantages they enjoyed, notably significantly better weaponry in the shape of steel weapons and firearms, superior military organisation, and the horse.

The result of the European conquests in the New World, initially by the Portuguese and the Spaniards, followed later by others including the French, English and Dutch, was for the New World and products produced there to become part of the system of world trade. At the same time voyages by European explorers, sponsored initially by the Castilian and Portuguese crowns, opened up a series of long distance oceanic trade routes. In 1497 Vasco Da Gama led the first expedition to round the Cape of Good Hope and then pass on to India. Others followed him, notably Amilcar Cabral in 1500 (who made landfall in Brazil on the way, probably accidentally), Sequira (who reached the strategically vital Straits of Malacca in 1511), and Perestrello (who reached Canton in South China in 1516). Then in 1519-22 there was the first circumnavigation of the globe by the expedition led by Fernando Magellan and completed after his death by Sebastian Del Cano. These voyages meant that there was now direct contact between Europe and other parts of the world by sea for first time. In particular it meant that for the first time there was direct maritime contact between Europe and both China and India, as well as South East Asia.

We should not believe though that this meant the appearance of a new world trade system with Europe and the Atlantic as its hub, as many have supposed. For one thing, the point of all of the early voyages, both the Portuguese ones Southwards and Eastwards into the Indian Ocean and those led by Spaniards and others along the coasts of the Americas, as well as the circumnavigation of 1519-22, was to gain access to the trade and products of the Asian economies and above all the lands around the Indian Ocean. The people who lived in those parts of the world felt (and had) no corresponding need, either to make contact with Spain and Portugal or to break into the

Atlantic trade. This reflected the reality that in the early sixteenth century and for many years thereafter the true core of world trade and production was in the lands around the Indian Ocean. It was there, above all in China and India, that the most valuable manufactured goods were produced and traded while South East Asia in particular produced the most sought after primary products in the shape of spices. The opening up of the route around the Cape and the exploration and conquest of the Americas and the Caribbean were important for the development of Europe but initially had little impact on the rest of the Old World. The Atlantic trade, including slaves, sugar and fur, was much less valuable and important from a worldwide perspective (including that of most Europeans) than the trade to and between China, India and South East Asia.

The Global Impact of the 'Great Discoveries' and the First World Monetary System

However, the relative unimportance of trade with the New World for most of the Old World does not mean that the opening up of the Americas and of the long distance sea routes had no impact on the greater part of Eurasia. In two ways it had a great, though indirect effect. The first was through what is often called the 'Colombian exchange' in which all kinds of products and plants were brought from the New World and distributed around the Old, mainly by the Portuguese and the Dutch. As well as tobacco, we may also mention the potato, the sweet potato, the chilli pepper and the tomato – to give just four examples. These obviously had a major impact on diet and cuisine – it is now hard to imagine Italian cooking without the tomato or Indian without the chilli pepper (or indeed the tomato and the potato). Even more significant though was the way new food crops such as maize and the potato and sweet potato made it possible to support households on much smaller areas of land, so leading to both population growth and important changes in agricultural organisation in many parts of the world, from Ireland to Russia and Poland, to China.

The other principal impact was via the one product from the New World that the Old World had an inexhaustible demand for. This was silver. Before the sixteenth century the world's major source of silver was Japan (which remained a significant source for a long time thereafter). In the sixteenth century, the Spanish discovered two enormous silver lodes, at Potosi in Bolivia in 1545 and at Zacatecas in Mexico in 1547. The result was a great flood of silver into the world trade system after 1550. This made it possible for the great Asian empires to create a uniform silver-based currency for their territories, particularly in the cases of the Ming and Mughal empires. The flow of silver around the world also lubricated trade and made whole economies much more liquid than had been the case before. One reason was that now trade was possible between parties where previously it had been difficult because one had nothing that the other wanted, except at a prohibitive rate of exchange. Everyone though would take silver, so now those parts of the world that ran a 'deficit' in primary products or manufactured goods with another part could make up the difference with silver.

This was less significant however than the basic fact of liquidity and the creation of a worldwide medium of exchange. Because silver was the monetary metal of China and India and the rest of the world wanted Chinese and Indian products, everyone would take silver. This meant that silver effectively became the world's money and the basis for the first truly global monetary system, even if it only applied initially to long distance trade. The effect of money is of course to make trade much easier by removing the need for barter and working out through a complex exchange process the rate at which any two products will exchange (grain for porcelain for example). Instead, when the relative value of all products is expressed in terms of the rate at which they exchange for one single commodity (money), it becomes easy to exchange and trade goods by using the intermediate commodity of money. The costs of trade itself in terms of things such as the time taken to work out and make the trade (transaction costs) are hugely reduced, so again many trades become profitable when they were not before. This also generates money prices that send signals to alert entrepreneurs as to where there are shortages or mismatches of supply and demand.

So the principal impact that the European conquest of the Americas had on the rest of the world came about through the way it led to the appearance from the later sixteenth century onwards of a monetary system based on silver that made possible a much more integrated world trade system than had existed even under the Mongols. The date at which we can say that there was finally a truly global circuit of goods and money was 1571, the year when the first of the silver bearing Manila galleons sailed across the Pacific from Acapulco to the Philippines, so connecting the New World to the Asian markets and the products of China and East Asia.

The New World Economy of the Sixteenth Century

In fact, all the indications are that long distance trade and economic integration were already recovering from the mid fifteenth century onwards, as the world began to slowly recover from the impact of the Black Death and began to come to terms with the challenges posed by the little ice age. A number of things fed into this. Populations began to recover and urban life to revive from the later fifteenth century in some areas and in most by the early sixteenth century. In many parts of the world there were important changes in the way that both agriculture and manufacture were organised, which made production more robust and less susceptible to crises than before. There was further slow improvement in technique in both as well. The flow of silver fed into this renewed system of trade and production and pushed its development. Most importantly, it meant that the trade system that was clearly in place by the 1580s was different from the one described by Janet Abu-Lughod in more ways than just including the New World.

By the later sixteenth century, the volume of trade and the part that trade played in economic life generally were both greater than they had been in the thirteenth century. Long distance trade in particular had grown in importance. Many of the trade routes and hubs were the same as they had been then, for simple reasons of geography. However, the trade circuits that Abu-Lughod was able to discern when looking at the thirteenth century were no longer so clearly identifiable. Instead there was much more direct connection between the various economic regions of the world, mainly through sea routes. The division of labour and the associated economic specialisation was now increasingly truly global, for a larger range of commodities than before. Also, this was no longer so clearly a world trade system built around cities. With changes in the organisation of manufacturing, rural hinterlands were far more integrated into longer distance exchange and the key units in the new system were increasingly regions such as the Low Countries or the Yangtze delta rather than cities.

If we look at the kinds of commodities that were traded in this new system and the distances over which they were normally exchanged, several other things will strike us. One is that there was a difference, often hard to distinguish, but there nonetheless, between the trade and exchange that took place primarily within one of the major trade regions and that conducted on a larger scale. The former often took place entirely within one of the major land empires that had grown up by 1550, whereas the latter crossed over the imperial borders. Most manufactures were in the former category but there was a significant and gradually growing list of exceptions that fell into the second. The most important of these exceptions were steel weapons, both edged and firearms, porcelain, and textiles, particularly silk and cotton. These goods that were traded over long distances were mainly luxury goods such as spices or porcelain on the one hand and primary products that were suitable for bulk transport by sea, such as grain, on the other.

Another point to note is the importance for trade and economic activity more generally of certain commodities in particular. As well as weapons, porcelain and textiles one should also mention commodities and products such as furs, salt, grain, iron, sugar (and sugar products such as molasses), spices, precious metals, high cost livestock such as horses and camels, and luxury goods such as jewelry and high cost clothing, fabrics and furnishings. One 'commodity' of increasing importance throughout the system was enslaved humans, normally Africans, which reflected the growing importance of unfree labour more generally after 1450. Another feature of the trade system was the central part played in it by a number of specific ethnic or religious groups, through diasporas of these groups being crucially important as middlemen. This phenomenon has been around for as long as trade has existed but it became much more prominent with the growth of long distance trade after 1450. The most important of these were Jews, Armenians, Lebanese (often described as 'Syrians'), Omanis, Gujeratis, Fukienese, Parsees, Maharatshis, and Zanzibaris. Later on Dutch, English, New Englanders and Cantonese joined the list.

Household Production and 'Proto-Industry'

These trade diasporas were important because their close familial, personal, and religious links enabled them to conduct trust based exchange over long distances. This in turn enabled them to coordinate economic activity over a wide area and a long distance. The reason for this was the central part played by merchants in the production, as well as the distribution, of goods at this time. The great merchants of this period combine a number of functions that have gradually become distinct since then, notably investment, management, retailing and marketing, and (frequently) tax collecting (via the institution of tax-farming). Above all though, they coordinated production. This was done through a way of organising manufacture that had sprung up in slightly different forms in various parts of the world in response to the economic and in particular agricultural slump between 1320 and 1450.

The common response in many parts of the world to the climactic pressures of the little ice age and the economic consequences of the Black Death was to move towards a more market based and cash driven form of agriculture, in which crops were produced for sale on a market as well as for local consumption. This had a number of effects, one of which was that while some households came to specialise in arable or pastoral farming of one kind or another, many more came to combine farming to a greater or lesser degree with manufacture. This meant a system where manufacture of a wide range of products, from clothing, to fabric, to household goods, took place in dispersed rural households. The key to this was the so-called 'putting out' system. In this a merchant based in a town would enter into agreements with a large number of rural households for the production of a given quantity of goods, often to a precise specification. He would provide the producer households with raw materials and tools with which to produce them and would then collect and market the finished products. The merchant was therefore the central figure, responsible for the distribution and marketing of the product, the capital investment in the form of the equipment and raw materials, and the organisation of labor through a series of contracts.

Obviously there were a huge number of variations on this basic model. Sometimes the producer households would provide the raw material, or even the equipment. The kinds of labor contracts could range from indentured or bonded labor, which was common in India for example, to a system of short-term contracts very close to wage labor. The degree to which manufacturing was combined with farming also varied widely, from households where farming was still the mainstay and manufacturing a supplement right through to cases where manufacturing occupied most of the time and any agricultural activity was residual, such as keeping a pig or chickens.

This way of organising manufacture and combining it to a greater or lesser degree with farming had a number of important consequences, especially as it went along with a movement towards more commercial agriculture. One was the appearance of regional specialisation, with most households in a region producing a particular kind of product that would then be sold outside the region itself. This happened both in farming and in manufacture. In farming regions would produce predominantly livestock or some kind of arable product such as grain, or specialised cash crops such as indigo or sugar. Thus, much of Poland and the Ukraine became specialist producers of grain for sale to Western Europe and the Ottoman Empire. In manufacturing whole regions would produce a particular kind of good, such as textiles or domestic product, which would then be distributed via the mercantile network. Thus parts of India and China, such as Bengal and the Yangtze delta, came to specialise in cotton fabric, while other parts of China came to focus on products such as iron utensils or porcelain. This whole way of organising manufacture is commonly known as proto-industry. The term is rather misleading, as it refers to a now discredited theory that sees it as a precursor to factory based industry, but the term itself has stuck.

Economic Innovations, and the Revival of Slavery

Just as competition between rulers after 1320 led to innovations in government and warfare, so the crisis of 1320 to 1450 led to developments in the organisation of commerce. As well as the system of decentralised and contract organised production described above, there were important developments and refinements in commercial institutions. Some were in the apparently boring yet vital subjects of accountancy and book keeping or insurance but the most significant were in the structure and legal organisation of firms. Many parts of the world saw the appearance of large, extended and multi-branched firms that combined trading, banking and finance with the kind of productive system described above. Firms such as the Medici and the Fuggers were well known European examples but they had counterparts in China, India, Japan, the Ottoman Empire, and Africa. As with military affairs, Europeans came to push these developments further than was the case elsewhere, mainly because of the need they faced to organise trade and production over very long distances and time spans because of their peripheral position in the world trade system. The most important innovations were made by the Dutch, especially the creation of the Dutch East India Company (the VOC) in 1602 and the invention soon after of the stock exchange and with it the modern capital market.

The other important new phenomenon that appeared in the aftermath of the crisis was the extension and revival of servile labor. This took the form of the use of unfree labor on large agricultural plantations and also in mines. The best known and most extreme case of this were the slave run plantations and mines of the New World but less extreme variants were found elsewhere in the world, notably in Eastern Europe and Russia, certain regions of India and parts of China. In these cases it tended to take the form of serfdom or bonded labor rather than outright slavery, but the common factor was that the labor of the peasant or worker was not under their own control and they were not free to do it or to leave it.

At the same time there was a widespread revival of slavery in the Islamic world, with a growing demand for slaves as household servants and for employment in artisan manufacture. Outside the Islamic world, unfree labor was used mainly in mining and the production of a range of cash crops. The best known were sugar, indigo, and cotton, but in some places serf or slave labor was also used in the production of grain and rice and it was also used in such areas of manufacturing as porcelain, brick making, and iron. The common elements in all of these cases were firstly that the product in question was being produced for sale a long distance away from its place of production and secondly a pressing need for a large and stable labor force that could be kept in one place for a prolonged period of time. In the case of outright slavery, mainly in the New World and the Islamic world, this led to the appearance from the mid to late sixteenth century onwards of large scale and organised slave trades. The best known was the Atlantic trade between West Africa and the New World but there was an equally significant trade in the Indian Ocean, between Africa and the Middle East and another making use of the trans-Saharan caravan routes that connected sub-Saharan Africa to the Maghreb, and to the Middle East via Egypt. The Barbary States of the Mahgreb also acquired slaves through warfare and by raiding the coasts of Western Europe – some two million were taken in this way from Europe between 1550 and 1750.

The Nature and Historical Place of the Renaissance World Economy

So the new economic order that emerged from the crisis of the medieval world was clearly different in a number of important ways from what had gone before. Some of these differences were matters of degree such as the higher level of economic integration and the further development of economic institutions. Others were more truly novel, such as the mercantile and 'proto-industrial' form of manufacture or the kinds of unfree labor that became widespread. As in the specific case of Ming China, we may say more generally that the kind of economy found in most settled parts of the world after 1500 was a highly commercialised and mercantile one, much more so than had been the case even in 1300. However, there were important and continuing differences between this kind of economic order and that of the modern world.

The most important difference was that this was still an economic order marked by extensive rather than intensive growth. Real growth rates when they occurred at all were low by modern standards, and intermittent. There were episodes of growth such as in China after 1580 and in the Dutch Republic in the early seventeenth century but again these did not continue. In general, the increase in production was matched by an increase in population. This in turn was intermittent, with a significant slowdown in many areas in the middle years of the seventeenth century and the rate of increase was not as rapid as that experienced in Song China, or much of the world after 1750.

Having said that, population did grow over the whole period from the later fifteenth century to the eighteenth and this eventually put the entire system under severe strain, as we shall see. Technological innovation was still ad hoc and its diffusion slow and sporadic by modern standards. Also, the economy was still relatively illiquid; and capital was much harder to pool and accumulate than is the case in the modern world, something reflected in very high interest rates, in other words a high cost of capital. Although society had become much more commercialised and market or exchange driven there was still not a true labor market as we would think of it. Wage labor and labor contracts that were easily terminable were rare: instead there were the kinds of contracts now found only among professional sportsmen and entertainers, while unfree labor or outright slavery were widespread. Firms, even large ones, were still almost all family based and the modern type of business corporation was just starting to appear.

What we should not do is think of this kind of economic order, found in much of the world after the recovery from the great crisis, as being somehow more 'advanced' than the medieval one it had replaced. In some ways it was because certain aspects of the medieval economy were enhanced or more prominent but other important elements of the medieval economic systems had diminished. Above all, we should resist the temptation of seeing the economic system or systems of the period between roughly 1450 and 1750 as being somehow a precursor or early form of the modern economy. The temptation, looking back from today, is to recognise and highlight those aspects of economic life that were similar to those found today and to retrospectively give them an importance that they did not have at the time. The unspoken assumption is that we are dealing with an evolutionary or developmental process and to highlight the elements that are supposed to have been progressive and part of the movement towards an end state, in this case the modern economy. Economic life, as it existed in this period was different from what it had been before during the Middle Ages, but also clearly different from what came afterwards and we should resist the temptation to see this as part of a continuous story of evolutionary progress either from what came earlier or what came afterwards. What we have here is another non-modern economy, different from that of both the ancient and medieval worlds but also from the modern and in no real sense an early or incomplete form of the latter.

We should also not think of economic life as a separate and distinct realm. In particular we should not think of it as clearly separate from the realms of culture and intellectual life, including the spiritual. In fact the case is exactly the opposite of this – the cultural developments of this period are all closely associated with economic activity such as trade and commerce of all kinds. The great crisis of the 'long fourteenth century' had produced turmoil and innovation in culture, art, ideas, and religious experience as much as in commerce, war and government. This is of course the period that histories of European civilisation commonly define as the Renaissance.

The Renaissance as a Global Phenomenon

The concept of the Renaissance was a nineteenth century one, first formulated by the Swiss historian Jacob Burckhardt in his book *"Civilisation of the Renaissance in Italy"*. He used the term (literally 'rebirth') to identify what he saw as a distinctive cultural and intellectual efflorescence that took place in Italy and spread from there to the rest of Europe. For Burckhardt the central feature of this was the rediscovery of the ideas and art of classical antiquity after the dark interlude of the Middle Ages, and their development into a new kind of society and culture (hence 'rebirth') which was the basis of modernity. This notion of the Renaissance thus came to occupy a pivotal place in the traditional narrative of 'Western Civilisation', connecting the modern world to the world of classical antiquity.

Certainly the period Burckhardt and subsequent historians have identified (broadly 1380 to 1560) did indeed see a great cultural and intellectual ferment. However the picture he painted needs to be amended in two ways. Firstly, the rediscovery of classical learning, while real, was less central and dramatic than he supposed. More importantly, looking at the wider global picture leads one to realise that the kind of phenomena Burckhardt identified also happened (in varied forms obviously) in other parts of the world. In other words what happened was not just a European phenomenon, a rediscovery of forgotten learning of Greece and Rome but rather a global event. The central element was not so much the rebirth of the ancient world in Europe but rather the global recovery from, and response to, the crisis of the 14th century and the continuing pressure of the little ice age.

Indeed, if we look at the cultural, intellectual and political history of the major civilisations at this time we can see certain common trends. Most obviously, there was a flowering of the arts and high culture and forms of cultural expression such as architecture, fine arts, music and literature. This involved the development and perfection of new forms and varieties of artistic expression and major innovations in technique. So for example in Islamic art there was the development of representational art such as portraiture and the miniature, and new architectural styles such as the Ottoman style of building as seen in the mosques and palaces of Istanbul. In Europe we can also trace the invention of perspective and more lifelike representation in paintings as well as the major changes in both the style and technique of architecture that we associate with people such as Alberti. All this was closely associated with trade and business, and it makes sense to think of art at this time as another branch of commerce – this was certainly how the artists of the time saw it, whether in Beijing, Florence or Istanbul and Agra.

Strangely however, this development of new style and technique went along with a backward looking focus on the achievements of the distant past, which was seen as more advanced and 'higher' than the recent past or the present. The nature and temporal location of the idealised past was varied from one place to another (it was the early years of Islam in most of the Islamic world, the pre-Islamic Sassanian period in Iran, China of the Tang and Han period in Ming China, the Gupta period in India, classical Greece and Rome or early Christianity in Europe). There was though a common pattern, of allying innovation in the present to a veneration of and yearning after the past.

This ambivalent view of the past frequently went along with the development of new forms of religious expression and consciousness. The upheavals of the fourteenth and early fifteenth centuries led many to both reject much of the past of their religious tradition while seeking to restore an idealised past variant of it. The common emphasis here was on a search for a more personal and authentic form of religious experience and a greater stress on both personal individual piety and the role of the lay individual (as opposed to the clergy or 'holy men'). This took many, often contradictory or exclusive forms. In some cases there was a search for an inclusive or syncretic from of religion which would reconcile religious differences. This was found in India for example in the shape of Sikhism or the *bakhti* movement in Hinduism. Japan saw an upsurge in the 'Pure Land' variant of Buddhism while the Islamic world witnessed a growth of Sufi movements and orders.

On the other hand there was also the spread of ideas that focused more on what was seen as a more pure and refined form of true doctrine and practice, often with a hostility to more accommodating or eclectic variants of the tradition from which they came. This was particularly true in both Christianity and the two main variants of Islam. In the latter, there was a revival of strict Sunni orthodoxy under the Ottomans while in Iran a sectarian form of Shiism became one of the foundations of the Safavid state. In Christianity, this found expression in both Protestantism after 1517 and a reinvigorated and more doctrinally explicit Catholicism. However, the world of the sixteenth and seventeenth centuries was not just one of religious enthusiasm and mysticism. Alongside the increase in piety and religious enthusiasm there was a growth of intellectual enquiry, materialism, and skepticism. This was particularly marked in Europe and China, less so in the Islamic world and India. An important aspect of this was the rise of the 'occult philosophy', which played a major part in the emergence of modern science.

One of the most commonly identified features of the Renaissance in the historiography of Europe is a 'discovery of the individual'. By this is meant a growth of individualism in the sense of a self-awareness or reflexivity, of the reflective acting person as a distinct individual rather than someone whose being was defined almost exclusively by their relation to others such as family, kin or superiors. This leads in art and philosophy to a focus upon the individual human being and their consciousness. This was manifested in a number of ways in the art and literature of the time through such things as the rise of true (i.e. accurate) portraiture and genres such as the diary and confessional autobiography. At one time it was common to decry this notion and people pointed out that a 'discovery of the individual' had been found in other periods of history as well, particularly the twelfth century. Nowadays the tide of fashion has moved back in the direction of taking this idea seriously. The point is that while intimations of a sense of self-awareness and individualism do indeed occur in almost any time and place if one looks hard enough, there are episodes when they are much more common and influential than is the case at other times. The fifteenth and sixteenth centuries are one of these and not merely in Italy. Thus the later Ming period in China witnessed the articulation of an individualist form of Confucianism that emphasised the unique qualities of each particular person.

The crucial feature though of this global renaissance is not just that we can discern common trends in the cultural, economic, and political history of all of the major civilisations. It is rather the degree to which these trends in all parts of the world were interconnected, so that developments in one part of the world can only be fully explained with reference to the contacts between that part of the world and elsewhere. No one part of the world was the source or origin or driving force from which the cultural phenomena described spread. Rather the increasing interconnectedness of the world led to a transmission and exchange of ideas and experience, which had a similar (but not identical) effect in each of the major civilisations. Some areas of mutual influence were more marked than others. The influence of China upon the rest of the world was considerable, that of the rest of the world upon China less marked (although it did happen, particularly under the later Ming (i.e. after 1550). The Islamic world, India and Europe were all much more interconnected and had a great effect on each other. These interconnections and mutual influences can be traced in a number of areas, notably in art, architecture, medicine, mathematics, and astronomy.

A consequence of this and of the increased trade contacts of the period was the way it led to people becoming much more aware of and interested in the nature and experience of other parts of the world, something that would ultimately undermine or threaten much traditional religion and belief. One aspect of this was renewed articulation of the idea of cosmopolitanism and a common human nature in all of the major civilisations. However, this period also saw increased hostile and unfriendly contacts between various parts of the world and the growth and articulation of exclusivist ideologies in all of the world civilisations, so forming a darker counterpoint to the harmonisation of interests brought about by trade. One reason for this was the inextricable connection between wealth and power. While most trade and exchange is voluntary not all of it is. Some falls into the category of 'offers that can't be refused' and in the absence of settled law the dividing line between trade and plunder is not always clear, while competition between economic actors may be settled by force as much as by quality or cost. The most important factor though is the complex relation between productive activity and political power. It is the former that provides the resources on which the latter feeds while power is needed to provide the order and stability that is needed for production to take place.

Trade and Political Power in the New World Order

The political order produced by the military revolution was one dominated by empires. By the 1560s five great land based empires had come to dominate most of Eurasia – China, Mughal India, Safavid Iran, the Ottoman Empire, and Russia. For the ruling classes of all of these empires trade and particularly long distance trade had become an increasingly important source of wealth, above all of liquid wealth, which was needed to sustain the new military establishments. Rulers welcomed trade and production but also sought to control it, so as to minimise its impact on traditional social arrangements. Their aim increasingly was to allow and even encourage trade within the territory they controlled so as to extract income from it while trying to tightly control trade with people outside their territory so as to ensure that they got as much as possible of any rent rather than their rivals. The vital question was that of the geographical area within which there was to be a free movement of goods. Was it to be the entire empire or state or rather a smaller more local area? This leads to two kinds of political struggle, firstly between local elites and rulers seeking to integrate local areas into a larger whole and secondly between the major players, over who controlled the main world trade routes and productive assets.

This was particularly the case for the other world players alongside the five great land based empires. These were the sea borne empires of the European powers, initially Portugal and Spain, later the Dutch and then France and Britain. These were empires of a different kind, with a different kind of governance to the great land based ones. These were empires based ultimately on naval power and control of the world's seas and its crucial passages and trade points. It was through this that they were held together and power was projected. An empire of this kind differed from a land based one in another fundamental way: its territories were not contiguous but separated from each other and the metropolitan power, in most cases by thousands of miles of ocean.

These empires, in spite of their metropolitan powers being economically marginal in global terms (or even because of that) came to play a large (and after about 1690 a dominant) part in the world's long distance trade. Although Portugal was first on the scene it was Spain (or more accurately Castile) that created the first sea based empire that was truly global in extent, one of which it could truly be said that it was an empire on which the sun never set. Later on, in 1611, the Dutch East India Company (the VOC) inserted itself into the politics of the East Indies and soon became the hegemonic power in that part of the world, creating a form of imperial rule that united most of the islands of South East Asia. This empire was not its main goal, which was rather to capture the trade in and around that part of the world and to exclude their main European rivals, the Portuguese (ruled since 1580 by their mortal enemy, Habsburg Spain). The empire came about as a political necessity in the pursuit of the main, economic, goal in order to prevent rivals from making political deals with local rulers that would exclude the VOC.

The European Divergence – No Hegemon Emerges

Why though had small, economically unimportant parts of the world in Europe come to play such a role in the imperial world system and economy of the renaissance world? The answer is something alluded to but not yet discussed, the way that the military revolution had worked out in Europe as compared to elsewhere in the world. Putting it bluntly, this was not inevitable, far from it. The great danger in the study of history is to think that the way things happened was the way they had to happen, that the actual outcome was the only possible one or at least the most overwhelmingly likely one. This is seldom the case. An extraterrestrial observer, comparing Europe and the Middle East in 1520 would have thought that Europe was likely to go the same way as the Middle East and see the emergence of a single hegemonic power. In fact, the observer would probably conclude that this was more likely than what had just happened in the Middle East where until 1516 there were two rival potential hegemons of apparently equal power (the Ottomans and the Mameluke Sultans of Egypt). In Europe by contrast, there was one very clear candidate for that status – the House of Habsburg in the person of the young Charles of Austria (1500 – 1558).

The Habsburgs were a German dynasty, originally from the Tyrol, who by a combination of marriage and good fortune had managed to become the dominant dynasty within the Holy Roman Empire, controlling Austria, Salzburg, Carinthia, Styria, Carniola, and Tyrol. As such they were a powerful dynasty but not markedly more so than others, notably their great rivals the House of Valois who ruled the French monarchy. However, by a series of dynastic accidents, by 1520 the young head of the House of Habsburg, Charles of Austria, had become the ruler of the largest empire in Europe since the time of Charlemagne and of an emerging global empire – the first of its kind in history. This put him in an immensely powerful position relative to the other rulers in Europe, including his nemesis and deadly enemy, Francis I of France (ruled 1515 – 1547).

Charles, in addition to the hereditary Habsburg dominions, came to control the lands of three other dynasties. The first and in many the most important inheritance was that of the house of Burgundy, via his paternal grandmother Mary. A cadet line of the house of Valois, the Dukes of Burgundy were a classic example of the kind of political entrepreneurs who sought to take advantage of the confusions of the later Middle Ages. By 1473 through a combination of marriage, conquest, treaty and purchase, they had acquired control of almost all of the provinces of the Low Countries, as well as other territories that by 1477 gave them a strip of territory running from the North Sea almost to the Alps. The aim of the last two dukes in particular (Philip the Good 1419 – 1467 and Charles the Rash 1467 – 1477) was to convert their domains into a kingdom and so recreate the 'Middle Kingdom' that had been created when Charlemagne's three grandsons partitioned his empire at the Treaty of Verdun in 843.

They might well have done so, had events and the personalities of the key players worked out differently, with profound results for the future political history of Europe. (Again, we should not assume that the political map that did emerge from the fourteenth and fifteenth centuries was the one that had to do so). In the event however Charles the Rash was defeated and killed at the battle of Nancy in 1477. His only heir was his daughter Mary and later that year she married Maximilian, the son and heir of the Habsburg Holy Roman Emperor Frederick III. Mary died in a riding accident in 1482 and Maximilian then ruled her lands as regent for their young son, Phillip the Handsome, until he came of age in 1496. In the meantime, in 1493 he consolidated all of the Habsburg German territories in his own hands and in the same year confirmed his son's rule over all of the Netherlands and the Franche Comte by the Treaty of Senlis. Maximilian remarried but had no further male heirs and so Phillip thus became heir to the lands of both the Habsburgs (from his father) and the Burgundian house (from his mother).

In 1496 Phillip married a young Spanish princess – Joanna. She was the third child of two remarkable rulers, Ferdinand of Aragon and Isabella of Castile. They had married in 1469 and when Isabella became Queen of Castile in 1474 and Ferdinand King of Aragon in 1479 the marriage brought about a dynastic union that united most of the Iberian peninsula. The marriage of Phillip to their youngest daughter while his sister married their oldest child and heir, Don Juan, was intended to seal an alliance between the houses of Trastamara and Habsburg that was aimed at the rising power of the house of Valois. Having defeated the Plantagenets in 1453 (and so finally ended the Hundred Years War) and then seen off the threat from the third party in that conflict, the house of Burgundy, the Valois, already rulers of the territories of the French monarchy, were looking to expand their power. In 1491 they acquired Brittany with the marriage of Anne, the last ruling duchess of Brittany, to Charles VIII and in 1494 he moved into Italy, pursuing claims to both Naples and Milan. This led to a series of wars in Italy with Aragon, as the Aragonese royal house already held the crown of Sicily and had its own claim to Naples.

However this defensive marriage alliance came to have dramatic results. In 1497 Don Juan died without issue. The following year his sister Isabella died in childbirth and her son died in 1500. This made Joanna the heir to the throne of Castile. In 1504 her mother died and she inherited the throne while Phillip became her consort (and effectively the ruler as the mental instability that was to gain her the unfortunate soubriquet of 'the Mad' had already become manifest). Phillip however died in 1506. Ferdinand then became regent in Castile as Joanna was incapable of ruling and her heir, Charles, was only six. Ferdinand himself remarried but was unable to sire an heir to the crown of Aragon, with the result that on his death in 1516, Charles, the son of Phillip and Joanna became king of both Castile and Aragon. He had already inherited the Burgundian lands in 1506 and when Maximilian died in 1519 he inherited the Habsburg lands in Germany. Later that year, after a bitterly contested and very expensive election he became Holy Roman Emperor and so took the title by which he is usually remembered, Charles V.

The Habsburg Failure

Thus by 1519 Charles had inherited the lands of the House of Burgundy via his paternal grandmother (Mary of Burgundy). This was the whole of the Low Countries plus the Franche Comte. He had acquired the lands of the Crown of

Aragon, via his maternal grandfather Ferdinand. This was Aragon (Catalonia, Aragon, the Baleares, and Valencia) plus Naples and Sicily, and subsequently Milan. He gained the lands of the Crown of Castile via his maternal grandmother Isabella. This was the rest of Spain, plus the empire conquered in the New World by conquistadores such as Cortez (who conquered Mexico in 1519 – 21) and Pizarro (who conquered the Inca empire in 1532 – 33). Finally, in 1526, following the death of Louis of Hungary at the battle of Mohacs, he inherited the crowns of Hungary and Bohemia.

This was a truly formidable inheritance and it brought much more than a string of titles or even extensive lands. The domains brought a large population and their production (i.e. a massive tax base) but in addition they brought other benefits. Aragon and Castile had created the finest army in Europe. Under their great commander, Gonsalvo de Cordoba they had applied more of the military revolution than anyone else. No troops anywhere in Europe were a match for the Spanish infantry and the Spanish army had a logistics and support system that nobody else could come near to matching.

The possession of the Low Countries, and particularly Liege, gave Charles control of the largest concentration of specialist gunsmiths in Europe so his artillery park was second to none. Domination of Italy gave the Habsburgs access to the financial expertise and wealth of the North Italians and the maritime power of the Genoese. The Low Countries was the other great centre of trade, commerce, manufacture and banking in Europe. The voyages of discovery over the Atlantic after 1492 had led to the creation of an enormous empire that controlled much of the resources of the New World. After the voyage of Magellan the Spanish controlled access to the Pacific and had a base in the Far East via their control of the Philippines. In terms of the world and European trading system the Habsburgs did not only control the two major centres of banking and manufacture in Europe (North Italy and the Netherlands). They also controlled the trade route from Northern Europe via the Baltic to Russia and Central Asia, and the North-South trade route from the North Sea down the Rhine and over the Val Telline pass to Genoa and the Mediterranean.

The question to ask is this. Why, given this amazingly strong hand, did the Habsburgs not become the hegemonic power in Europe in the way the Ottomans did in the Middle East or the Mughals in India? It was not for lack of trying. Quite apart from the natural tendency of political power to seek to expand until checked it seems that from at least the 1550s the strategic goal of the Habsburgs was to create what one contemporary called "ane universal empire". They failed to do this for a number of reasons. The key factors were the survival of France as a rival great power (a close thing) and their failure to crush rebellion in a key territory, the Netherlands.

The first phase was the reign of Charles V. The counterpoint to his amazing inheritance was the continued power of the house of Valois. The French monarchy remained a large, powerful and compact rival and a serious obstacle to any hegemonic position (much as the Mamelukes were for the Ottomans before 1517). The central feature of European politics for the first half of the sixteenth century was the struggle between Habsburg and Valois in the persons of Charles V and Francis I. This was fought principally for control of Italy and the Low Countries, with most of the fighting initially in Italy. The conflict had started in 1494 with the invasion of Italy by Charles VIII of France and resumed soon after Charles V had defeated Francis I in the election for Holy Roman Emperor in 1519. The fighting, in Italy and elsewhere, was almost continuous, with official hostilities in 1521-26, 1526-30, 1535-38, 1542-46 and 1551-59. Charles V was victorious in most of the campaigns and gained a stunning victory at the battle of Pavia in 1525, when he captured Francis I.

However he was unable to gain a decisive victory over either Francis or his successor Henri II (1547 – 1559), much less the kind of total triumph that Selim I had gained over the Mamelukes. A crucial reason for this was that in addition to confronting the Valois in Italy he had to face several other threats. In the Holy Roman Empire he faced the challenge posed to his authority and that of the church by the Protestant Reformation, which broke out shortly before his election as emperor when Martin Luther nailed his Ninety-Five Theses to the church door at Wittenberg in 1517. Despite a series of campaigns and an apparently decisive victory at Muhlberg in 1547 he was unable to finally defeat the German princes who had supported Luther. Even more serious was the threat he faced from the Ottoman Turks. Following their victory at Mohacs they had conquered most of Hungary and in 1529 they besieged Vienna. Although they were unsuccessful in this, conflict between the Habsburgs and the Ottomans continued with warfare in both central Europe and the Mediterranean. Moreover, despite his title of 'Most Christian King', in 1542 Francis I entered into an informal alliance with Suleiman the Magnificent against their mutual foe Charles V.

In 1556, exhausted and worn out by a lifetime of fighting and travelling, Charles V abdicated. He broke his huge empire up, leaving the traditional Habsburg lands and the largely formal title of Holy Roman Emperor to his brother Ferdinand. The rest went to his son Phillip II of Spain (1556 – 1598). However, Phillip inherited the parts of the Habsburg Empire that brought all of the advantages, as described earlier. Moreover the position of the Habsburgs was if anything stronger within a few years of his taking over the reins. By this time, the overseas empire in the New World was established and after the 1550s began to generate a significant flow of silver via the annual plate fleet from Havana to Cadiz. In 1559 the long struggle for control of Italy finally concluded with the treaty of Cateaux-Cambresis, The terms of this treaty marked a decisive victory for the Habsburg side in every point of contention and left them as the paramount power in Italy, with only Venice retaining any significant independence.

The French Religious Wars
and the Dutch Revolt

However, it was a chance event that yet again opened up the prospects for Phillip and his house. Shortly after the signing of the treaty of Cateaux-Cambresis, Henri II died as the result of an accident in a joust. He left behind four young, weak, and truly strange children to rule a kingdom deeply divided by the spread of the Reformation. The result was a progressive collapse of royal authority and a savage struggle for power between two great noble houses and their clients, the house of Guise and that of Bourbon-Chatillon. As these were identified with the two sides of the Reformation (the Bourbons with the Protestants or Huguenots, the Guises with Counter-Reformation Catholicism) this gave the struggle an added dimension hence the name given to them – Les Guerres de Religion – the Wars of Religion. Essentially there is continuous warfare with brief truces in France from 1562 to 1598. The result was to eliminate France as a great power and leave the way clear for the Habsburgs. However they then faced another obstacle. This was a revolt in a vitally important territory – the provinces of the Netherlands that they had inherited from the Burgundians.

The Netherlands were the most economically developed of Phillip II's domains and strategically vital, but also the most politically troublesome. The Dutch had reacted to the death of Charles the Rash by extracting concessions from Mary and Maximilian and following the abdication of Charles V they resisted the attempts by Phillip and his ministers to reform the government of the Netherlands so as to increase the power of the central administration and the burden of taxation. In 1567 revolt broke out in the Netherlands. This was put down by local forces loyal to Phillip II but in a momentous decision he decided to send an army to the Netherlands under the Duke of Alva to sort out the Dutch once and for all. Alva imposed sweeping reforms and a reign of terror, marked by the execution of two of the rebel leaders, Egmont and Hoorn. In 1572 a second revolt broke out, led by another of the leaders of the original rebellion, William the Silent, the Prince of Orange. This was crushed in most of the Netherlands, thanks to the failure of French support to materialise as a result of the Spanish sponsored seizure of power by the Guises at the Massacre of St Bartholomew's Eve.

However the Dutch rebels held out in Holland and Zeeland despite savage and bloody fighting, while their fleet – the so-called *Guex de Mer* (Sea Beggars) – operating out of the Huguenot stronghold of La Rochelle were able to cut the connection between Spain and the Netherlands via the Bay of Biscay and the English Channel. This meant that the Spanish had to rely upon the much slower and more costly 'Spanish Road' from Milan via the Val Telline and the Rhine. Meanwhile they faced a revived threat from the Ottomans, who gained a major victory at Djerba in 1560 and captured Tunis in 1574 and Cyprus in 1570, while laying siege to Malta in 1565. At the same time Phillip II's financial position deteriorated and as a result he was unable to pay his army in the Netherlands. In 1576 the outrages committed by the desperate and unpaid Spanish troops led to a third revolt, which involved all of the Netherlands.

However, at precisely this point in the later 1570s the tide turned again, in favour of the Habsburgs. The flow of silver from the New World really accelerated and solved their acute financial problems, at least temporarily. After their naval defeat by the Habsburgs at the Battle of Lepanto in 1571 the Ottomans were forced to turn their attention eastwards to deal with the Iranians. Even more dramatic were the events in France. There the monarchy was so reduced by the civil wars and the incapacity of the last Valois monarchs that by 1585 the monarchy had effectively lost control of most of the kingdom. In the Netherlands Phillip II now had an outstanding general, Alexander Farnese, the Duke of Parma. Between 1580 and 1587 he reconquered more than half of the Netherlands (roughly modern Belgium). This culminated in 1587 with the capture of Antwerp, the largest city in the Netherlands, following a siege that was a masterpiece of that kind of warfare. Meanwhile William of Orange, the inspirational leader of the revolt, had been assassinated in 1584.

The Turning Point, 1582 – 1592

So the critical turning point for European and in significant ways world history (because of its impact on later events) was the decade of 1582 to 1592. In those years Phillip II played for the ultimate prise. Had he succeeded in his twin aims, of suppressing the Dutch and either dismembering the French monarchy or reducing it to client status, he would indeed have achieved a dominant position in Europe with no power realistically able to check him and the military revolution in Europe would have had the same result as elsewhere. However, in going for everything he failed in both of his major objectives.

Firstly, Phillip II tried to consolidate his apparent victory over the Dutch by invading and conquering England in 1588 via the 'Invincible Armada' which would have given him domination of the Northern Seas, as well as control of England's wealth and resources. He saw this as both an opportunity and a strategic necessity. In 1585 Elizabeth I had finally entered the war in the Low Countries on the Dutch side through the Treaty of Nonsuch. Then in 1587 her cousin and heir, Mary Queen of Scots, had been executed. This opened up the opportunity for Phillip, as overthrowing Elizabeth would no longer bring a pro-French ruler to the English throne. The Armada came close to success and had it managed to transport the Spanish army from Gravelines to Kent no amount of patriotic rhetoric would have helped Elizabeth's forces against Parma's veterans. However, at a crucial point the naval superiority of the English, culminating in an attack by fire ships and combined with a change in the wind, forced the

Armada to run round the eastern side of the British Isles. The Armada fatally distracted Parma from pushing home his advantage over the Dutch and gave them time to regroup.

Meanwhile in France, the state of the French monarchy went from bad to worse. In 1584 the Duke of Anjou, the youngest of Henri II's four children and the heir presumptive to the childless Henri III, died and this left his cousin and head of the Huguenot faction Henri of Navarre as the heir to the throne. The Catholic faction headed by the Guises refused to accept his right and entered into the Treaty of Joinville with Phillip II. (It was this and Parma's successes that finally provoked Elizabeth into the treaty of Nonsuch). Then in 1588 a mass uprising by the Catholic League of the Guises drove Henri III out of Paris in the 'Day of the Barricades'. Later that year Henri III treacherously murdered the Duke of Guise at Blois, an action that destroyed any remaining support for him in Paris and the North and East of France. At this point the French monarchy barely controlled a few strongholds along the Loire, and France seemed in imminent danger of succumbing to the Habsburgs. Then, in 1589 Henri III was murdered in his turn, by a Catholic assassin. This meant that Henri of Navarre became King, as Henri IV. He proved to be one of France's greatest rulers and brought the wars of religion to an end by firstly, becoming a Catholic ("Paris is worth a mass" as he said), secondly defeating the Guises despite intervention by Parma on their behalf, and thirdly by promulgating the Edict of Nantes which guaranteed limited freedom of worship to the Huguenots. This meant that France re-emerged as a great power whereas a few years earlier it had looked as though it would break up or fall under Spanish supremacy, like Italy.

Meanwhile the Dutch, on the ropes in 1587, were able to recover while the Armada and the war in France distracted Parma. William the Silent's son, Maurice of Nassau, proved to be an outstanding general and military theoretician and he was able to recapture the key fortresses of Breda and Geertruidenburg and drive the Spaniards south of the Rhine and Maas. At this point the financial burden of the wars proved insupportable once more and in 1609 the Habsburgs were forced to sign the Twelve Year Truce with the Dutch. They had missed their chance.

Arguably though, the Habsburgs had one final try at a dominant position in Europe. Following the reunification of the ancestral Habsburg lands by Ferdinand of Styria in 1618 he became Holy Roman Emperor Ferdinand II and allied himself with his Spanish cousin Phillip IV, in an attempt to complete the unfinished task of Phillip II. The result was the Thirty Years War of 1618 to 1648, which laid waste large parts of Germany and came to involve almost every power in Europe. Towards the end of the war France, under the leadership of Cardinal Richelieu, intervened directly on the anti-Habsburg side. French forces inflicted devastating defeats on the Spanish at Rocroi and Lens, which marked the end of Spanish military superiority in Europe. The war between

France and Spain finally ended with the Peace of the Pyrenees in 1659, which marked the end of Spain as the premier great power in Europe.

Even more importantly, in 1648 the Treaty of Westphalia which ended the Thirty Years War formally recognised the permanent division of Europe into distinct sovereign states, that is to say that there was no hegemon or true supranational power, and set up a set of rules to govern relations between them. The so-called 'Westphalian System' remains the basis of international relations to this day. This and the (largely contingent) failure of the Habsburg project together had enormous and far-reaching effects over the longer term. Why though had things worked out the way they had?

Reasons for the Different Outcome of the Military Revolution in Europe

In the first place one has to put sheer chance. The very formation of the great empire of Charles V was itself brought about by a series of dynastic accidents. Had this not happened France under the Valois would have remained the most likely candidate for a pre-eminent position and it would not have suffered from the problems that faced Charles V and Phillip II, of trying to rule and coordinate geographically scattered territories, each with their own interests and institutions. Despite this the Habsburgs came very close to ultimate success. Had the Armada landed an army in England its success would have been assured and the Dutch cause almost certainly doomed. Had any number of events taken a different form, the outcome of the Wars of Religion could have been much more favourable to the Habsburg cause than what did happen, the reappearance of the French monarchy as a major rival and obstacle.

In addition though the events in Europe were partly shaped by what happened elsewhere. A major reason for the inability of both Charles V and Phillip II to achieve a final and conclusive victory was that they were distracted by having to face several threats and foes at the same time, which prevented them from concentrating all their power for a decisive blow at critical moments. Here the contrasting example of the Ottomans is instructive. Selim I was able to attack his major rivals in the Middle East because he did not face a serious threat in the Balkans, due to the incapacity of the last Hungarian rulers. Having eliminated the Mamelukes and checked the Safavids for a long period he and Suleiman the Magnificent could then turn their attention to the Balkans and the Mediterranean, free of any worries about their rear. Only after the Safavids recovered in the mid-sixteenth century did the Ottomans face the same kind of problems that the Habsburgs had faced since the 1520s. It was the threat from the Ottomans and the need to attend to the Mediterranean that distracted Phillip II's attention from the Netherlands at a number of crucial moments, particularly in the 1560s and 1570s.

Another factor was the simple fact that in Europe several powers introduced the new military techniques at the same time. Once any power had done so, and particularly once it had adopted the new system of fortification, it became very difficult to gain a decisive victory in any war. The more time that passed, the more difficult it became for any one power to gain a clear military advantage over either its major rival or a coalition of hostile powers. The events elsewhere in the world at this time (and also at other times in comparable situations) demonstrated that if one of a number of roughly equal competitors gained an early advantage then this could set off a positive feedback in which that power gained an ever increasing lead over its rivals to the point where it achieved a position of clear dominance. In Europe the outcome was the alternative one where because no power gained a decisive advantage early enough (before many others had a chance to adapt their military policy) or the powers that did were not able to press home their advantage quickly enough, the dynamics led to a set of roughly evenly balanced powers, with a tendency for a blocking coalition to emerge to check any power that seemed to be on the verge of gaining that elusive lead.

This pattern dominated Europe's internal relations after 1648. Thus, in the 1690s a blocking coalition of England, Austria and the Dutch Republic formed to check France under Louis XIV when it seemed that the French monarchy would gain a dominant position through absorbing the Spanish monarchy's dominions after the death of the last Habsburg King of Spain, Carlos II. There are two explanations for the more rapid and widespread adoption of the new military techniques in Europe and the consequent persistence of division there. One again is chance and contingency, with accident and the fate of war causing a critical delay, essentially the story told above.

The other is more structural. According to this medieval Europe had produced political units with a much clearer territorial and institutional identity than was the case in other parts of the world, especially the Middle East and most of India. Consequently, the government apparatus at the disposal of European rulers was more powerful and effective than that of their counterparts elsewhere, not in terms of the quantity of resources over which they ruled, but in terms of their ability to mobilise them and to do so at a higher level of cost effectiveness (that is the proportion of total output that needed to be taken in taxation to mount a given level of military force was less). This meant, according to this theory that it was easier for European rulers to consolidate their power within their dominions and adopt the new military techniques and so this happened more rapidly and extensively than elsewhere, with the consequence that the window of opportunity for a potential hegemon to emerge was much narrower.

The Consequences

These two arguments are not mutually exclusive so the debate is rather over which should bear the greater explanatory weight. What are not in doubt are the outcome by 1648 and its significance. Even then however its full importance is often not realised. What were the consequences then of the distinctive outcome of the military revolution in Europe, in the context of the world of empires and the economic order described earlier?

One specific consequence of the events described was the emergence of the Dutch Republic. Although there had been earlier intimation, such as Venice, this was a new kind of polity, one where the ruling class were merchants rather than aristocrats, and which had a distinctive culture, which supported and espoused mercantile bourgeois values rather than aristocratic or clerical ones. For contingent and pragmatic reasons it adopted a policy of religious toleration and (relative) free expression. The Dutch Republic played a central role in the intellectual revolution of the seventeenth century and also made several hugely important innovations, in military affairs, finance, and business.

Another result, already alluded to, was that in Europe the military revolution continued whereas it came to a halt in other parts of the world. Elsewhere, once the hegemonic empire had appeared and consolidated its position, internal war and conflict within its territory came to an end. Although the various great empires still faced clashes on their borders and wars with each other they were generally too large and powerful to fear complete defeat and dismemberment so the incentive to improve and adapt the military system was low. By contrast Europe, divided between several states of roughly equal power and others that while not great powers were still militarily formidable, continued to experience internal wars on an almost continuous basis. Because of its geographical location it was also in direct contact with two of the major land empires (Russia and the Ottomans), both of which were active participants in its affairs. Consequently there was continuing military innovation after 1580, at which point it had stopped in other parts of the world. The result was a gradual but ultimately clear cut shift in the balance of military power. By the 1690s European powers were militarily superior to all of the world's other empires and states on sea and all but the Chinese on land. By 1750 they had a clear superiority over the rest of the world.

Another specific result of the wars of roughly 1520 to 1648 was that Europe remained not only politically but also religiously divided, as the Reformation was not undone while Catholicism survived. Although each individual state was a confessional state with an established form of Christianity as the official religion and penalties for dissent, this meant that Europe as a whole was intellectually pluralistic. This, together with the reaction of intellectuals and the educated to the religious disputes of the period, was a major factor in the other great change to take place in Europe during this period, an intellectual revolution that brought about a fundamental intellectual rupture in the period after 1690.

The great consequence however was that ruling classes in Europe faced quite different incentives as compared to their counterparts in Asia. They were now part of a system of constant and intense competition, as the states that they controlled had to compete with other similar ones in a meta-system of the rules of international relations. Moreover this was not simply military competition. Although warfare and military preparedness was the central element at this time, the cost of war and the need to generate cash to fund it meant that increasingly states and their rulers were engaged in economic competition as well. Each ruling class sought to maximise the wealth and production of the areas it controlled or, to put it another way, to capture as large a proportion of the wealth of the planet and its trade system as possible. This meant that it was not in their interest to check economic or scientific advance because any state that did so would lose out in the competition. The lack of a single hegemonic power meant that nobody in Europe was in a position to do what the Ming Emperors did in China and deliberately stop innovation, no matter how much they might have wished to. It also meant that there was a sustained pressure on rulers to reform their administration and finances and this eventually led to a change in both the way government was understood at the level of theory as also its actual practice.

All of these changes were to work out over the longer run. Although they arose by 1648 or even the 1590s, their full effects were not felt until the 1750s and later as they interacted with the way that the economy described at the start of this chapter had developed by that time. Before looking at how that happened however, we need to look at something that also happened in Europe at this time and which was both related to and encouraged by the continued division of Europe. This was the intellectual upheaval already alluded to, which while apparently esoteric, also had extensive practical implications.

Further Reading

The Impact of the expansion not just of Europe but also the Islamic world, and the way these together created a world trade system is captured in the essays in Michael Adas (ed.) *Islamic and European Expansion: The Forging of a Global Order*. (Temple University Press, 1993). The earlier system of old world trade and its completion by the Mongol Empire is the subject of Janet Abu-Lughod *Before European Hegemony: The World System AD 1250 – 1350* (Oxford University Press, 1989). She identifies twelve overlapping regional circuits, which together made up a system that covered most of the Old World. A key part of this was the overland routes that collectively formed the Silk Road. This is covered in a number of books, including James A. Millward *The Silk Road:*

A very Short Introduction (Oxford University Press, 2013), Valerie Hansen *The Silk Road: A New History* (Oxford University Press, 2012), and Xinru Liu *The Silk Road in World History* (Oxford University Press, 2010). The collapse of key institutions of this Medieval trade system as part of the great crisis described in the previous chapter is covered in works such as Raymond De Roover *The Rise and Decline of the Medici Bank 1397 – 1494* (Beard Books, 1999), and Edwin S. Hunt *The Medieval Super-Companies: A Study of the Peruzzi Company of Florence* (Cambridge University Press, 1994).

The central place of the Indian Ocean and its trade and commerce in the post-Medieval world trade system is the central element in Andre Gunder Frank *ReOrient: Global Economy in the Asian Age* (University of California Press, 1998), which draws on a wide body of scholarship. The key work is that of K. N. Chaudhuri, most notably *Trade and Civilisation in the Indian Ocean: An Economic History from the Rise of Islam to 1750.* (Cambridge University Press, 1985). Other work on this topic includes Milo Kearney *The Indian Ocean in World History* (Routledge, 2003), Patricia Risso *Merchants and Faith: Muslim Commerce and Culture in the Indian Ocean* (Westview Press, 1995), Edward A. Alpers *The Indian Ocean in World History* (Oxford University Press, 2014) and Ashin Das Gupta *The World of the Indian Ocean Merchant 1500 – 1800: Collected Essays.* (Oxford University Press, 2001).

The way that the world that grew out of the crisis was one of empires is the theme of John Darwin's *After Tamerlane*. Another work on that topic is Marjorie Wall Bingham *An Age of Empires 1200 – 1750.* (Oxford University Press, 2005). The relationship between trade and power in the new trade system with long distance maritime routes gaining importance and acting as one of the ways power was exercised is the subject of the essays in the two outstanding collections edited by James D. Tracy (ed.) *The Rise of Merchant Empires: Long Distance Trade in the Early Modern World 1350 – 1750* (Cambridge University Press, 1993) and *The Political Economy of Merchant Empires: State Power and World Trade 1350 – 1750* (Cambridge University Press, 1997). The point that comes out of the essays, on a wide range of topics, is that Europe, while it played an important part, was not the centre of this system and was not anything like the centre or location of the most valuable activity or production. Two other works on this topic are David Ringrose *Expansion and Global Interaction: 1200 – 1700* (Longmans, 2000), and Jerry H. Bentley *Between the Middle Ages and Modernity: Individual and Community in the Early Modern World.* (Rowman & Littlefield, 2007). The second looks at what was Bentley's central interest, the interaction and meeting of different cultures and the effect this had on identity.

The impact of Europeans on the New World and of the New World in turn on its invaders and conquerors have led to enough studies to fill a fair sized library. The biological history of these events and the impact of the new plants brought from the New World to the Old by Europeans (above all by the Portuguese) are perhaps the most dramatic and important, not least for the effect they had on global trends later on in the eighteenth century (for which see chapter VII below). The major work on this is that of Alfred W. Crosby, in particular *The Columbian Exchange: Biological and Cultural Consequences of 1492* (Praeger, 2003 1ˢᵗ pub. 1973), and *Ecological Imperialism: The Biological Expansion of Europe, 900 – 1900* (Cambridge University Press, 2004). Another valuable work is Noble David Cook *Born To Die: Disease and the New World Conquest 1492 – 1650* (Cambridge University Press, 1998).

Another very significant effect of the integration of the Americas into the world trade system by Europeans was the transformation of the world's monetary systems by the massive influx of New World silver, which led to the appearance for the first time of something like a true global money system. The best introductions to this are Dennis O. Flynn *World History and Monetary History in the Sixteenth and Seventeenth Centuries* (Variorum, 1996), Dennis O. Flynn & Arturo Giraldez (eds.) *Metals and Money in an Emerging World Economy* (Variorum, 1997) and William Shaw *The History of Currency 1252 – 1894* (Adamant Media 2005). A study of a non-European system is Sevhet Pamuk *A Monetary History of the Ottoman Empire* (Cambridge University Press, 2004).

The plantation economies of the New World and the slave trade that grew up to support them have again been the subject of a massive number of books. One of the best general surveys is Philip D. Curtin *The Rise and Fall of the Plantation Complex: Essays in Atlantic History* (Cambridge University Press, 1998), while Robin Blackburn *The Making of New World Slavery; From the Baroque to the Modern 1492 – 1800* (Verso, 1998) is a substantial survey of the New World slave system. A recent work, which explains the part that Africa and Africans played in all of this (including an active role in parts of the trade) is John Thornton *Africa and Africans in the Making of the Atlantic World 1400 – 1800.* (Cambridge University Press, 1998). The central place of one particular product (sugar) in this system is the subject of Sidney W. Mintz *Sweetness and Power: The Place of Sugar in Modern History* (Penguin, 1986). For the definitive disproof of the idea that slavery, the slave trade, and colonial exploitation were the source of Europe's later take off see Patrick O'Brien "European Economic Development: the Contribution by the Periphery" *Economic History Review* 35 1982 pp 1 – 18, and Paul Bairoch *Economics and World History: Myths and Paradoxes* (University of Chicago Press, 1993) particularly pages 57 to 125.

The historiographical concept of the Renaissance was of course first articulated by Jacob Burckhardt in his classic work of 1860 *The Civilisation of the Renaissance in Italy,* which like all great works of historiography is still worth reading. The Penguin edition of 1990 is a good one. The global nature of the cultural and intellectual movements of that time is described in Jerry Brotton *The Renaissance Bazaar: From the Silk Road to Michaelangelo* (Oxford University Press, 2002). This should be supplemented by Jerry Brotton & Lisa Jardine *Global Interests: Renaissance Art Between East and West* (Cornell

University Press, 2000), Charles H. Parker *Global Interactions in the Early Modern Age, 1400 – 1800* (Cambridge University Press, 2010), and Timothy Brook *Vermeer's Hat: The Seventeenth Century and the Dawn of the Global World* (Bloomsbury Press, 2009). Lisa Jardine *Worldly Goods: A New History of the Renaissance* (Macmillan, 1996) is also useful. For a look at the cultural history of parts of the world outside Europe at this time look at Athar Abbas Rizvi *The Wonder That Was India Vol. II: A Survey of the History and Culture of the Indian Sub-Continent From the Coming of the Muslims to the British Conquest, 1200 – 1800* (South Asia Books, 1999), and Anna Contadini & Claire Norton (eds.) *The Renaissance and the Ottoman World (Routledge, 2013).*

Habsburg and particularly Spanish power in the period between 1500 and 1648 is the subject of John Edwards *The Spain of the Catholic Monarchs 1474 – 1520* (Wiley-Blackwell, 2001), William S. Maltby *The Reign of Charles V* (Palgrave Macmillan, 2004), the same author's *The Rise and Fall of the Spanish Empire* (Palgrave Macmillan, 2008), and Harald Kleinschmidt *Charles V: The World Emperor* (History Press, 2004). It is worth looking at another classic work of historical writing in Roger Bigelow Merriman's *The Rise of the Spanish Empire in the Old World and the New*, first published between 1918 and 1934, now available in an ebook edition. The contemporary version of this is Henry Kamen *Empire: How Spain became A World Power 1492 – 1763* (Penguin, 2002). The great contemporary historian of the Spanish Habsburgs and their struggle with the Dutch is Geoffrey Parker. *The Grand Strategy of Philip II.* (Yale University Press, 2000) puts the Spanish Empire into a global context and explains the aims and strategies of Philip II and the fears of his contemporaries. *The Dutch Revolt.* (Penguin, 1989) and the ten essays collected in *Spain and the Netherlands, 1559 – 1659* (Fontana, 1990) tell the story of the nemesis of the Habsburgs in their failure to defeat their rebellious Dutch subjects while *The Thirty Years War* (Routledge, 1997) looks at the later stage of that conflict and the wider struggle that grew out of it. Parker summarises much of his work in *Success is Never Final: Empire, War and Faith in Early Modern Europe.* (Basic Books, 2006). The other outstanding recent work on the Thirty Years War is Ronald G. Asch *The Thirty Years War: The Holy Roman Empire and Europe 1618 – 1648* (Palgrave Macmillan, 1997) while Pieter Geyl *History of the Dutch Speaking Peoples 1555 – 1648* (Phoenix Press, 2001 1st pub. 1932 & 1936) is another detailed history of the conflict. The critical role of events in France is a major theme of Parker's work and is also well covered in R. J. Knecht *Francis I* (Cambridge University Press, 1984), Mack P. Holt *The French Wars of Religion, 1562 – 1629* (Cambridge University Press, 2005), and R. J. Knecht *The French Religious Wars, 1562 – 1598* (Osprey, 2002).

The society and culture that appeared in the seventeenth century Dutch Republic is described in Jonathan Israel *The Dutch Republic: Its Rise, Greatness, and Fall 1477 – 1806* (Oxford University Press, 1995), Michael North *Art and Commerce in the Dutch Golden Age* (Yale University Press, 1999), Simon Schama

An Embarrassment of Riches: An Interpretation of Dutch Culture in the Golden Age (Vintage, 1997), and Jan De Vries *The First Modern Economy: Success, Failure, and Perseverance of the Dutch Economy 1500 – 1815* (Cambridge University Press, 1997). The way these Dutch ideas and practices then spread to Britain in 1688-90 is the subject of Steve Pincus *1688: The First Modern Revolution* (Yale University Press, 2009), and Lisa Jardine *Going Dutch: How England Plundered Holland's Glory* (Harper Collins, 2011).

The later war in Europe that checked any later possibility of a hegemon is covered in James Falkner *The War of the Spanish Succession, 1701 – 1714* (Pen & Sword, 2015). Peter Padfield *Maritime Supremacy and the Opening of the Western Mind: Naval Campaigns that Shaped the Modern World 1588 – 1782.* (Overlook, 2002) looks at the naval aspect of the conflicts that brought about European divergence. The global conflict of the mid-eighteenth century is the subject of Daniel Baugh *The Global Seven Years War 1754 – 1763: Britain and France in a Great Power Contest* (Routledge, 2011).

Chapter VI: The Scientific Revolution and the Shaping of the Modern Mind

ONE of the main questions examined by contemporary historiography is that of the origins of modern science. At one time there seemed to be a clear and generally agreed account but more recently matters have become much less clear yet at the same time more intriguing. Certain points though are not in doubt. One is that this is a hugely important question because science and scientific discoveries and their application are so crucial to the distinctiveness of the modern world. Another is that contemporary science as an activity and enterprise is different in important ways to what went by that name or that of 'natural philosophy' in times past. Sometimes this distinction is made by speaking of 'modern science' but increasingly the prefix is dropped and we simply think of science as a particular way of understanding and investigating the material world, one that came into existence in a particular place and time.

This obviously poses the question of when and where science as we understand the term appeared and why it did so at that time and in that place. This is of course one part of the more general question about the origin of modernity and so is connected to related parts of that larger question, such as the appearance of modern population growth, sustained intensive economic growth, and the modern sense of self. In this case though the answer has for a long time seemed straightforward and obvious, that modern science first appeared in Europe in the seventeenth century through something generally known as 'the Scientific Revolution'. There is a long established body of historiography that recounts a story of how this came to pass, with a well known set of events and important figures. However recent research has made this narrative increasingly problematic.

This has meant that an increasing number of historians deny that there was such a thing as a Scientific Revolution in seventeenth century Europe, with the location, the time and the thing itself all called into question. The problem with that is that clearly something *did* happen in Europe at that time, something that had a profound effect because if we look at the understanding of the natural world of educated Europeans in the mid to later eighteenth century and compare to that of their contemporaries elsewhere and their forbears some two hundred years earlier we can see a massive, radical alteration. That is, a change not just in content, in terms of what was known and understood, but at a deeper level, in terms of how knowledge itself was understood and the physical world was conceived.

The traditional narrative clearly has problems; both in terms of its content and the way change in this area of intellectual life was portrayed. The critics of this account also face difficulties, partly because of assumptions that they share with the view they are criticising. The shared fault is too much focus on knowledge and theory rather than on method, and on specific parts of knowledge about the world rather than the system of knowledge as a whole and its qualities. Another is to see some things as being consequences of the change when they were causes as well, in a process that became self-reinforcing. The question to ask and try to answer is what did actually happen in the intellectual life of Europe in the seventeenth and early eighteenth centuries and what brought it about? The answer given here then raises another question, that of why the effects (which were ultimately world changing) took such a long time to work through in so many areas of life and knowledge.

Was There a Scientific Revolution?
The Traditional Narrative

The traditional account of the scientific revolution was first put together as early as the eighteenth century. The account is mainly about the sciences of astronomy and cosmology and the replacement of the traditional Ptolemaic cosmology by the Newtonian one. There is also an account of anatomy and medicine but it is astronomy and 'mechanics' (the study of moving objects and their relations) that holds centre stage. The starting point is the vision of the cosmos shared by all educated people up to the seventeenth century. The dominant ideas were ones that had originally been formulated by Greek thinkers, mainly in the Hellenic period (3rd century BC to 1st century AD) and then developed by Muslim, mainly Arab, thinkers during the 8th to 10th centuries. In astronomy and cosmology the key figure was Ptolemy (Claudius Ptolemaeus) who had summarised the predominant view in his *Almagest*. The equivalent figure in medicine and biology was the second century Roman writer Galen. For physics and mechanics in particular the founding figure was the Greek philosopher Aristotle.

These ideas had been much elaborated and developed by Islamic thinkers who had developed several new areas, notably optics, and the study of materials and their qualities through the science of alchemy (an Arabic word of course). In cosmology the key notion was that of a very large but finite universe with a stationary Earth at its centre, with seven 'planets' (Moon, Mercury, Venus, Sun, Mars, Jupiter, Saturn) moving around it in circular orbits. In medicine the key idea was that of the four 'humours' (blood, phlegm, bile and black bile) which determined one's temperament (Sanguine, Phlegmatic, Choleric and Melancholic respectively) while in the study of matter it was thought all substances were composed of four basic elements (fire, water, earth and air) with four combinations of the two qualities of hot or cold and wet or dry.

The traditional story tells how the dominant Ptolemaic cosmology was first challenged in 1543 by the work of the Polish canon Nicolaus Copernicus (1473 – 1543) in his work *The Revolutions of the Celestial Orbs*, in which he argued that the Sun was the centre of the universe with the Earth and other planets orbiting around it but still in circular orbits. Discoveries were then made using the new technology of the telescope by Tycho Brahe (1546 – 1601) and Galileo Galilei (1564 – 1642), which tended to support the hypothesis of Copernicus and undermined the traditional picture in other ways, notably through Galileo's discovery of the moons of Jupiter in 1610 and Tycho's identification of a 'new star' (a supernova) in 1572. Meanwhile, in 1609 and 1619 Johannes Kepler (1571 – 1630) fundamentally altered the debate by formulating the three laws of planetary motion which stated that planetary orbits were elliptical not circular and that planets did not move at a constant speed but at a variable one depending on how close to the Sun they were. Finally in 1687 Isaac Newton published the *Principia Mathematica* in which he formulated the three laws of motion and the law of gravitation and created a comprehensive system that would survive until the 1900s when it was subsumed within the larger and more comprehensive Einsteinian cosmology. Newton also fundamentally altered our understanding of light and optics.

Elsewhere medicine was revolutionised by the work of people such as Andreas Vesalius (1514 – 1564), who moved away from the Galenic model of anatomy with the publication of the *De Fabrica Corporis Humani* in 1543, and William Harvey, who discovered the dual circulation of the blood in 1628. In addition to his work in astronomy Galileo also fundamentally undermined the traditional Aristotleian mechanics, most famously by showing that heavy objects did not fall faster than lighter ones, and put forward a novel set of ideas about motion and force in his *Discourse on the Two New Sciences* published in 1638. This work was then incorporated into the Newtonian system in the *Principia*. In chemistry there was a radical breakthrough by Robert Boyle (1627 – 1691) with the publication of *The Sceptical Chemyst* in 1661. Further developments in physics came from people such as Torricelli and Christian Huygens (1629 – 1695). The discovery of the microscope led to the sudden discovery of microorganisms and the cellular structure of living tissue by Robert Hooke (1635 – 1703), Marcello Malphigi(1628 – 1694), Antony van Leeunwenhoek (1632 – 1723) and others. All of this is often supposed to have contributed to a rapid surge of technological innovation that soon led to Europe taking a clear lead in technology over the other major world civilisations.

Criticism of the Traditional Account

In recent years this narrative has come under increasing fire. Initially criticism focused on the final aspect of the traditional narrative, in which the Scientific Revolution led to European societies gaining a clear technological advantage over their non-European counterparts. A series of scholars, beginning with Joseph Needham, argued that European societies were not markedly more advanced technologically than those in other parts of the world until after 1780, if not even later. More significantly, historians of science and technology argued that there was no real connection between scientific knowledge and technical or practical knowledge until the middle of the nineteenth century. Therefore, even if there had been a major breakthrough in scientific understanding in the seventeenth century, there was no feeding through of the new understanding into practical affairs and technology until about 1850. Instead, advances in technology before that time depended rather upon the activities of craftsmen and inventors, who were often lacking in formal education and scientifically ignorant.

The more fundamental criticism however was that directed against the central part of the narrative, the well known story of growing knowledge about and understanding of the physical world, above all in matters of astronomy and physics. The argument was that in matters such as astronomical knowledge and understanding of the motions of the planets, Europeans such as Copernicus were only reiterating arguments made earlier by Middle Eastern and Indian astronomers, so that there was no actual increase in knowledge. This point was made with even more force in the case of areas such as medicine and optics. Another point made concerned the nature of scientific thought and understanding at this time. Since the 1930s it had become known that Newton was an alchemist and magician as much as a modern scientist and simple research will show that he was not alone in this combination of interests. Kepler for example was an astrologer as well as astronomer and indeed it was the desire to be able to cast more accurate horoscopes that drove him to formulate the laws of planetary motion. So even as late as the 1690s the distinction between science and magic was not clear and so it is not clear in what way there was a breakthrough in scientific understanding of the world at this time.

Faced with this, some have gone so far as to argue that there was no such thing as a Scientific Revolution, that this is simply a heuristic concept intended to guide and direct research, which has now outlived its usefulness. However, this also goes too far. In the first place there were genuine breakthroughs in understanding and knowledge. Most important was Newton's formulation of the laws of motion and the principle of universal gravitation, which was a hugely significant increase in both knowledge and theoretical understanding. The work of the microscopists such as Malphigi and Leeuvenhoek was also genuinely unprecedented. Even more significantly, no matter what we may be able to say about the world view, methodology and way of thinking of figures such as Newton and Kepler, if we look at Europeans of less than a hundred years later such as Laplace we can see that there had indeed been a shift in understanding, from a magical and religious way of thinking about the world to a scientific one.

So something clearly did happen. What though was it? It clearly was not a 'Scientific Revolution' as traditionally understood, for most of the points made by the critics are correct. The crucial thing was not so much a breakthrough in knowledge of any kind as in the way that knowledge and enquiry themselves were understood. In other words it was not that educated Europeans in 1700 knew more about any area of knowledge than they had in 1550 or than their contemporaries in China, India or the Middle East. (Although in both cases they did). It was the way they understood that knowledge that had changed, along with their understanding of how it had been discovered and how it might be extended.

Joel Mokyr's Argument

A recent work that helps to resolve this problem is *The Gifts of Athena*, by Joel Mokyr. In this work Mokyr concerns himself with what he calls 'useful knowledge', that is knowledge about the human and natural worlds that enables human beings to make more productive or effective use of their own effort and the material environment in which they live. He argues that useful knowledge is of two kinds. The first is 'propositional knowledge', which consists of formal propositions or descriptive statements about the world and the natural order, and the nature and qualities of human beings. These are what philosophers call 'truth statements' because they make claims about the world that purport to be true in some meaningful sense. Mokyr points out however that the actual truth or falsity of the statements in question is a secondary matter when considering the effect they have on human action and behaviour at any given time – what matters for that is not whether they are actually true but whether they are *believed* to be true, in other words the degree to which their truth is a matter of consensus. As he concedes, given this, it is normally social pressure and power that will tend to determine which propositions are held to be true or more likely to be true at a given time and also which ones are regarded as important or trivial. In other words, historically it is power and authority that tend to ultimately shape what is regarded as the body of true and important propositions. This is particularly true when propositional knowledge is not subject to check and correction by empirical or practical experience or by truly open discussion.

The second type of useful knowledge for Mokyr is what he calls 'prescriptive' knowledge. At any time this consists of a set of instructions, that is a knowledge or understanding of how to do things so as to bring about a given result that can be expressed in formal verbal instructions or written down and then followed so as to arrive at the desired result. Examples would be the prescription of what to do so as to create a steel sword or to produce silk or grow a particular crop successfully. In other words, this is 'how to' knowledge. The point is that this kind of knowledge can exist in the absence of any kind of understanding of exactly why following it produces the desired outcome. This is because it is not necessarily or inevitably linked to the first kind of knowledge.

For most of human history in fact the two kinds of knowledge are not connected except in an accidental, ad hoc way. This had important practical consequences. It meant that because there was little or no theoretical understanding of why prescriptive knowledge worked (i.e. generated beneficial outcomes) there was no clear idea of how to go about generating new prescriptive knowledge, other than by random experimentation which was costly (because it meant investing time and effort with no guarantee of any return) or by accident, which was slow and cumbersome. It also meant that there was no feedback from practical experience and prescriptive knowledge to theoretical propositional knowledge. This meant that propositions that while believed to be true were actually empirically false (such as the humoural theory of medicine) would continue to be adhered to and were not subject to disproof or correction by empirical evidence. This in turn meant that to the extent that prescriptive knowledge *was* understood at all by reference to propositional knowledge, the understanding would often be false and misleading.

A Change in the Nature of Knowledge: The Old World-Pictures

The key is to understanding this is the way knowledge was formed and understood in traditional, non-modern, societies. Knowledge of both kinds, but particularly the first sort, was a social phenomenon as much as an abstract matter. There was a close connection between propositional knowledge and the established social and political order and systematic propositional knowledge in particular was an essential support for and justification of the position of dominant groups. Tradition and the appeal to the past and the intellectual inheritance that came from it was hugely important, particularly for settling debates and determining which propositions were clearly thought to be untrue or trivial. Religion and religious beliefs or propositions were absolutely central to the body of propositional knowledge, in a way that is not true in the modern world. Consequently theoretical or propositional knowledge had a sacred or numinous quality and was not merely a matter of the mundane and quotidian, the natural. Instead a crucial part of all intellectual traditions and bodies of propositional knowledge was beliefs and propositions about the supernatural and transcendent. These were thought of as foundational, as being the essential basis for propositions about the physical or natural world. This also meant of course that to question certain propositions was not merely mistaken but impious.

In this context the activity and debates of scholars and intellectuals led to the development over time of elaborate and worked out intellectual traditions and systems of thought or to put it another way, coherent systems of propositional knowledge. These were often used to make sense of prescriptive knowledge but were not themselves subject to correction by it. The intellectual traditions often coincide with major civilisations, indeed they may be said to define them, if a civilisation is understood as a system of shared and mutually understood symbols and cultural practices and the institutions that embody them. Intellectual traditions or systems of this sort are not eternal, they can cease to exist in a meaningful sense for a number of reasons. In the centuries after the breakdown of antiquity we can clearly discern at least four and maybe five such systems. These are the Christian, Islamic, Indian, Chinese and Buddhist. (Some would argue that the Christian one should increasingly be divided into two while others would conflate the Christian and Islamic into a single Jewish/Christian/Muslim one). Obviously these all differ from each other in terms of the content of the propositions they consist of, as well as being internally diverse and complex. However each can be recognised as a coherent and self-referential system. Moreover they have certain common qualities.

One has already been mentioned, the central part played in them by propositions that refer to supernatural or transcendent entities. Such propositions are by their nature unverifiable and incapable of disproof by concrete experience. Another is that these systems of thought and knowledge purported to give a total and comprehensive account of reality, of what is and of what can be known. That is not to say that they were thought to be complete, on the contrary, it was well appreciated that there were considerable gaps. However it was thought to be theoretically possible to fill in these gaps and have a set of propositions that was complete. This meant that the body of knowledge was immensely large but ultimately finite. The aim of scholars and investigators was to fill in these gaps and so make the picture more complete. The outlines and defining features, which the scholars then filled in and fleshed out, were supplied by a combination of revelation (often in the form of an inspired text), tradition and the works of a select and very small number of system builders such as Confucius or Aristotle.

As well as being total and comprehensive, the major traditions of knowledge all had the quality of being systematic and internally interconnected. They were holistic. That is, the truth of any particular proposition within the system was both dependent upon and also gave rise to (was determinative of) the truth of all of the other propositions. The body of propositional knowledge was thus not a collection of truth statements that were only loosely or distantly connected to each other. Rather they formed a systematic and organised whole. This means that taken as a systematic whole, the body of organised propositional knowledge gave rise to what scholars call a 'world picture' in which everything was connected in a meaningful way to everything else and nothing could be properly understood or grasped in isolation. In one sense this is simply a truism but the various traditional world pictures went beyond that level to one where there were close and meaningful connections between things that we would now see as separate and unconnected in anything but the most basic and distant fashion.

We can see how this works in the case of the Christian and Islamic traditions (or the single Jewish/Christian/Islamic one if that is how we think of it). These both combined a set of propositions derived ultimately from religious revelation and its interpretation, with another set taken from the defunct tradition of the classical Greco-Roman civilisation, which had been partly absorbed and incorporated by its two successors. Propositions about matters as varied as astronomy, climate, medicine, biology, and physics were all directly connected. Thus planets and stars were connected to a person's qualities, character and actions, and propensity to particular illnesses. These in turn were related to physics and the understanding of matter through the idea of the four elements of fire, water, earth, and air, which were connected to the four humours. These in turn were all connected to particular constellations or planets. The notion of microcosm and macrocosm meant that human society or the individual human being, were seen as smaller versions of the cosmos as a whole with connections between elements of each end of the scale. Thus disturbances in the heavens (such as the appearance of a comet) had a direct connection to disorder in the human world.

This was a world where everything was linked to everything else, by an elaborate web of correspondences and connections. The various intellectual disciplines were thought of as branches of philosophy and were explored using philosophical reasoning. Empirical investigation was used but rather as a supplement. Above all, for all three monotheistic faiths, these systems were God centred. As he was the creator and governor of everything so his creation (even if marred) reflected his qualities and his will. This meant that the ultimate key to greater understanding of the world was through the study of God, hence the position of theology as the 'Queen of the sciences'. (The term 'science' in the pre-modern world meant any kind of knowledge that could be gained by a process of structured, abstract study and was contrasted to the category of 'art' which meant a kind of knowledge that could be gained by practical experience and emulation). This also meant that for an educated person in either civilisation it was very difficult, if not impossible, to be an atheist because without a belief in an active God nothing made sense and the whole system of knowledge fell to pieces.

This had important implications for the way knowledge was understood and its social position. It meant that this was an ethical as well as a factual system. The way the world worked and the nature of human beings and their place in it were seen as having moral import. Statements about the physical nature of the world were not morally neutral, which is one reason why the religious authorities concerned themselves with them. The great problem was that to undermine one part of the system or to call it into question was to threaten the system as a whole. It was thought that the alternative to the elaborated world picture was mere chaos and randomness or radical ignorance. This had ethical implications but also political ones, because of the way the system of knowledge legitimated and upheld the established social and political order and indeed authority in general. This meant that although debate and disagreement obviously happened, its scope had to be limited. Even more importantly, the evidence of experience could not be allowed to subvert established beliefs if they were held to be significant or central to the system, so in such cases empirical evidence was trumped or overridden by what was simply 'known' to be true because of religious revelation or longstanding tradition.

The Role of Authority, and 'Ages of Reason'

It is this that accounts for the central role of authority and arguments from authority in traditional systems of propositional knowledge. There had to be a way of finally settling disputed points and of protecting the system against the unsettling and solvent effects of enquiry and experiment because to challenge the system in a significant way was impious and to allow it to be undermined was to open the door (it was thought) to mere chaos. Certain authors or texts were held to have a definitive authority, which meant that an appeal to them could settle an argument if it could be shown that one position contradicted the clear meaning of the text of the authoritative writing. Of course in many cases the meaning of the authoritative text was ambiguous which meant that resort was then had to exegesis and hermeneutics, that is to arguments about the meaning of the text and how to apply it to the issue in question. Here what finally counted was the decision of an authoritative institution (in the Christian case) or the general and settled consensus of the learned (in the Jewish and Islamic case) as to what the correct reading was.

That is why so many of the intellectual debates of the pre-17th century in both the Christian and Islamic world turned on the correct interpretation of scripture with appeals to the Bible and Quran to settle disputes in subjects such as astronomy, physics and medicine. The authorities were of course the Bible or Quran and secondly the writings of certain classical authors, notably Aristotle and Galen. What was not open was to question the truth or validity of these texts or to claim that there was any other, superior authority or source of knowledge. Of course it was possible to use reason, argument and logic to resolve disagreement and this was done wherever possible in all of the traditional civilisations. However such methods often had the dangerous consequence of generating radical scepticism and despair of actually knowing anything with reasonable certainty or alternatively materialism and a rejection of the transcendent, which was regarded as even more dangerous. So ultimately it was a decisive move in debate to show that an argument or finding, no matter how robust, contradicted the recognised authority. This was held to show that despite appearances, the argument or finding must be faulty. In this way for example the arguments of Al-Ghazali defeated those of Averroes and the other Islamic rationalists because the theses of the latter led to propositions (such as that of the eternal existence of the world) that contradicted the general understanding of scripture. The ultimate move was to assert the primacy of faith or intuition over reason and evidence.

This picture does need to be qualified in one important respect however. As we have seen, in the areas of economic activity and of technique (of prescriptive knowledge in other words), there are repeated historical episodes in which the interaction of human beings through trade and commerce leads to a process of economic and technological innovation and practical investigations that increase the extent of prescriptive knowledge. The manifestations of this are intensive economic growth and innovations in technique. However these efflorescences are either suppressed by action on the part of elites or simply peter out and fall foul of diminishing returns. One reason for this is that because of the institutionalised disconnect between propositional and prescriptive knowledge the improvements in technique are not properly understood, so they do not generate further innovation. There is a corresponding phenomenon in the realm of ideas and knowledge, which we may term intellectual efflorescences or 'Ages of Reason'. These are episodes of open enquiry and experimentation, extensive debate, and scepticism about tradition and authority. They are best thought of perhaps as a process of spontaneous change and development together with a loss or weakening of control by those with power or authority. That is why they often coincide with episodes of political disorder or competition.

Historically we can make out a number of such 'Ages of Reason'. Examples include the Warring States period of Chinese history as well as both the Song period and the latter years of the Ming after about 1580, the so-called Hellenic period of classical history after the death of Alexander, the twelfth century in Christian Europe, and the eighth and ninth centuries under the Abbasids in Islamic history. Just as episodes of intensive growth are not sustained, so these kinds of intellectual explosions prove to be short lived. Eventually they are terminated. Sometimes, as in the Chinese cases, this is primarily due to action by the ruling elites and their intellectual allies to articulate and enforce an orthodoxy, if necessary by harsh sanctions. In other cases it happens mainly because of developments in the field of ideas itself, as scholars recoil from the radical implications for social order and established beliefs of letting enquiry continue.

The Islamic case is the best example of this phenomenon. Under the early Abbasids and in particular under the Caliph al-Ma'mun (786 – 833) there was a growth of interest in Greek philosophy, through figures such as al-Kindi (801 – 873). This led to the appearance of a school of rationalist theologians, the Mutazilites, and of Islamic philosophers who explored the ideas of classical Greek thought, especially those associated with Aristotle. This however led to ideas that called many central Islamic beliefs into question, such as the notion of miracles and divine intervention in and knowledge of particular events in history (as opposed to general rules). This provoked a reaction in the shape of the Asharite school of theology, named after its founder al-Ashari (874 – 936). They emphasised orthodox ideas and in particular the absolute and unknowable will of God.

The counter to this was the work of ibn-Sina (Avicenna, 980 - 1037), which sought to combine reason and revelation into a harmonious whole, that is to save both the structured system of knowledge and the ideas and methods of philosophy. This was subjected to devastating attack by al-Ghazali (Algazel 1058 – 1111) in *The Incoherence of the Philosophers*. He argued that the enquiries of the philosophers could not yield any certainty or true knowledge but would lead only to epistemological chaos and that they would inevitably contradict the revealed truths of Islam. In general his arguments carried the day, despite powerful resistance from ibn-Bajjah (Avempace, d. 1138) and Ibn-Rushd (1126 – 1198), better known in the West as Averroes. In fact Averroes went much further than Avicenna in asserting the claims and conclusions of reason as opposed to authority and this is one reason why he lost the intellectual argument.

In Western Christendom Thomas Aquinas played a similar role to Avicenna and created a synthesis of Greek philosophy and Christian revelation which was successfully defended against critics such as Thomas Bradwardine (who argued a position similar to that of al – Ashari) The arguments of Averroes were taken up by a minority tradition within Christendom but within the Islamic tradition he and the other rationalists suffered a crushing defeat – so much so that many of his works only survive in Latin translation. By the thirteenth century the age of reason in the Islamic world had come to a definite halt. The system of knowledge had not only defended itself against the threat posed by philosophical enquiry by absorbing and limiting it (as happened in Christianity and Judaism) but had actually rejected it.

The Challenge of Scepticism and the Response

This scheme enables us to understand better what actually happened in Europe between about 1550 and 1690. The period after about 1520 was one of increased contact with the rest of the world, and a growth of trade and economic integration, due in part to the impact of American silver on world trade. It was also a period of intellectual exploration thanks in no small part to those increased contacts, particularly with the Middle East and the lands around the Indian Ocean. At the same time the Reformation shattered the institutional unity of the Christian church after 1517. By about 1550 it had become clear that the division would not be resolved peacefully.

Moreover a central element of the Reformation, and the main reason why Protestants did not go the way of earlier heretics, was the alliance between religious dissidents and secular rulers. The conflict between Catholic and Protestant thus became combined with the competition between the new states that had emerged from the military revolution. The role of the Habsburg power under Charles V and Phillip II as the champion of Catholicism added to this, although things were complicated by the history of the French monarchy as a power hostile to the Habsburgs yet still Catholic. The years between 1550 and 1559 thus saw a conflict between the Habsburgs and their rivals, which as we have seen ended in the failure of the former to realise a hegemonic position and the eventual emergence of the Westphalian system of competing sovereign states, and a series of bitter religious conflicts, fought within as well as between states. Certainly one way of understanding this century is to see it as an age of competing fanaticism.

However it was also an age of growing scepticism and doubt. This had a complex relationship to the clash of religious enthusiasms and the states that supported them. Scepticism had entered Western thought in the fifteenth century with the rediscovery of classical sceptical philosophy and increased interest in the ideas of Muslim rationalists such as Averroes. Initially all sides of religious disputes used sceptical arguments in order to attack the positions of their opponents and cast doubt on them. However it also increasingly became the position of those who were repelled by the fanaticism and bitterness of these disputes and the political disorder and cruelty they engendered. This was particularly true in France, given the savagery and disastrous effects of the Religious Wars after 1559. Seeing such passionate certainty on opposing sides and the intolerance that resulted, many were driven to doubt that certainty or rather the grounds for it. Greater contact with and knowledge of the rest of the world also led to doubt as people wondered why the beliefs and claims of their own civilisation should have any greater claim to truth than those of others.

The key event in the growth of radical scepticism was the rediscovery of the writings of the second century Greco-Roman philosopher Sextus Empiricus (c160 – 210), above all his *Outlines of Pyrrhonism*. This was published in a Latin translation in Geneva in 1562 (the Greek original was published in 1621) and soon became one of the most influential works of the time. Sextus argued that we could not be sure of the validity of claims to knowledge regardless of whether these were based on the evidence of the senses, reason, or revelation. He concluded that given the uncertainty of knowledge there were no good grounds for holding any belief, whether positive or negative. One should rely instead upon habit, custom, and convention.

His ideas were taken up and advocated by a number of people, most notably Michel de Montaigne (1533 – 1592) who presented this kind of argument in several of his *Essays*, particularly the *Apology for Raymond Sebond*. One result of scepticism, which Montaigne exemplified, was a much greater sense of self awareness and subjectivity as people turned to the one thing they could speak of with some confidence, which was themselves and their own thoughts and feelings. This was also connected to religious developments through the increased importance in both Protestantism and Catholicism of the idea of individual conversion and personal belief which led to greater introspection and awareness of ones own life as a distinct narrative – the confessional autobiography which appeared at this time as an established literary form being an important result of this.

So alongside the competing certainties of Catholic and Protestant was a growing trend of scepticism and pragmatism. In political thought this led to the Machiavellian or *politique* tradition, which argued for politics as an end in itself, rather than as an activity that was part of a wider moral order. More generally the rising scepticism led to doubts about whether anything could be known for certain and therefore about the claims for knowledge made in the existing system of propositional knowledge. This kind of crisis of scepticism had happened before in history and had usually resulted in either conventionalism and reliance upon tradition (the argument being that although one could not be certain of anything the best thing to do was to follow the conventions, customs and traditions of one's own place) or the enforcement of an orthodoxy. Both of these responses happened and in particular there were vigorous attempts to enforce and uphold the traditional system of knowledge and its associated sciences. However this was made problematic by the continued political and religious division of Europe, and the way that the military revolution and the new kinds of government it had brought about had intensified competition between elites. Unlike in China or the Ottoman Empire or Russia there was no single authority that could settle and enforce an agreed system.

A Change in the Nature of Knowledge: The Appearance of Critical Rationalism

Faced with the apparent choice between authority and radical doubt, thinkers in the early seventeenth century came up with another way of resolving this problem. This was moderated scepticism or critical rationalism. This came in two varieties, associated with the two thinkers who first articulated them, Francis Bacon and Rene Descartes. The common idea to both was that propositions can be believed to be true but in a tentative way and that the degree of tentativeness can vary according to how well founded the proposition is thought to be. The difference between the two varieties is over how one determines the extent to which a proposition is well founded, or to put it another way, over what the foundation of tentative knowledge is held to be.

Descartes argued that the way to establish knowledge on a firm foundation was to take a premise that was self-evidently true (in his case the famous *cogito*) and to then derive conclusions from it by a process of logical reasoning and testing of those conclusions by experience. Bacon's argument was that we should draw conclusions about the nature of the world from the accumulated evidence of the senses but that these conclusions should always be subject to challenge and revision (on the basis of "You never know, you could be wrong"). This means in both cases that there is no room for the appeal to authority or tradition as a way of settling an argument. Instead arguments are settled by a combination of reasoned argument and empirical investigation (NB not abstract reasoning on its own) designed to test whether a theory (i.e. a tentative hypothesis) can be <u>disproved</u>. To the extent that it is not the degree of tentativeness is reduced. Among other things this necessarily entails freedom of speech and discussion and of investigation and the publication of the findings of investigation since this is how theories are tested.

This way of thinking about knowledge did more than square the circle of the conflict between authority and scepticism. It transformed the way that propositional knowledge of the world was thought about and understood. Above all there is no longer an idea of knowledge as being a single, interconnected, enormously large but still finite system. Instead knowledge is fragmented, non-systematic and infinite. The body of propositional knowledge no longer starts with an idea of the system as a whole or with propositions that are metaphysical and concerned with the nature of existence as a whole. Rather it begins with propositions that can be made on one basis or another about specific and particular things. These are then built up and linked together to form larger structures of propositions and knowledge about categories or types of experience. This is a bottom up and piecemeal notion of knowledge rather than a top-down and holistic one. The system of correspondences and connections that tied together the world pictures of knowledge systems in traditional societies is gone and the only connection that exists between different aspects of the world, such as human biology and the structure of the solar system is basic and elementary and certainly not causal or explanatory.

Moreover, knowledge was no longer seen as something definite and certain or final, rather it was thought of as something that was in a process of constant amendment and revision. In knowledge as in economic life there is a process of creative destruction in which discrete facts (reasonably secure propositions about particular things) are put together to form larger theories. These are then tested and this process will both reduce the tentativeness of many of the propositions while at the same time casting doubt on others and increasing their tentativeness. Eventually the larger scale hypothesis will be discarded or amended and may be replaced by or incorporated into another one. This does not mean that there is no progress in knowledge however as the new way of putting together facts will explain more (incorporate a larger number of discrete facts) or will explain things better (in a way that is more internally coherent or parsimonious, i.e. requiring fewer entities or assumptions). This is however an open ended process with no final conclusion.

There is also a displacement of authority as the basis for knowledge. There is no longer an ultimate authority that can be appealed to in the shape of a text or institution or consensus as a way of settling disputes. All truth claims about the world are subject to question and possible amendment or refutation. The findings of experiment and physical investigation generate facts or simple propositions, which form the basis and elements of the larger hypotheses. They cannot be simply ignored or ruled out because they contradict a larger, supposedly authoritative system of propositions. This also means that there is no need for revelation or a series of propositions about metaphysical entities or the transcendent to provide a foundation for knowledge as that is now founded on statements about the specific, concrete, and particular. This also means that knowledge loses its inherent moral quality and becomes ethically neutral – it is only the use or effect of that knowledge that is subject to moral judgment. As later history was to show this way of thinking was to have profoundly subversive effects. Above all it displaces God from the centre of things and either removes him entirely or makes him a remote and uninvolved figure, no more than a 'first cause'. Thus Laplace, when asked by Napoleon why he had no mention of God in his great work *Celestial Mechanics* (1799 – 1825), could answer "Sire I had no need of that hypothesis" – a statement that would have been literally unthinkable two hundred years earlier.

The Consequences of the Revolution in Knowledge

This means that this way of thinking about knowledge does two things that were not present before, or not to anything like the same degree. The first is the creation of new knowledge. The second is that it establishes a two way link or connection between the two kinds of knowledge that Mokyr identifies, the propositional and the prescriptive. The process of churning and recombining the elements of propositional knowledge is combined with the incorporation of knowledge of the prescriptive kind, discovered initially by ad hoc experimentation and investigation. Because it no longer has to conform and be fitted in to a structured system of propositions it can be used to amend and alter the complex hypotheses and so correct mistaken propositions. Thus the argument that is now made is "Proposition X cannot be true, no matter what its authority because if it were true such and such would follow or not be possible and that is contradicted by the evidence of this or that practical investigation". In turn this creates an epistemic or theoretical understanding of why the prescriptive knowledge generates useful results and suggests ways of extending or refining that practical prescriptive knowledge. In other words the two kinds of knowledge are combined and each feeds into and encourages the development of the other through a research agenda that is generated by their interaction.

So the true intellectual revolution in Europe between 1550 and 1690 was this. Two processes were going on side by side, not unconnected by any means but still distinct. One, which has attracted most attention, was a process of physical investigation, by experimenters and inventors. A great deal of this was driven by considerations of commerce and war and was as much about practical benefits as theoretical knowledge, a point made by Lisa Jardine in her work *Ingenious Pursuits*. All of this threw up findings that were novel (such as the discovery of the moons of Jupiter and microscopic animals) and could not easily be fitted into the traditional system or world picture.

However it was not the case that these investigations were clearly driven or inspired by what we would now call scientific ideas and ways of thinking. Many were inspired by magical thinking and theories, which had been enormously elaborated and synthesised since the fourteenth century. Along with these investigations there was a great deal of more abstract speculation, often by the same people as in the cases of Galileo and Tycho. Initially at least, many of the new theories did not work as well in practical terms as the established knowledge that they challenged. Thus the Copernican model of the solar system was not as successful at predicting planetary motions as the Ptolemaic one – until Kepler made the crucial move of abandoning the idea of circular orbits. Initially the mechanics and models of motion put forward by Galileo did not work as well as the traditional Aristotelian model – the critical moment here was Newton's formulation of the three laws of motion.

The second process was the more purely philosophical one of the growth of scepticism and the creation of the new ways of thinking about knowledge described earlier. This meant that ideas and findings were not rejected as incompatible with the existing systematic body of knowledge, because the focus had shifted from the general and the transcendent to the concrete and particular, while the larger claims of the existing system were now held to be true tentatively and so subject to amendment or replacement. This meant that the process of investigation and theorising continued until the integrity of the existing system was radically undermined and significantly new propositions came to be accepted.

At the same time the division of Europe, both politically and intellectually, made it very difficult for rulers to successfully check or suppress this process. In addition the increasing practical results and benefits of enquiry and experimentation, particularly in areas that were relevant for warfare such as ballistics and navigation meant that rulers actually had a direct interest in actively encouraging it, given the continuing and intensified competition they faced. The result was that from the mid seventeenth century onwards rulers set up bodies such as the Royal Society in England in 1660 to stimulate scientific investigation. The spread of critical rationalism also undermined the authority of the traditional world picture more generally. This meant that the process of enquiry was not stopped or contained but continued: this time an 'Age of Reason' was not terminated.

Another European Exception: Why?

So there had been a radical change, in the way many educated people thought about knowledge itself and, as a consequence of that, in the attitude they took to empirical findings and unorthodox ideas. There was a move from a structured system of given truths, sanctioned by tradition and the authority of religion, to one that was open ended, constantly changing, and relatively unstructured, driven by a combination of empirical investigation and rational argument. The difficult question to answer is that of why the impact of this revolution in thinking was so patchy and consequently so slow in many areas and why it took so long for the feedback loop between propositional and prescriptive knowledge to become established. One reason was the relative lack of an institutional framework for scientific investigation before the mid nineteenth century, not least because institutions of learning proved to be conservative and resistant to many of the new ways of thinking (despite Newton's holding a chair at Cambridge). The main reason however was probably intellectual inertia more generally. The traditional world picture proved to be very robust not least because of its intimate association with the Christian religion and it took a long time for many areas, such as medicine to undergo the kind of upheaval that had affected astronomy.

However, subsequent events have shown that the new way of thinking about knowledge, modern science if you will, is radically subversive of traditional beliefs. The experience of the last three hundred years has shown that it has a corrosive and solvent effect upon traditional systems of belief and worldviews, drastically undermining their credibility because of its own capacity to generate more and greater beneficial practical outcomes than traditional systems of belief. The modern scientific way of thinking about knowledge is not respectful of sentiment, hopeful aspiration, faith, or mere belief, no matter how passionately these are held. It disenchants the world. However, it and the processes associated with it gradually become an enormously powerful way of generating new knowledge and of bringing about practical results that are beneficial to human life. This starts slowly, just as sustained intensive growth does, but like that, it accelerates as time goes on.

The important thing to grasp is that although this first appears in Western civilisation it is not an organic product or continuation of earlier, long standing trends in the intellectual history of Christian civilisation. Rather, although it drew on that earlier history it came to mark a radical break from it, a decisive historical rupture. Moreover it drew upon and in a very real sense derived from earlier thinking in the Islamic world. The ideas of Muslim rationalism, as expounded by people such as Averroes and Avempace were defeated in the Islamic world but passed on into Western culture, where they were developed and were successful. This is true both at the general level and in the case of specific theories about the natural world. Thus the ideas of Copernicus about a heliocentric solar system and those of Galileo about mechanics are so close to ones put forward earlier by Muslim thinkers, even in matters of mathematical detail, that we must suppose either an extraordinary coincidence or the transmission of the ideas and their reception, although as of now we have no idea of how this might have happened. The point however is the one made earlier, that a truncated 'Age of Reason' in one part of the world was able to play a role in a later one in another part of the world which was not truncated in the same way.

Why though did this happen in seventeenth century Europe or to put it another way what made seventeenth century Europe different from the earlier Middle East, Song or late Ming China, or Europe itself in the twelfth and thirteenth centuries? In Song China we see the same kinds of intellectual movements and experimental investigation that are to be found in Europe between 1550 and 1690, with the same connection between commerce and war on the one hand and technology and scientific experiment on the other. The same set of phenomena reappear in Ming China during and after the reign of the Wan-Li emperor and we can also see them in the Islamic world in the ninth century and subsequently. There seem to have been two vital differences. The first was the greater resilience of traditional intellectual systems in the earlier episodes and their successful resistance to the subversive effects of enquiry and argument.

Thus Asharite orthodoxy triumphed over rationalism in the Islamic world, more traditional varieties of Confucianism defeated the more materialist and rationalist variants in the Chinese case. An important part of this was the way that scepticism in philosophy was not checked and moderated, but rather followed to a radically sceptical epistemology. This made empirical investigation and rationalist argument both appear to be useless, since neither could lead to any degree of certainty. The only alternatives appeared to be conventionalism (accepting the authority of tradition and convention) or fideism (relying upon faith and revealed truth), as Al-Ghazali argued. In Europe this did not happen. In part this was because of the successful articulation of critical rationalism as a response to the problem of complete scepticism. That in turn however was probably made possible by the religious divisions within Europe after 1517 and the way that all sides of the debates came to employ sceptical arguments as a weapon in controversy. At the same time the results of enthusiasm and passionate conviction alienated many thinking Europeans from definite certainty and dogma. It is no coincidence that the great centre of the new way of thinking in seventeenth century Europe was the Netherlands, which was also the place with the freest press and the widest degree of religious toleration.

The other critical difference was the political division of Europe described in the previous chapter, which distinguishes Europe from the Chinese case (though not the Islamic or probably the Indian). Rulers may have wished to enforce an intellectual orthodoxy and frequently made moves in this direction but they were limited in their ability to do so by the continued competition they faced and the incentives this created. It became increasingly obvious that there were considerable benefits from freer enquiry and technological innovation, both directly in terms of military effectiveness and indirectly through the increased wealth and hence revenue that these brought. The new kind of state system brought about by the military revolution in Europe went along with a new kind of intellectual system, a new way of thinking about knowledge and how to acquire and organise it. After 1690 these came together, to transform the relationship between Europe and the rest of the world. They also meant that the processes and phenomena that began to manifest themselves throughout the world as the eighteenth century progressed would have a unique outcome in Europe and its offshoots.

Further Reading and Bibliographical Essay

The two best introductions to the intellectual world of educated Europeans as it was before the Scientific Revolution are E. M. W. Tillyard *The Elizabethan World Picture: A Study of the Idea of Order in the Age of Shakespeare, Donne, and Milton* (Vintage Books, 1959), and C. S. Lewis *The Discarded Image: An Introduction to Medieval and Renaissance Literature* (Cambridge University Press, 1964). Another key and classic work is Arthur O. Lovejoy *The Great Chain of Being: A Study of the History of an Idea* (Harvard University Press, 1976 1st pub. 1933)

A good example of the 'classic' account of the Scientific Revolution is Herbert Butterfield *The Origins of Modern Science* (Free Press, 1997). For more recent work see among many other works, John Henry *The Scientific Revolution and the Origins of Modern Science* (Palgrave Macmillan, 2002), Steven Shapin *The Scientific Revolution* (Chicago University Press, 1998), H. Floris Cohen *The Scientific Revolution: A Historiographical Enquiry* (Chicago University Press, 1994), Margaret J. Osler (ed.) *Rethinking the Scientific Revolution* (Cambridge University Press, 2000), and David C. Lindberg & Robert S. Westman (eds.) *Reappraisals of the Scientific Revolution* (Cambridge University Press, 19900. Particularly useful is the work of Toby E. Huff as in *The Rise of Early Modern Science: Islam, China, and the West* (Cambridge University Press, 2003), and *An Age of Science and Revolutions, 1600 – 1800* (Oxford University Press, 2005). A recent work that incorporates much of the new arguments while asserting very firmly that there was indeed a Scientific Revolution is David Wootton *The New Science: A New History of the Scientific Revolution* (Harper Perennial, 2016). For the subject of medicine in particular, go no further than the same author's *Bad Medicine: Doctors Doing Harm Since Hippocrates* (Oxford University Press, 2007). Brian Vickers *Occult and Scientific Mentalities in the Renaissance* (Cambridge University Press, 1986) explores the complex relationship between magic, and science at that time and earlier.

For studies of science in other civilisational traditions and their influence on Europe as well as in the other direction see George Saliba *Islamic Science and the Making of the European Renaissance* (MIT Press, 2007), Benjamin Elman *A Cultural History of Modern Science in China* (Harvard University Press, 2006), and his *On Their Own Terms: Science in China 1550 – 1900* (Harvard University Press, 2005). The original for studies of this kind is Joseph Needham *Science in Traditional China* (Harvard University Press, 1982).

The crucial part played by the response to scepticism is the theme of Richard H. Popkin *The History of Scepticism: From Savonarola to Bayle* (Oxford University Press, 2003). This is also covered in Richard H. Popkin (ed.) *The Pimlico History of Western Philosophy* (Pimlico, 1999). One book that explores the changing idea of knowledge as a systemic whole is Alexandre Koyre *From the Closed World to the Infinite Universe* (Johns Hopkins University Press, 1968).

The key work of Joel Mokyr on this subject is *The Gifts of Athena: Historical Origins of the Knowledge Economy* (Princeton University Press, 2002). Another work with a similar theme is Lisa Jardine *Ingenious Pursuits: Building the Scientific Revolution* (Abacus, 2000). The connection of the Scientific Revolution with both the subsequent Enlightenment and even later economic modernisation is the subject of Theodore K. Rabb, *The Last Days of the Renaissance: The March to Modernity* (Basic Books, 2006), Thomas L. Hankins *Science and the Enlightenment* (Cambridge University Press, 1985), and Margaret C. Jacob *Scientific Culture and the Making of the Industrial West* (Oxford University Press, 1997).

CHAPTER VII

The Enlightenment and the Advent of Modernity

The World After the Fourteenth Century Crisis

THE breakdown of the medieval world and its economic systems in the great crisis of the fourteenth century had led to a transformation of the Old World civilisations rather than their collapse. One aspect of this was the emergence in most parts of the world of large empires, based on the new military techniques that had appeared during the political disorder of the fourteenth and fifteenth centuries. At a global level the main empires controlled most of the major civilisations and increasingly expanded at the expense of less complex societies, including the Central Asian nomads who by the sixteenth century had lost their former military advantage. The main land based empires were all sufficiently large to not fear conquest by one of the others but there was intermittent conflict in areas where they met, as in Mesopotamia between the Ottomans and Safavids or Manchuria between Russia and China.

Alongside these land based empires were a series of oceanic or sea borne empires, based on new maritime technologies developed by the previously marginal Europeans. In Europe itself however the military and political competition had a different outcome, due to the failure of a hegemonic winner to emerge, with the appearance of a system of states that were indeed generally larger and more powerful than their medieval predecessors but in a condition of continuous competition against each other. This was to have significant consequences in a number of ways. It played an important part, as we have just seen, in the reshaping of the mental world of educated Europeans by the 1690s and it was to make the response of European elites to economic developments in the course of the eighteenth century crucially different from that of elites and societies more generally elsewhere.

A Pre-Modern Economy?

The other main result of the great crisis of the 1320 to 1450 period was a transformation of the economic system in most parts of the world. As explained before, the kind of economy that we find in most parts of the world after 1450 was different in important ways from both the medieval one and the modern. It was much more commercialised and market driven than the medieval, with households much more integrated into a market exchange system than had been the case then. Once the world trade system recovered after the later fifteenth century the degree of economic integration between different regions of the world and the volume and importance of long distance trade were both much greater than before. Large scale slave labour now played a prominent part in the world wide division of labour and the slave trade was a very important one. We should not fall into the trap of seeing this as somehow a progression from the medieval kind of economy and above all we should not see it as a proto-modern economic order, one that was steadily developing into a modern kind of economy.

The economic system of the world as a whole and of most parts of it had modern features such as an extensive and increasingly monetised market that drove and organised an ever larger share of production but it differed from the kind of modern economy that began to emerge at the end of the eighteenth century in a number of basic ways. Economic growth was still generally not much greater than that of population so there was little or no real rise in living standards and what there was happened very slowly. This was still a predominantly rural economy with the great majority of the population involved in agriculture, either full time or in combination with some other activity. Production both for direct consumption and for the market was carried out mainly in households or small workshops attached to households and the family was integrated with the productive process in a way that is no longer generally true. Technology was generally stable, with slow and piecemeal innovation. The modern, corporate form of business organisation was rare, even for large enterprises, and capital markets were marginal. This kind of economy was a market economy but not a capitalist one, it was one where production was mainly organised through domestic rather than factory production, it was predominantly rural and family based and it did not have the economic and technological dynamism characteristic of modernity.

The General Crisis of the Seventeenth Century

In the central decades of the seventeenth century this new world order experienced a series of setbacks and political upheavals. This took the form everywhere of economic recession, a slowdown or even a reversal of population growth, and a fiscal and political crisis, brought about by the relentless growth of taxation and elite spending. The common underlying factors were twofold. The first was a sharp intensification of the global cooling of the Little Ice Age, which reached its peak in the seventeenth century and consequently a worldwide decline in agricultural yields and a series of devastating famines. The second was the way that the ever increasing demands of the new military establishments and other forms of elite spending led to a rise in taxation and an acute crisis of state finance. Faced with rising taxes at precisely the moment when they were under pressure from the worsening climate, productive classes throughout Eurasia resorted to armed resistance. This was not a simple matter of elites versus masses however, as there were also severe divisions within elites over public policy and the nature of government, and between local and national or imperial elites.

This 'General Crisis' as some historians have called it, manifested itself in a whole series of rebellions, civil wars and outright revolutions right across Eurasia, with the culmination in the 1640s and 1650s. There were enormous peasant uprisings in Russia and a political crisis at the centre in 1648. The three British kingdoms were torn apart by civil war after 1637, culminating in the execution of the King in 1649. Elsewhere in Europe the Spanish monarchy saw rebellions in Milan, Naples, and Catalonia while between 1648 and 1653 the French crown was rocked by the upheavals of the Fronde which led to the young Louis XIV having to flee Paris at one stage. In other parts of the world things were equally dramatic and turbulent. In China a series of peasant uprisings culminated in the revolt led by the self styled 'Dashing Prince' Li Zu-Zheng. In 1644 he captured Beijing and the last Ming emperor hanged himself in the gardens of the imperial palace. There was a major uprising in Japan in 1637-8, which led the Tokugawa shogun to adopt the policy of isolating Japan from the rest of the world. In India a series of revolts and a growing fiscal crisis led to the overthrow of the Mughal emperor Shah Jehan in 1657 and the seizing of power by his son, Aurangzeb. The Ottoman Empire was paralysed by Janissary revolts and a breakdown of central administration between 1648 and 1656. As one contemporary put it, these were times of universal shaking.

However it became clear by the 1680s at the latest that that the outcome in most of the world was the triumph and consolidation of the gunpowder empires. In China an army commander, Wu San-Kuei sought assistance from the Manchu leader Dorgon to regain Beijing from Li Zu-Zheng. The Manchus defeated Li Zhu-Zheng and went on to conquer China between 1644 and 1661 and established the Qing dynasty, which would rule China until 1911. After the suppression of a major rebellion in 1674-81 their rule was consolidated. They restored and further developed the system of government created by the early Ming emperors. In the Ottoman Empire the period of disorder came to an end with the accession to power of the Grand Vizier Mohammed Koprulu in 1656. On his death in 1661 he was succeeded as grand Vizier by his son Ahmed and the family were to effectively rule the Empire on and off until 1711. The Koprulus restored order and introduced a series of reforms that revived the power and effectiveness of Ottoman central administration. In Russia the period of instability ended in the 1680s, and definitively with the accession of Peter the Great in 1689.

In Europe the various rebellions were defeated and absolutism was consolidated, with one very significant exception. This was the British Isles, where the period of instability came to an end by 1692 with the establishment not of an absolute monarchy like those found in most of the Continent, but a constitutional one in which much of the constitutional and representative government of the Middle Ages survived. In general though, the crisis of the mid seventeenth century saw the consolidation of the new political and economic order that had emerged over the previous century and a half. It would survive in every part of the world until the last two decades of the eighteenth century and in many places for a hundred years after that.

The one major exception outside Europe was India. Here the structural problems of the Mughal state were not resolved. The reign of Aurangzeb did see an effort to restore the power of the Mughal state. A part of this was to resume a policy of aggressive expansion, into the southern part of India beyond the Deccan. This involved an arduous and protracted struggle but by the end of Aurangzeb's reign in 1707 the Mughal empire had reached its greatest extent and included all of the subcontinent apart from its southernmost tip. However his reign and policies proved to be disastrous for the Mughal state and he left it in an extremely fragile condition. The wars were both bloody and enormously expensive and put ever greater strain on the central treasury. Aurangzeb himself was suspicious and cruel but above all he was a religious fanatic. In 1669 he abandoned the tolerant policy followed since Akbar and began persecution of the Hindu majority along with a campaign of iconoclasm that destroyed many temples. Ten years later he imposed the jizya poll tax on his non-Muslim subjects, partly to defray the costs of the wars. The result was a succession of rebellions above all by the Mahrattas between 1659 and 1680 under their charismatic leader Shivaji. By the latter date they had become effectively independent of the Mughal central authority. Meanwhile there were uprisings elsewhere while the Sikhs became increasingly militant and a threat to the empire's power in the Punjab. Consequently, the Mughal state proved unable to deal with its problems and in the decades after 1707 it disintegrated, so here the hegemonic empire collapsed. This had important geopolitical consequences, as we shall see.

The Appearance of Economic Policy

Within Europe in particular, the 'General Crisis' and its aftermath also saw the emergence of something quite novel, although we now take its existence for granted. That was public (i.e. government) economic policy. Previously governments and rulers had not had the capacity or administrative machinery to engage in what could meaningfully be described as an economic policy – a general sentiment in favour of greater prosperity and more trade does not count. The only possible real exception had been in China under the Song. A great deal of legislation that we now view as economic regulation (such as the Roman emperor Diocletian's price edict or the medieval English Statute of Labourers) was primarily about maintaining social stability, above all a stable social hierarchy and organisation, and it did not have an explicit economic goal or purpose.

Indeed rulers in most parts of the world before the seventeenth century lacked the very idea of an economy or of trade as an abstract category of analysis rather than as a concrete activity and they certainly did not see the promotion of trade and wealth accumulation as one of the functions of government. The continuing and intensifying military competition within Europe meant that boosting the revenue base became ever more pressing and simple conquest and acquisition of territory was no longer enough by itself. The result was the gradual appearance from the early seventeenth century onwards of theoretical analyses of trade, production and wealth, and advice to rulers on how to make their domains and subjects more productive, and how they might capture a larger share of the wealth so produced. This meant that as time passed the new kinds of states that had resulted from the military revolution in Europe were engaged in economic competition as much as military and diplomatic.

The form this took was what later came to be called 'the mercantile system' or, when thought of as an economic theory, mercantilism. The two central notions were firstly that wealth could be increased and secondly that the way for any particular part of the world to do this was by capturing wealth at the expense of other areas. Trade and production were thus seen as being about competition between states rather than cooperative exchange between individuals. The aim became to fence off an area of the planet's surface and allow free trade within that area but not between those living within it and those outside. Trade of that kind was seen as an aggressive policy often only one step away from war and aimed at capturing a larger share of the trade that went across political borders, which was seen as ultimately a fixed quantity. This meant conflict over where the 'fences' were to be drawn, that is over exactly which areas of the planet were to be inside a fenced off area and on what terms. One type of conflict was that between local elites, who wanted the unit of free exchange to be a smaller one and those elites connected to a larger state who wanted it to coincide with the entire political unit. This was particularly the case in Japan, which was interestingly the one area outside Europe where the mercantile system really took root. Another was that between different ruling groups, over which fenced off area a specific territory and population should belong to.

The policy that resulted from this had the following main elements. Firstly a combination of free trade within a state or empire with tariffs and prohibitions on trade across its boundaries, secondly a system of colonies, that is dependent settlements the inhabitants of which were (in theory) not allowed to trade with the rest of the world other than via the 'mother country' and which were supposed to produce primary products such as raw materials in exchange for manufactured goods, thirdly a system of state subsidies and privileges for favoured mercantile interests, fourthly direct state action to encourage or even finance and run key areas of production, with the aim of reducing imports and capturing a section of what was seen as a finite market, and finally a system of privately owned but state backed trading companies for trade with other parts of the world, particularly those a long way from the state in question. The main form that state support took was the granting of a monopoly in trade to a particular part of the world, along with actual military support in some cases.

This full range of policies was found only in Europe and although it began to take shape in the 1590s only really arrived after the 1650s. The pioneers in this as in other respects were the Dutch. Outside Europe this kind of policy was also found to some degree in Japan. Elsewhere although elements of it were to be found in the great empires there was much less of a conscious policy and above all there was not the dynamic element found in Europe that derived from competition between relatively small metropolitan states. Empires such as China or the Ottoman Empire were so large that their rulers did not see the need to push for a larger share of trade revenue in the way that their European counterparts did. However, as mentioned in Chapter Five, the element of trying to fence off an area of the planet and encourage trade within it while regulating trade between it and the rest of the world was universal. Despite this the period after 1550 and particularly after about 1680 saw a noticeable increase in the volume of long distance world trade and in economic integration and specialisation which also came to involve more and more sectors of the economies, despite the efforts of rulers.

A Population Surge

The decade of the 1690s saw the last years of the acute phase of the Little Ice Age. After the 1700s, although by most calculations the Little Ice Age did not fully end until the 1850s, the planet began to warm up and severe adverse weather conditions became less frequent. This was one factor behind the increasingly rapid growth of population experienced by most parts of the world after 1720 at the latest (Africa was the major exception). Another was the impact of food plants introduced to the old world from the new, above all the potato and the sweet potato. These made it possible to support a household on a much smaller area of land than before and so enabled a much higher population to survive on the same area of land. Alongside this were innovations and improvements in traditional Old World crops such as rice, as well as the increase in production on a global scale brought about by increased regional specialisation. The effects of these were felt in many parts of the world and led to significant increases in population in regions as far removed as Ireland, Poland, the Yangtse delta and Bengal.

The final major factor behind the growth of world population, just as in the twelfth and thirteenth centuries, was the growth of output generally. Just as in the earlier period a positive feedback loop was created in which increases in population led to increases in output (which were amplified by such factors as the new crops and the increases in productive efficiency that resulted from the more extensive trade connections between different parts of the world) and this increase in output in turn led to a growth in population as people married earlier, had more children, and had more of those children survive. These new people then in turn brought about more output and exchange and so on. However, this cycle of growth was still not intensive over the long to medium run or in the world as a whole because population and output kept pace with each other. Moreover, just as in the thirteenth century, there was a growing tendency for population to outrun the growth of production and come up against Malthusian checks.

The figures for world population growth in the 1650 to 1750 period are certainly impressive. During this period world population as a whole grew from four hundred and fifty to around eight hundred million and so reached a level about twice as high as that reached in 1300. During this time there was so far as we can tell no growth or even a decline in Africa while the Americas were still thinly populated compared to the Old World and so the bulk of the increase came in Eurasia. It was Qing China that saw the most rapid growth with its population almost doubling between 1650 and 1750 while there was also rapid growth in India. Japan and the Ottoman Empire also experienced growth but at a slower rate. Asia as a whole saw a rise of fifty four per cent, from three hundred and thirty million in 1650 to four hundred and eighty million by 1750, representing an annual growth rate of 0.4. Europe's population also grew dramatically but not as rapidly, from one hundred million in 1650 to a hundred and forty million in 1750, a growth of forty percent at an annual rate of 0.3. It was also China and Europe plus Russia that saw dramatic territorial expansion during this period. European powers continued to expand their colonial territory and populations in the Americas while Russia expanded right across the northern part of Eurasia to the Pacific. China under the Qing meanwhile more than doubled in size and came to incorporate Tibet, Mongolia and Sinkiang (Manchuria was of course the original domain of the dynasty) while in the South-West there was a continued expansion of Han Chinese population into the provinces of Yunnan and Sichuan. By the early eighteenth century the Chinese empire had reached its largest ever extent and population.

Just as in the thirteenth century, this sustained growth in population began to exert pressure on both the productive and the political orders, which intensified as the eighteenth century progressed. Along with the economic developments of the time this created a combination of problems and opportunities. Pressure of population on natural resources caused problems such as growing land hunger but also created opportunities for entrepreneurs in both agriculture and manufacturing. At the same time increased population and economic activity had a number of gradual intellectual and cultural effects which took much the same form everywhere but were amplified in Europe by the continuing consequences of the intellectual revolution described in the previous chapter. Everywhere there were movements for intellectual, cultural and political reform. These were obviously specific and local in many ways but they also had shared features, above all an interest in both intellectual and economic/technological innovation. At the same time these reform movements typically had both a backward and a forward looking aspect.

Reform Movements Outside Europe

One of the earliest of these movements took place in the Ottoman Empire, in what came to be known as the 'Tulip Period' of Ottoman history between 1718 and 1730, which saw a notable flourishing of Ottoman high culture, with important innovations in areas such as representational art, poetry and literature in general, along with a borrowing of various forms from other parts of the world, particularly Western Europe, and a movement to reform the institutions of Ottoman state and society. Qing China saw both significant economic development, particularly in the Yangtse delta, and the provinces of Guangdong and Fukien, and also a lively intellectual life. This saw both the systematic collection and publishing of enormous reference collections of traditional Chinese works and the articulation of ideas for radical reform of the centralised imperial administration and of Chinese society more generally by thinkers such as Dai Zhen (1724 – 1777). Chinese culture was not significantly influenced at this time by other parts of the world but had a great influence elsewhere with Europeans for example much influenced by Chinese design and ideas. Japan under the Tokugawa was the scene of both dramatic economic development and a body of new thinking, much of which involved a revival and reform of the Japanese variety of Confucianism.

The intellectual ferment of the eighteenth century typically combined the following elements: innovations in culture and the arts, often deriving from contacts with other parts of the world; the articulation of new ideas about society, social life and government which led to proposals for concrete change and reform in all of these areas; at the same time, an increased interest in the past and often a deliberate intention to reform the present by reviving past institutions or more accurately to reshape the present so as to make it conform to an idea of a past period. All of this is found in Europe as in China, Japan, India, and the Ottoman Empire. The intellectual history of eighteenth century Europe, like its economic history, needs to be seen as a part of a wider global whole, even if only at the level of coincidence and mutual influence. However, in both areas the developments were more dramatic and ultimately brought about the destruction of the old order and the appearance of something new – modernity.

Within Europe – the Enlightenment

It is conventional to refer to the intellectual history of Europe in this era by the name the main movement gave itself – the Enlightenment. This was the European case of the wider phenomenon described above. However it was more extensive and radical, and ultimately had a greater impact than its counterparts elsewhere. One reason was that it followed on from and in some ways was the product of the intellectual revolution described in the previous chapter. Moreover the context in which it occurred also gave it a distinctive quality. This was a civilisation that no longer had a political or religious monopoly power and was becoming increasingly pluralistic. Another factor was precisely that European civilisation was more open to and influenced by the rest of the world than was the reverse. This reflected the position of Europeans as middlemen between other civilisations and the way that initially they felt the need to borrow from what they regarded as more advanced cultures, above all the Chinese.

So much has been written about the Enlightenment that the books on this topic would fill a fair sized library by themselves. It has also become fashionable in some circles to criticise it and its ideas as dangerous and the source of much of the ills of the contemporary world. This critical view has a long pedigree and ultimately springs from a hostility to the modern world as such. Much of the recent criticism though is simply misguided and misunderstands what was actually going on in the writings of many Enlightenment thinkers. In particular it is profoundly wrong to see the Enlightenment as a defence of traditional European civilisation and a slighting of other civilisations from an arrogant, 'Eurocentric' perspective. In fact the reality is almost exactly the opposite.

The Enlightenment as an intellectual movement began in the years between 1690 and the 1720s with what one well known work called the '*Crisis of the European Mind*'. This derived from the cataclysmic effects on the traditional view of the world of the collapse of Christian unity into savage religious wars following the Reformation and the undermining of the traditional view of both cosmology and the nature of knowledge by the Scientific Revolution. What is important to realise is the degree of discontinuity in intellectual history that it represents and the degree to which, as it developed, its principal target was the traditional civilisation of Western Europe and its central element, the Christian faith. Indeed as time passed it turned into a fundamental assault upon the most basic assumptions of traditional Western Christian civilisation. This did not happen to anything like the same extent elsewhere in the world – the counterpart movements in the Ottoman Empire,

Japan and China were all more about the reform and refurbishment of their own civilisational traditions.

A common type of Enlightenment writing, particularly in the earlier part of the eighteenth century, was accounts by travellers of other parts of the world or of Western civilisation by actual Europeans but presented as being the view of a traveller from another part of the world (one well known example was the *Persian Letters* of Montesquieu). The accounts of other parts of the world were often straightforward reportage but sometimes were simply fictional. In these cases the real subject was Western society, which was described reflexively, by giving an account of a contrasting social order. In all of these works in general, the viewpoint of a citizen of another civilisation or the description of it was used to criticise Western civilisation and hold it up for inspection.

The key concept in these and subsequent works was that of civilisation, which meant a particular state or condition of society and was defined in part by contrast to the other two supposed kinds of social order, savagery (no agriculture or settled life), and barbarism (agriculture, cities but little or no art and culture, simple living conditions, and plain or coarse manners and ways of behaving). The things that marked out a given society as being in one or another of these categories were numerous but the main ones were thought to be the level of cultural expression and achievement, the level of wealth and economic development, the style of life and manners, the level of knowledge and understanding of the world as shown by both scientific and technological achievement, the degree of social complexity in terms of institutions and division of labour, and not least, the extent to which intellectual life was dominated by reason and free enquiry rather than faith and superstition. Progress meant movement from one stage to another.

Initially at least Europe was not seen as being more civilised than the Ottoman Empire, Iran or India, and certainly not as being as civilised as China. The early Enlightenment thinkers saw the immediate past of their own culture as belonging to the class of barbarism with Africans and Native Americans as savages and Europeans, Muslims, Indians, and Chinese as civilised with the Chinese in particular at a higher stage of civilisation than either Europeans or Muslims. By the 1800s Europeans had come to see themselves as more civilised than the other main cultures of Eurasia.

Crucially it was the main features of the traditional Christian Western civilisation, which their own time had inherited from the Middle Ages that were seen as evidence of the relative lack of civilisation on the part of Europeans and movement away from these came to be defined as improvement and progress in the direction of a greater degree of civilisation. Above all economic development and technological innovation and the decline of revealed religion from a central place in intellectual life were thought of as being the markers of progress in this direction. Thus the important thing to realise about the Enlightenment as a movement, particularly in its 'mature' phase after 1750, was that insofar as it was a critical movement its main target was not the rest of the world (much of which for a long time was seen as better or more advanced than Europe) but the traditional past of Europe, particularly the medieval and religious past which was contrasted unfavourably to both the ancient and the modern.

As an intellectual movement the Enlightenment was enormously varied and complex. Its leading figures came from many parts of Europe and not just France or Scotland as some might suppose. Despite the great variety there were a number of common ideas, in addition to the social and historical one of civilisation and these ideas and their development and application to particular topics can be traced through the course of the eighteenth century and the writings of the major figures.

In the first place was empiricism and critical rationalism: reason and dispassionate enquiry were seen as being better routes to knowledge than tradition, authority, revelation or emotion. True knowledge was to be found by empirical investigation and tests, not by intuition, revelation, intuition, or the reliance upon authority or revealed 'truth'. This meant that everything should be subject to question and critical scrutiny – a position that ultimately was incompatible with the notion of the sacred. This was closely connected to the second main notion, that of materialism: a belief (in many cases) that only matter existed i.e. a denial of the reality of the category of the spiritual and more generally an emphasis upon material progress and comforts as opposed to non-material ones.

What followed from both of these was scepticism in the shape of hostility to organised religion, particularly Christianity, and to religious dogma generally. This took the form of deism (belief in a God while rejecting actual revealed religion) or increasingly, outright atheism (something many historians argue was not possible for educated persons before the 18th century). The first systematic statement of atheism was D'Holbach's *System of Nature,* published in 1770. This went along with universalism, that is the idea that the truths discovered by reason and investigations were timeless and not confined to one part of the world. In other words they were true for all people in all times. This also meant that underneath their apparent variety human beings shared certain common essential qualities – it is this that underlies the concept of universal (as opposed to specific and particular) rights, the rights of man rather than the rights of Englishmen, Frenchmen etc.

Perhaps the most dramatic break with past thought and the idea that now seems most unexceptionable was that of eudamonianism. This is a technical term meaning that the end of life is happiness or human flourishing, that is the maximum possible realisation of the potential of each human being (from the Greek *eudemonia*) – a view captured in the American Declaration of Independence. According to this the aim of life is happiness here and now in the material world. (This is in marked contrast to earlier views, which saw the end of life as service to God and happiness as ultimately something to be realised in the afterlife). This in turn was linked to hedonism, the idea that physical pleasure and comfort are good. This meant regarding 'luxury' (what we would call affluence or prosperity) as a good thing, rather than as being morally corrupting. There was a great deal of internal debate on this point among enlightenment thinkers and many continued to adhere to the idea that 'luxury' was corrupting but with time this became very much the minority opinion.

Perhaps the best known Enlightenment idea was optimism, the belief that the world and human life could be made better rather than simply being accepted as a fate given by God, and that the long term course of human history was for things to get better, in contrast to the view that the world had been made perfect so that change meant decay and deterioration. Applied to public affairs this meant humanitarianism, the notion that it is possible to bring about improvement in the conditions and prospects for human beings by concrete action and public policy, with these being guided by reason and understanding. Enlightenment views of society were less clear but two notions tended to come to the fore as time passed. One was individualism, not in the sense of the advocacy of what would later pass under that term but rather an emphasis upon the individual human being in social analysis rather than on human beings as members of categories or classes. Society was increasingly seen as composed of self-governed, decision-making individuals, in contrast to the older idea of society as an organic interconnected body made up of households and lineages rather than individuals. The other idea was that of sensibility which meant the ability to put oneself in somebody else's position and imagine their feelings. This was seen as the basis of moral conduct and benevolence (as for example in Adam Smith's *Theory of Moral Sentiments*) and was associated with the gradual move to more refined or gentle ways of behaving which was a key marker of progress because it indicated the degree to which the 'passions', associated with people's lower nature and the barbarous past, were being subjected to the intellect.

While these ideas were shared there were others that we associate with the Enlightenment but which were the subject of vigorous debate, such as that of spontaneous order, the idea that order and structure in human affairs could arise as an unintended consequence of human interaction and not because of any design or purpose, whether divine or human. Another controversial topic was that of providence. Most Enlightenment authors rejected the traditional Christian idea of divine providence and it suffered a massive blow among educated Europeans with the great Lisbon earthquake of 1755. Many though continued to believe in a form of the idea but assigned it to the constitution of the natural world, often as created by the distant and remote creator of the deists (often apostrophised as Nature).

These ideas were all profoundly subversive of traditional thinking and had extensive implications for public policy. They meant that traditional institutions and ways of living were held up to scrutiny and criticism rather than being regarded as part of a divinely created natural order. However this did not stop them being taken up, to some degree at least, by rulers, via the phenomenon of 'Enlightened despotism'. There might be broad agreement about what the ends of government should be and as to what would constitute an improvement in social conditions but a strong disagreement over how to bring this about. This can be seen in a number of areas but most clearly in 'political economy' (as systematic thinking about economic affairs came to be called). Essentially the division that emerges is one between those who emphasise the inevitability and vital importance of power and its use for bringing about improvement and others (such as Adam Smith in the *Wealth of Nations*) who stress the dangers of power and rely rather upon the natural inclinations of human beings and the kind of results that come about spontaneously as a result of their interactions. This debate, which is clearly underway by the last three decades of the eighteenth century, continues to this day and is one of the defining features of the modern world.

Counter Enlightenment

In addition, we should not forget that the Enlightenment faced strong opposition from a whole range of thinkers who defended the traditional order and way of thinking against their assaults or rejected its conclusions. Historians speak of a 'Counter-Enlightenment', a reaction against it that began in the later eighteenth century and continued into the nineteenth but in fact there had been sustained resistance to and criticism of its arguments from the start. Much of this is forgotten however, partly because of the tendency of historians to give more attention to those seen as the 'winners' and also because much of the earlier anti-Enlightenment case is often inaccessible and difficult to modern readers because of its reliance on modes of argumentation that now seem strange or beside the point, such as a reliance on biblical citation and exegesis, or traditions of political thought that are no longer current, such as classical republicanism. In addition to these thinkers we can also identify a third body of ideas, beginning with Rousseau, which takes much of the Enlightenment's views as its starting point but rejects many of its central positions (such as the beneficence of civilisation). This anti-Enlightenment (and by extension anti-modern) tradition also continues up to the present day.

The most striking contrast to the rest of the world however, is that Enlightenment ideas and arguments were ultimately not defeated or suppressed. In the battle of ideas the defenders of the traditional positions were not able to gain a decisive victory over them. Political elites often sought to suppress what they (correctly) saw as subversive notions, through such means as censorship and the persecution and imprisonment of individuals but they were unable to carry this through, not least because many members of the elites supported the ideas and rulers often adopted some parts of them and the agenda they generated. Above all though Europe gained from the intellectual and political pluralism and competition that was the result of the way the Reformation and the military revolution had worked out there. In contrast, elsewhere in the world movements for intellectual and institutional reform ran up against both the way the rulers of large empires often acted to maintain the traditional order and a wider resistance to change on the part of many social groups. Thus in the Ottoman Empire the opposition of the ulema meant that a printing press using Arabic script was not set up in Istanbul until 1727, and on the death of its founder Ibrahim Muteferrika in 1745 printing ceased and did not resume until 1783. (There were printing presses in the Ottoman Empire run by Jews and Christians from an early date but these did not publish works in Arabic script). In China the arguments of reformers such as Dai Zhen were rejected by the majority of scholars, who instead devoted themselves to the production of massive compilations of classical works, while the emperors firmly upheld the traditional view of the organisation of government and social life.

Economic Innovation – An Enlightened Economy

So in Europe the kinds of intellectual development that were a common feature of the eighteenth century world were more radical and extensive than elsewhere. Alongside this intellectual revolution was an economic one. In Europe the pressure of population and economic development on the productive system led to a process of innovation that eventually transformed it. Taken singly the innovations were small and they happened in a piecemeal fashion but they were cumulatively massive in their effects. Most importantly, they were pursued despite their disruptive effects on traditional social order, particularly the family, and the ruling elites were unable or unwilling to stop them, at least in certain parts of Europe and above all in Britain. As with the Enlightenment there is an enormous literature on this topic and many learned controversies but there is also a surprisingly wide range of agreement on the key elements.

The central element was sustained innovation in agriculture. It was here that the consequences of rising population and the pushing of the existing system of production to its limits were most keenly felt, just as in the later thirteenth century, because this was still the sector that employed the majority of the working population in the early eighteenth century. The main result was declining returns in agriculture, above all to labour. The period between 1700 and 1850 saw a response in a continuous series of innovations in several parts of Western Europe but in Britain in particular which all had the effect of raising agricultural productivity significantly before 1750 and by an unprecedented amount after that date. This was a rise in productivity per acre but even more importantly it was a rise in labour productivity so that fewer and fewer people were needed to produce more and more food. This made it significantly different from the kind of increase in output that results from farming a given area of land more intensively through greater labour input – a process with natural limits.

The innovations included such things as enclosures of common access pastureland, increasing specialisation in production, the adoption of new crops and new farming methods such as greater use of lime and fertiliser and the switch to the four field rotation system, mechanisation of various activities which may be said to have started with Jethro Tull's invention of the seed drill in 1701 and later the adoption of the threshing machine in 1786, the deliberate selective breeding of livestock and plant varieties, and the adoption of improved tools such as the horse drawn hoe (another of Tull's inventions) and new forms of the iron plough such as the 'Rotherham' plough, first used in 1730. Another important feature of agricultural development in Britain was a process by which small farms were increasingly consolidated into medium sized ones – this reflected the existence of a true commercial market in land.

Another result of the changes in agriculture was a change in the distribution of labour in the economy with a marked shift out of agriculture and into manufacturing. This led many households to completely abandon any involvement in the agricultural sector, sometimes this meant moving from full time farming to manufacture, in other cases it meant households that combined domestic manufacture with some farming abandoning the residual agricultural element. This shows up in various ways, including the timing and pattern of weddings (because people with a significant involvement in farming tended to marry at certain times of the year due to the highly seasonal nature of agricultural work). It is important to realise that this shift started well before any move to factory production – in fact outside textiles and iron there was no real move to factory production before 1850. Rather it meant a move towards working in the home full time or, increasingly, in small workshops, which could be attached to the home but often were not.

The changes in agriculture and the movement into manufacturing meant that there was a slow but steady change in the organisation of work. Increasingly it was less family and household based and less organised through indentures or domestic service. Instead there was a growth in short term contract wage labour, which often meant higher income but less security. It also meant that the labour market became increasingly responsive to fluctuations in demand and the overall level of economic activity. Within the workplace there were innovations in the way that work was organised, especially an increase in the division of labour, of which Adam Smith's famous account of the pin factory is a good example. This increasingly structured division and organisation of work was often incompatible with a family and household organised system of production, simply because there were often not enough people in any one household to carry out all of the stages of production simultaneously. Of course it was possible to have different households carrying out the various stages of the divided labour or to have the entire process done in one household but with the various stages done at different times but both of these were less productive and more costly than the kind of division described by Smith.

This change in the organisation of work was linked to innovations in the organisation of manufacturing production as a whole. Interestingly there was no clear movement in the direction of one form of organisation or of large enterprises as opposed to small ones, unlike after 1850. Instead there were innovations that led to a wide range of organisational forms appearing with some dominant in one particular industry or sector but not in others. In iron and textiles there was a move to relatively large firms organising production through large plants, with a significant measure of vertical integration. In other sectors such as metalware and household products generally there was a move to smaller workshops, often federated or coordinated by merchant retailers while artisan household manufacture was still important in other areas. The point is that there was a pattern of increasing innovation and experimentation. What was no longer found was a control of the structure and organisation of production by institutions such as guilds or merchant federations with the backing of law and political power. This was in marked contrast to the situation in the Ottoman Empire, where the guilds controlled entry to various trades and regulated such matters as prices, organisation, quality of products and terms of employment, or China where since the Ming much activity had been controlled and regulated by state supported merchant syndicates.

The best known feature of the economic life of eighteenth century Britain (and of other parts of Europe as well) was of course technological innovation. This clearly started before 1750 (so, for example the Newcomen steam engine was invented in 1712) but became more sustained after 1750 – as Joel Mokyr puts it technological innovation was unusual before then but the rule thereafter. The list of innovations in such areas as metalworking, textile production, pottery, and civil engineering is enormous. The best known are the ones often regarded as revolutionary such as James Watt's invention of the condenser steam engine in 1776 but the ones that had the greatest impact in terms of increasing productivity were those that improved existing technology or filled in gaps such as Watt's own later refinements to the steam engine or Henry Cort's perfection of the metal rolling mill to produce bar iron in 1784. In many cases these innovations, particularly the early ones, only brought European manufacture up to the level reached by the Chinese as far back as the Song dynasty. Thus the introduction of coke as a fuel for blast furnaces by Abraham Darby in the 1710s reproduced experiments made under the Song while breakthroughs in ceramics only enabled the Europeans to reproduce the kind of porcelain that the Chinese had been producing (and exporting to Europe in huge quantities) for centuries. However the critical difference is that the process of innovation continued and became more rapid rather than slowing down.

The final area of innovation was in investment and financial institutions. Historians often speak of a 'financial revolution' at the very end of the seventeenth century, one that was started by the Dutch and then taken up and further developed by the British. As with many other innovations the original motive behind much of this was inter-state competition and the need to find ways of financing military expenditure. The three main recognised elements of this were the bill of exchange, which became part of the medium of exchange due to its status as a negotiable instrument and also became a source of credit; a capital market in which shares in an enterprise were freely tradable and transferable; and perpetual bonds and annuities (gilts) issued by governments against future tax revenue. Some of these were of relatively long standing by the 1700s – the bill of exchange was known to medieval merchants and the phenomenon of tradable securities in an enterprise that also enjoyed limited liability was invented by the Dutch with the creation of the VOC (Dutch East India Company) in 1605. Such institutions were also long established in other parts of the world, above all China. The phenomenon of tradable government debt however was genuinely novel and marked a revolution in state finance. Moreover, just as with the other innovations described the point was not so much their novelty as the way that they were elaborated and developed and continued to do so, often in the face of intense hostility.

All of these phenomena developed in Britain after 1700, despite opposition from some circles, which led to measures such as the Bubble Act, passed in 1723 after a speculative boom in shares, which banned the creation of limited companies. What slowly but steadily emerged was a market in credit and investment, initially centred on London with other independent local markets and a larger independent one in Scotland, but which by the later eighteenth century had become a national market, at least for some kinds of business and an international market for state finance. This process involved the appearance of a number of financial institutions, most notably the stock exchange in London, 'country banks' in the provinces (which were an important source of investment for manufacturing enterprise), merchant banks, and latterly joint stock banks. It is important to realise how genuinely novel this was. Markets had existed in various forms for thousands of years but a market in investment of the kind that developed in eighteenth century Britain was something quite new. It undoubtedly played a part in one of the most significant developments of the time, which was the decline in the cost of capital in Europe and Britain in particular compared to the rest of the world.

In the seventeenth century the cost of capital in Europe had been comparable to what it was in China or the Middle East and was very high by modern standards. This high cost had a number of causes – the lack of capital accumulation in general, the degree to which much of the capital that existed was appropriated by rulers and used for war or other non-productive activities, and the way in which much of the capital was scattered in small amounts that were costly and difficult to mobilise or was tied up in relatively illiquid forms. Capital markets began the process (which still continues) of reducing the last two problems by creating mechanisms that collect and pool small capital sums and make it easier to convert illiquid assets into liquid and tradable ones. To the extent that this, along with other developments, led to sustained growth it started a benevolent circle in which investment created more capital, which reduced the cost of investment and so led to more capital being accumulated. The problem of appropriation however is still with us.

Innovations in Government and Science

Alongside innovations in economic life we can also discern the start of a transformation of government and political power. At the level of theory and abstract philosophy this can be traced as far back as the 1590s, which saw the first formulation of a theory of the state as an institution with defined attributes, above all that of sovereignty, as opposed to the idea of government as a kind of function or role carried out by certain people (or more accurately, certain families). In the eighteenth century this idea was elaborated by a number of thinkers, above in the German states, where they acquired the nickname of Kameralists. Their crucial innovation was to work out what became known as the 'police power' of the state, the idea that a central function of rule or power was to have a responsibility for the 'general welfare' of the population. Exactly what this entailed became the subject of warm argument. In practice this began to lead slowly but surely to a change in the organisation and functions of government, which again accelerated after 1750 and even more so after 1800. Some would have it that this change in government was a cause or at least a necessary condition for the kinds of economic innovation described earlier. Others would argue that political developments of this kind were an epiphenomenon and purely a consequence of economic processes that both made a new kind of government possible and led to its emergence as a response. The reality surely is that both of these arguments are true and the modern state as it began to appear at this time was both a contributory cause and a result of the steady transformation of European societies at this time.

The other change to note in eighteenth century Europe was the continuation of the Scientific Revolution, or rather its spread to new areas of knowledge. Again this started after 1690 but became much more noticeable after 1750. The study of materials was the area that saw the most important breakthroughs. Here we see the effective emergence of both metallurgy and chemistry as disciplines and the decisive supplanting of alchemy and the older model of the nature of substances along with another fragmentation of the knowledge system, as understanding of materials was no longer connected to ideas and propositions about such matters as human psychology, social order and the nature of the heavens. The century also saw the spread of scientific method to biology with a key date being the publication by Carl Linnaeus of the *Systema Naturae* in 1758, which created the modern system of taxonomy. Geology also began to emerge as a science with the work of authors such as Buffon (1707 – 1788) and began to undermine the traditional biblical models of the age of the Earth. There were also the first faint intimations of real breakthroughs in medical knowledge and understanding, although here real progress did not come until after 1850.

Why Innovation Continued in Europe

So, in the eighteenth century the development of economic life and the growth of population led to pressure on both the intellectual and productive order of traditional societies. The result everywhere was twofold. Firstly, it led to the appearance of intellectual and cultural movements that sought reform and questioning of the established intellectual and political order (even if this was often cast in terms of restoring an idealised past). Secondly it produced innovation in economic organisation and practice, i.e. in the productive activities of human beings. These innovations were a response to economic incentives above all the need to sustain or increase returns in the increasingly commercial and market based economy of the time as it began to push up against structural and systemic limits, so creating both problems and opportunities. Europe in general and Britain in particular were initially not that different from other parts of the world. However there proved to be one difference that became apparent after 1750: in Britain and some other parts of Europe the innovations continued (as did the intellectual exploration) and began to generate yet more innovation in a self-sustaining process. Elsewhere this was not the case.

Why though was this so? The point is that the kinds of commercial and technological innovation described above were very subversive of traditional established social, economic and political institutions and ways of life and this became increasingly apparent the longer the process of innovation continued. Changes in agriculture undermined the stable order of rural society for example. Several of the changes mentioned tended to subvert the economic role of the household and to disrupt the traditional life cycle, in which domestic service played a key part. The appearance of true national markets for both a wide variety of everyday goods and investment disrupted both established social relations and local institutions such as guilds that controlled and regulated productive activity of all kinds. In other parts of the world innovations did not continue because of the way that they threatened the established order. This was because of both action by elites to protect the existing order, even if it meant choking off economic development, and the consequences of wider social and cultural conservatism. In the Ottoman Empire for example the ulema blocked intellectual enquiry and the government upheld the powers and privileges of the guilds that blocked economic innovation. In Qing China movement of labour out of agriculture and into the growing manufacturing sector was blocked by the persistence of strong family ties and the reluctance of households to abandon a connection to agriculture while the state supported the merchant cartels and maintained a whole series of regulations that limited innovation.

There was of course much opposition and resistance to change in Europe as well, which became more intense as the innovative process continued. European states also had privileged groups and regulations designed to preserve a status quo and inhibit change and innovation. However the ruling elites were not able or ultimately willing to act in a way that would effectively arrest the connected processes of cultural/intellectual and economic transformation, particularly in Britain. Eventually this became an inescapable and self-sustaining process but the initial reason was undoubtedly the state system and the kinds of incentives it created for elites, which made it very difficult for them to check change without suffering a loss of their competitive position, and which also by virtue of Europe's division meant that there was no single authority to even try and uphold the old order. In Britain there was the additional element of the distinctive outcome of the crisis of the mid seventeenth century, which had created a different kind of polity, one that was prepared to allow a much greater scope to private initiative and where political power was checked and restrained in ways that were not found elsewhere.

What happened was that for the first time an episode of intensive growth, innovation both technological and economic, and scientific speculation was sustained in the long run, rather than being cut off by the action of power or smothered by the resistance of traditional social institutions and practices (or more realistically a combination of the two). The obvious comparison is with Song China where something very similar had happened before being cut short by the Mongol conquest and the Ming restoration. The two episodes shared many features, above all the way in which ruling groups had allowed the process of spontaneous change and discovery arising from the interactions of people to take its own course and had even increasingly sought to encourage it for reasons of their own. Another common feature was the way that the process produced a change in the nature of government and the ruling elite – there are suggestive similarities between the ideas of modern administration that were being developed in eighteenth century Europe and the reforms introduced by Wang An-Shih in twelfth century China. In other parts of the world the pressure for change died away or was suppressed as the eighteenth century went on and the result was that the existing economic and social system continued in the form it had broadly had since the fifteenth and sixteenth centuries. In Europe by contrast development did not just take place within the confines and structures of the existing system but came to transform and ultimately destroy and replace it.

The Crisis of the Later Eighteenth Century and the Breakthrough of Modern Innovation

This was to produce sharply contrasting outcomes in the years after about 1800. In Europe and its offshoots there was for the first time (apart from Song China) a period of sustained intensive growth. Initially this was not very rapid by contemporary standards but it <u>was</u> sustained and the effects of compounding mean that even low rates of growth have striking results if they continue for long enough. This was the start of a process that resulted in a twelvefold growth in real average incomes between 1780 and 1990. The growth of population, which accelerated after 1780, was absorbed by the growing manufacturing sector and actually drove the economic growth in many ways. This went along with an unprecedented degree of urbanisation such that by 1851 Britain had become the first society in history where a majority of the population lived in large towns and cities. By contrast, in both China and India population growth continued but without systemic improvements in agriculture or any significant movement of labour from agriculture to manufacturing, much less to factory production – instead the existing system of decentralised domestic production combining agriculture and manufacture and making extensive use of indentured labour continued. The result was that by the 1850s China in particular was facing a Malthusian crunch, with severe malnutrition, land hunger and overexploitation of marginal land.

The breakthrough or eruption of modernity thus happened (or was allowed to happen) in some very specific places. It was not even all of Europe but rather certain regions within the European sub-continent that experienced it. It happened initially in North-West Europe and particularly in Britain, soon followed by the Low Countries, France and parts of Germany (the Rhineland). Another vital feature was that once it had continued for a time the collection of phenomena that we call modernity was not only self-sustaining. It also showed a long term tendency to spread rather than remaining confined to certain regions. In fact, the longer it continued the more it became apparent that other ways of organising society, politics and economic life were no longer viable (in the way that the initial invention of agriculture in the Fertile Crescent ultimately doomed hunter-gatherer societies in most parts of the world). In this it was different from the earlier case of Song China (although we might argue counterfactually that had that earlier episode been sustained it would also have spread). One reason why modernity has tended to spread since 1800 is undoubtedly the greater interconnectedness of the various parts of the world and the way in which as the world economy has developed withdrawing from it has come to involve increasingly severe costs, to the point where few ruling groups are prepared or able to do so. However, as the next chapter shows, it is also the outcome in part of war and politics.

To return to a point made in Chapter Four, we should always beware of assuming that the course historical events actually took was the one they inevitably had to take. Just as the actual development of China after the Song was not predetermined, so it was not inevitable that the breakthrough to modernity would happen and then be sustained in the 1750 – 1850 period. Nor was it certain that it had to happen in Europe. The factors mentioned such as political division and the intellectual revolution of the seventeenth century made it much more likely that it would happen there but there were other candidates in the later eighteenth century. In particular it could have happened in Qing China, or more accurately in some parts of China, above all the Yangtse delta, which by the 1770s was every bit as developed as Britain. Kenneth Pomeranz has argued that a simultaneous breakthrough to modernity in the Yangtse delta and Britain failed to happen only because the reserves of coal in China were remote and hard to access for geological reasons so that the cotton industry of the Yangtse delta was unable to adopt energy intensive and labour saving machinery in the way the British were. The problem with this argument is simply that the importance of fossil fuel powered machinery in the early stages of industrialisation is overstated as most of the early part of that process was powered by water. More likely the critical difference was that Britain was a sovereign political entity while the Yangtse delta was a region of a single empire, one that was also highly centralised. Even so, we should not regard either outcome as inevitable.

The point to note is that the birth of modernity in Europe was neither peaceful nor uncontested. Indeed the years after 1770 were the most turbulent that many parts of the world had experienced since the great crisis of the mid seventeenth century over a hundred years earlier. Today the stereotype of the eighteenth century is that of an age of artistic refinement and elegance, and a world of stability and traditional order in comparison to the upheavals that came later, above all after 1789. In fact this is to misunderstand what was going on in most parts of the world to an ever greater degree as the century went on.

As mentioned earlier there was a steady growth of world population after the later seventeenth century. At the same time there was a growth in output and in the volume and extent of trade. However, as has already been pointed out, this growth was of the traditional extensive kind. There was no systematic and sustained innovation in most of the world. The key factor, particularly in Asia, was what has come to be called 'the Industrious Revolution'. This was an intensification of the exploitation of existing resources including land, which was farmed ever more intensively using the new crops such as the potato. The principal feature however was a major increase in the number of hours worked and in the proportion of time available that was used for productive labour (hence 'industrious revolution'). However because output per unit of land or per hour of work did not increase and even began to decrease because of diminishing marginal returns, there was no intensive growth. That is, there was no increase in total factor productivity and hence no increase in total wealth per capita.

As the century went on it became ever more difficult to simply increase output by increasing inputs of time and land. At the same time the windfall benefits of the new crops and of the growth in trade brought about by the integration of larger parts of the world began to wear off. Population however continued to increase. The result, just as in the thirteenth century, was that global population began to push up against structural Malthusian limits and the complexity of social and political arrangements began to approach or go beyond the maximum level that was sustainable given the limits of the productive system. So for example urbanisation in several parts of the world reached the maximum level that could be supported given the difficulty of supplying and feeding urban populations. Land hunger and increasing pressure on land and on peasant populations became more marked with pressure on food supplies and increased subdivision of land to the point where the ratio of land to households was reaching its sustainable minimum. All of this made the political order ever more fragile and led to a series of massive political upheavals.

In India the collapse of the Mughal state by the 1750s led to widespread conflict and disorder including serious unrest in many parts of rural India. It was this state of political deliquescence that provoked the French and British to intervene increasingly in Indian affairs, each driven by the fear that the other would otherwise gain control of the lucrative India trade. Eventually the British came out on top in this competition and consequently became the paramount power in the sub-continent, through the East India Company. China meanwhile saw a whole series of massive peasant and anti-Manchu rebellions such as the White Lotus uprising in 1795 – 1804 and the Eight Trigrams rebellion in Shantung province in 1786-8. The first of these is estimated to have led to several hundred thousand deaths during the eventual suppression of the revolt. There were also several large scale revolts by non-Han populations in the Southwest provinces, in 1735 – 36 and in 1795 to 1806. These were the most serious and damaging such events since the comparable uprisings in the mid to late seventeenth century a hundred years earlier.

Slightly later the very early nineteenth century saw increasing unrest in the Ottoman Empire and major upheavals in Sub-Saharan Africa, particularly in Southern Africa, which saw a series of major wars and population displacements. Globally, there were a series of what can truly be called world wars between the various European powers, particularly Britain and France. The first of these was the Seven Years War of 1756 to 1763 followed by the War of American Independence in 1775 to 1783. There were also a series of major wars between the Ottomans and Iran on the one side and Russia on the other.

However it was Europe and the wider Atlantic world that saw the greatest upheavals. Crucially these took a slightly different form to the ones found elsewhere in the world. In other words, the growing Malthusian crisis of the later eighteenth and early nineteenth centuries took a different form and had different results in those parts of the world as compared to elsewhere. This was because of the different kind of state system there and the way it changed the calculations of elites and rulers, as well as the intellectual revolution that went along with that. Between 1755 and the early 1820s there were revolutions and political upheavals all around the Atlantic in Europe, North America and Latin America. These began with the revolution of 1755 in Corsica against Genoese rule, led by Pasquale Paoli, who introduced the first constitution to reflect Enlightenment ideals. The French Revolution of 1789 was of course the most dramatic and best known of these late eighteenth and early nineteenth century revolutions. Another was the American Revolution, a genuine revolution despite efforts by some today to present it as a conservative 'tidying up or preservation'. The same period also the appearance of the first ever organised anti-slavery movement (along with several massive slave revolts, one of which in Santo Domingo became the first successful slave revolt in history), as well as the first organised movement for women's emancipation. Historians such as Palmer and Godechot have argued that these were all part of a more general 'Atlantic Revolution'.

The years between 1750 and 1850 saw in fact a bitter struggle in most of Europe, and in the Americas. The conflict was over two issues. Firstly that of whether the modern world as it was emerging was something desirable or a disaster to be checked or reversed and secondly over what kinds of form and features the new world that was emerging would have. It was the outcome of that struggle that first consolidated and established the emergent modern world in the face of its opponents and then ensured that the world we now live in would be one with some features and not others. Between 1770 and 1850 there were two generations of conflict, in which the side that sought to check or reverse the eruption of modernity was conclusively defeated and in a way that had vitally important consequences.

Further Reading

The economy of Europe in the 1550 to 1750 period is well covered in Jan De Vries *The Economy of Europe in an Age of Crisis, 1600 – 1750.* (Cambridge University Press, 1976), and Peter Musgrave *The Early Modern European Economy* (Palgrave MacMillan, 1999). The way that this economy was still dominated by institutions that inhibited innovation is clearly described in Sheilagh Ogilvie *Institutions and European Trade* (Cambridge University Press,

2011), and Laurence Fontaine *The Moral Economy: Poverty, Credit, and Trust in Early Modern Europe* (Cambridge University Press, 2014). Two useful studies are S. R. Epstein *Freedom and Growth: Markets and States in Pre-Modern Europe* (Routledge, 2000), and John Day *Money and Finance in the Age of Merchant Capitalism 1200 – 1800* (Wiley-Blackwell, 2008). The idea of 'proto-industry' is described in Sheilagh Ogilvie and Markus Cerman (eds.), *European Proto-Industrialisation: An Introductory Handbook* (Cambridge University Press, 1996). The development of this economy up to the later eighteenth century (and even beyond then) by processes that intensified its workings without producing the sustained intensive growth seen later is set out in Jan De Vries *The Industrious Revolution: Consumer Behaviour and the Household Economy, 1650 to the Present* (Cambridge University Press, 2008)

On the huge impact on world population at this time of the new plants brought from the New World, above all the potato, see Redcliffe N. Salaman *The History and Social Influence of the Potato* (Cambridge University Press, 1985 1st pub 1949), Larry Zuckerman *The Potato: How the Humble Spud Rescued the Western World* (North Point Press, 1999), Henry Hobhouse *Seeds of Change: Six Plants that Transformed Mankind* (Shoemaker 7 Hoard, 2005).

For the seventeenth century 'General Crisis', see Geoffrey Parker & Lesley M. Smith (eds.) *The General Crisis of the Seventeenth Century* (Routledge, 1997) and Geoffrey Parker *The Global Crisis: War, Climate Change, and Catastrophe in the Seventeenth Century* (Yale University Press, 2014). The growth of a new way of thinking about government in the aftermath of the General Crisis, which gained pace in the eighteenth century, is the subject of Martin Sepple & Keith Tribe (eds) *Cameralism in Practice: State Administration and Economy in Early Modern Europe* (Boydell, 2017).

The global trade and political relations of the eighteenth century are set out and examined in Jurgen Osterhammel & Niels P. Peterson *Globalization: A Short History* (Princeton University Press, 2005), Philip D. Curtin *The World and the West: The European Challenge and the Overseas Response in the Age of Empire* (Cambridge University Press, 2002). China's massive expansion and aggressive imperialism under the Qing is described in Peter C. Perdue *China Marches West: The Qing Conquest of Central Asia.* (Belknap Press, 2005).

One work that looks at the interplay between Europe and Asia from the Asian end is Donald Keene *The Japanese Discovery of Europe 1720 – 1830* (Stanford university Press, 1969).

The transformation of manufacturing in Britain in the later eighteenth and early nineteenth century has had an industry of research and writing devoted to it. Some of the best accounts, which make clear the complexity of the process and the way that the well known story of the mechanisation of cotton manufacture and its move to factories was only one part of a more complex process, are Maxine Berg *The Age of Manufactures 1700 – 1820: Industry, Innovation and Work In Britain* (Routledge, 1994), E. A. Wrigley *Continuity, Chance and Change:*

The Character of the Industrial Revolution in England (Cambridge University Press, 1990), Jeremy Black *Eighteenth Century Britain 1688 – 1783* (Palgrave Macmillan, 2001). Emily Nacol *An Age of Risk: Politics and Economy in Early Modern Britain* (Princeton University Press, 2016) is good for the innovations in finance, insurance and investment at this time and earlier

As with the industrial revolution, there is an industry of books devoted to the Enlightenment. Introductions to the huge topic are James Schmidt (ed.) *What is Enlightenment? Eighteenth Century Answers and Twentieth Century Questions* (University of California Press, 1999), Roy Porter *The Enlightenment* 2nd edition (Palgrave Macmillan, 2001), and Peter Hans Reill & Ellen Judy Wilson (eds.) *Encyclopaedia of the Enlightenment* (Facts on File, 1996). The earlier work of Paul Hazard is still hugely important as setting much of the frame for subsequent discussion, and in making the fundamental point of a clear discontinuity in European thought at this time. A good English edition of his work in two volumes is Paul Hazard *The European Mind 1680 – 1715* (Pelican, 1964 1st pub. 1935) and *European Thought in the Eighteenth Century* (Pelican, 1965 1st pub. 1946). Another classic work, still well worth reading, and which also makes the point that it was traditional Western Christian civilisation that was the object of both analysis and critique is Peter Gay *The Enlightenment: The Rise of Modern Paganism* (Norton, 1995), and *The Enlightenment: The Science of Freedom* (Norton, 1996). A good collection of primary sources is Isaac Kramnick *The Portable Enlightenment Reader* (Penguin, 1995).

Recent work has recaptured the radical and subversive quality of much Enlightenment thought and here the key and monumental work is that of Jonathan Israel, so far extending to the following works: *Radical Enlightenment: Philosophy and the Making of Modernity, 1650 – 1750* (Oxford University Press, 2002), *Enlightenment Contested: Philosophy, Modernity and the Emancipation of Man 1670 – 1752* (Oxford University Press, 2006), *A Revolution of the Mind: Radical Enlightenment and the Intellectual Origins of Modern Democracy* (Princeton University Press, 2009), *Democratic Enlightenment: Philosophy, Revolution, and Human Rights 1750 – 1790* (Oxford University Press, 2011). Another work that brings out this quality in the specifically British context and makes clear the connection with both science and business is Roy Porter *The Creation of the Modern World: The Untold Story of the British Enlightenment* (Norton, 2001). The critique of traditional Christian Western ideas is examined in the essays in Christopher Nadon (ed) *Enlightenment and Secularism: Essays on the Mobilisation of Reason* (Lexington, 2015). Two other works that should be read and which defend the continuing relevance of these ideas as well as making the connection to both science and trade are Anthony Pagden *The Enlightenment: and Why it Still Matters* (Random House, 2013), and Timothy Ferris *The Science of Liberty: Democracy, Reason, and the Laws of Nature* (Harper Collins, 2010).

The view of the upheavals of the later eighteenth century as an inter-connected Atlantic Revolution is first put forward in Robert R. Palmer *The*

Age of the Democratic Revolution: A Political History of Europe and America 1760 – 1800 (Princeton University Press, 1959), and *The Age of the Democratic Revolution, Vol. II: The Struggle* (Princeton University Press, 1970). The best work for the co-originator of this analysis, Jacques Godechot, is *France and the Atlantic Revolution of the Eighteenth Century, 1770 – 1799* (Free Press, 1965). A recent work that revives and extends this way of looking at the later eighteenth century is Jonathan Israel *The Expanding Blaze: How the American Revolution Ignited the World, 1775 – 1848* (Princeton University Press, 2017). The amazing career of Pasquale Paoli is described in Peter A. Thrasher, *Pasquale Paoli: An Enlightened Hero 1725 – 1807* (Archon Books, 1970). The period and its upheavals is also covered in the magisterial work by C. A. Bayly, *The Birth of the Modern World 1780 – 1914* (Blackwell, 2004).

CHAPTER VIII

The World We Live In – For Now?

THE so-called 'Atlantic Revolution' of the late 18th century was only one early part of a longer process – the eruption or explosion of modernity. The terms eruption and explosion capture what happened. Essentially pressure from many small instances of innovation and change built up and eventually burst through restraints, whether institutional, cultural, political or intellectual. The result was a transformation of the world economy and of society in certain parts of the world – the pressures also occurred elsewhere but were contained in most places. The changes that took place in this eruption were not only economic or technological, although these are the aspects that have received the most attention. They were also political and social, often the product of intense political conflict. The period between the Corsican revolt of 1755 and the end of the Atlantic Revolution in the later 1820s saw the first clear articulation of modern ideologies and of recognisably modern political argument. The basic argument at and since that time has been over whether modernity is a good thing or not and secondarily over what form modernity should take.

The first of the two debates was initially that between the classical left and right. The terms left and right as political labels derived originally from the seating of members of the National Assembly in the first phase of the French Revolution, with the supporters of the Ancien Regime on the right and the advocates of reform and revolution on the left. Thus, initially the right were those forces opposed to modernity, which sought to uphold or restore the Ancien Regime and to resist or reverse the rise of modernity while the left were those who to a greater or lesser degree favoured the changes that were taking place and sought to encourage them. Broadly speaking the left drew upon and descended intellectually from the Enlightenment of the eighteenth century while the right were a continuation of the opposition to the Enlightenment and the later Counter-Enlightenment.

However this was never a straightforward matter and increasingly there were figures on both sides who saw themselves as upholding some part of the Enlightenment tradition. One reason for this was the common phenomenon of people who support change up to a point but resist it when they feel it has become excessive or who support change in some areas but not in others. There was also a clear difference between the British case and that of the rest of Europe. In Britain there was little or no real fundamental opposition to the new modern order, at least after the defeat of the British old order in 1829-32 and maybe not even before then. Consequently the kind of radical anti-modernist argument made on the Continent was not so common in Britain and much less politically effective. The same was true to an even greater degree in the United States and Canada. On the Continent (and also in Latin America) a very clear part of the division between classical left and right was that between secular radicals on the one hand and the forces of established religion on the other, above all the Catholic Church. For the first two thirds of the nineteenth century that institution remained obdurately resistant to the new order of modernity (and in some ways still does).

Pro-Modern and Anti-Modern Thinking

In contemporary intellectual life the pro-modern and pro-Enlightenment arguments are very familiar and often taken for granted or assumed to be true. They essentially derive from the core Enlightenment ideas set out in the previous chapter. The arguments of the anti-modernist position, particularly in the form in which they were put by the classical right of the early nineteenth century in Europe, are much less familiar and are often simply ignored. This is a mistake for two reasons. In the first place the arguments are often powerful and penetrating. The most effective critiques of all varieties of modernity have come from this source. Secondly they have had and continue to have considerable influence, particularly in societies that are undergoing the early stages of the transition to modernity, as Western Europe and the Americas were between 1770 and 1850.

We can trace a tradition of anti-modern thinking back as far as the early 18th century when modernity first began to appear. This hostile response to modernity has reappeared in every society that has experienced its advent. It can be found in the Islamic world, China, Japan, Russia and Latin America, as well as in Europe. The form and content of this response, that is the arguments made and the analysis presented, are remarkably similar no matter where they are found. This point is made by a number of authors, notably Stephen Holmes in *The Structural Features of Anti-Liberal Thought* and by Ian Buruma and Avishai Margalit in *Occidentalism*. However both of these works have problems. Holmes identifies modernity with just one of its main ideologies (liberalism), which leads him to conflate moderate pro-modern arguments with those of the thoroughgoing anti-moderns. Buruma and Margalit accurately describe the main elements of anti-modern thought but see it as a Western creation (paradoxically because hostility to the West is, they think, one of its main elements) that has since been spread to other parts of the world by the West. In fact while there is an element of this, anti-modernism tends to appear spontaneously wherever the move to modernity occurs and is best understood as the universal response of defenders of traditional society to the challenge of modernity. Initially anti-modern thought seeks to restore a past state of affairs (often an imagined or idealised one) and to resist or turn back the tide of modernity. After a while it becomes clear that this is not possible or practical and a politics of this kind becomes no more than a pose or affectation, a kind of nostalgia. The response is to sharpen the critique while at the same time arguing for a kind of politics and economics that combines modern technology and economy with a pre-modern set of social and political arrangements.

Classical anti-modern thought has the following core elements. These are found in movements that are otherwise as distinct as Ultramontanist Catholicism, Integralism, Traditionalism, Panslavism, Japanese nationalism, and contemporary Islamism. These arguments have been put by thinkers as different in other ways as Joseph De Maistre, John Ruskin, Pius IX, Sayid Kutb, and Friedrich Nietzsche.

The argument is firstly that the modern world is excessively rationalistic and is too concerned with reason at the expense of religion, feeling and tradition. Secondly, the modern world is too individualistic and promotes a rootless, atomistic individualism. It destroys the traditions and sense of rootedness of people, producing a transient, deracinated population with no clear sense of identity. Modernity leads to a moral corruption with an emphasis on self-fulfilment rather than virtue. In particular it leads to sexual immorality (defined to include such things as sex outside of marriage, homosexuality and masturbation). Thirdly, it is dominated by the city rather than the more natural and rooted life of the countryside and by industry rather than agriculture. As such it cuts human beings off from what is natural and instead confines them to the artificial.

The most frequent argument is that the modern world is materialistic and obsessed with money at the expense of higher, spiritual values and concerns. It is irreligious and atheistic and denies the divine, spiritual and sacred. It elevates the mundane, trivial and domestic values of the bourgeois at the expense of the heroic and self-sacrificial values of the warrior or sage. Indeed it removes any opportunity for heroism or self-sacrifice and lauds the materialistic, petty and trivial. Modernity promotes an obsession with material comfort and convenience (*Komfortismus* in the words of one leading anti-modernist) at the expense of heroism and glory. Linked to this is the argument that the modern world elevates the feminine at the expense of the masculine while at the same time it corrupts the true position and nature of women with a misleading notion of female 'liberation'. Finally, it denies the reality and necessity of hierarchy and distinctions and instead asserts an impossible egalitarianism.

In general the argument is that the modern world is impious and unnatural. Impious because it denies the divine and elevates the material and human and seeks to transform the world and human nature rather than accepting a divine order – this is the sin of hubris, the vaunting pride that provokes the wrath of the gods in the shape of the implacable goddess Nemesis. Unnatural because it denies the true given nature of human beings or seeks to transform it and thus creates a society that is incompatible with the real nature of human beings (this is commonly based on the idea of human nature as defined by a Creator but need not be).

These arguments against modernity or for a pessimistic view of its nature and prospects are contrasted to the optimistic view of those who see modernity as progressive and liberatory, a view first formulated in the Enlightenment. So ever since the 18th century there has been a debate between supporters and critics of modernity. One way of understanding this is as a debate between those who think that modernity is a 'good thing' and those who see it as a 'bad thing'. Another aspect of it is the division between those who evaluate ideas, policies and institutions in terms of their ability to satisfy human needs and promote human happiness in the material world and the here and now and those who evaluate them by the degree to which they confirm to a set of timeless and divinely inspired principles. In this way of thinking the aim of human life is not happiness here in the material world but service to God or some transcendent order, and happiness in another world. (The argument is that the pursuit of happiness in this world is self-defeating and that happiness is found by not actively seeking it).

The Triumph of Modernity and Liberalism

In practical terms the years between 1770 and 1850 in Europe saw intense, often violent, political argument between these two worldviews. While overall this was about how to respond to the emergent modernity it was fought out over a number of more concrete political issues. The first, and by far the most important for many of those involved, was over the issue of the separation of church and state, or to put it another way, the privatisation of religious belief. One side (the right) held that religion was by its nature and necessity a public matter and a central concern of government (as well as being in some sense its foundation), the other (the left) that religion was a private matter for the individual conscience and no concern of government. It is important to realise just how novel the second position was. That the religious beliefs and practices of the people were perhaps the central concern of the secular power had been widely accepted for centuries at least. The argument of the modernists was not for religious toleration: this was something that had been widely practised before in many times and places. Under a regime of religious toleration religious opinion was still a matter of government concern, toleration was the policy adopted by certain governments with regard to this concern. The argument of the classical left was that religious opinions were no more the concern of government than ones taste in socks, a truly radical innovation.

Connected to this was the argument over freedom of thought and expression, including freedom of speech and the press. The traditional view was that one of the functions of government was to regulate these, in order to prevent the diffusion of dangerous or heretical ideas that could cause dissension or social harm, bring down God's wrath or even worse condemn those holding them to an eternity of unimaginable suffering in Hell. The opposed view, which can be traced back as far as the mid seventeenth century, was that there should be open debate, freedom of expression and that this was the best (or even the only) way to discern the truth. Another debate that may seem abstruse now was that over legal and social equality (meaning equality of social status and esteem not wealth) as opposed to the principle of social hierarchy and degree, upheld by a whole body of laws and practices and which had been a central feature of the old order. One argument that is still very much with us today was over political economy and in particular the issue of free trade versus protection. This was actually the 'point issue' for a wider debate that pitted free exchange, allowing individuals to exchange and contract with each other free of hindrance, against the notion that economic exchange should be controlled and regulated in the interests of a higher good. The case for free exchange also meant abandoning the attempt to 'fence off' a particular part of the world's economic activity and so also implied the end of empires – or at least the economic justification for empires and colonialism.

The main issue of pure politics was that of the nature of government. The classic pro-modern left supported constitutional and rule bound government (the *RechtsStaat* as it was known in German) based upon consent, contrasted to the idea of an absolute government based upon prescription and tradition that existed as part of a divinely created and sanctioned order. In other words, was government instrumental and rule bound (as the US Declaration of Independence declared) or something that was part of the constitution of things and ultimately independent of temporary human wishes? The two final issues were over the abolition of slavery and unfree labour such as serfdom more generally and the emancipation of women, meaning their being given legal equality with men.

In all of these areas the ultimate outcome was a victory for the pro-modern side and defeat for the anti-modern. This took longer in some areas than others (the emancipation of women being particularly drawn out) but it happened in each case. The victory was so total that to argue the classic anti-modern case in many parts of the world now is to immediately declare oneself to be at best an eccentric. (This has not stopped many from doing that, of course). The concrete result was to ensure the consolidation and continuation of the emergent modern world and the supplanting of the old order in state, society and economy. It also meant in the last two cases that the modern world would be organised in one way rather than another. There is nothing in the inherent nature of modernity that means that slavery should not exist or that women should have legal equality with men and there have been political figures and movements that have supported the modern world in other respects but have also argued for slavery and female subordination. In these cases the eventual outcome was as much of the internal arguments of the pro-modern side as that between them as the anti-modern right.

Internal Arguments and the Three Conversations of Modernity

Indeed, as mentioned earlier, there have been two kinds of argument going on since the advent of modernity in the latter part of the eighteenth century. Alongside the one just set out is a more complex one among those who broadly think modernity to be desirable (or at any rate unavoidable). This is over what precise form modernity should take, given its basic core features. The main issue, since the later eighteenth century has been over the role, organisation, and extent of government and political power but there are others, in particular there have been disagreements over certain aspects of the modern world that some otherwise pro-modern observers have decried or had misgivings over. The pro-modern camp, or to put it another way, those thinkers from Smith onwards who emphasise the need for satisfying human wants in the material here and now (a list that includes people such as Marx but also Herbert Spencer) therefore have many disagreements among themselves over how to do this.

In the aftermath of the French Revolution the three main traditions of modern thought are articulated explicitly for the first time and subsequently become self-aware intellectual traditions. These are liberalism, modern conservatism, and radical egalitarianism (including but not exclusively socialism). All of these are post Enlightenment ways of thinking that derive from aspects of Enlightenment thought and accept its basic premises. (This is true even for the conservative variant – we should remember that Edmund Burke was a Whig and not a Tory and an exponent of pro-modern thought on matters such as economic affairs, as well as a critic of revolution. He was also one of those who rejected an important part of the modernist position, in his case its opposition to religious establishment and support for a secular state – the conservative view is also that of those who broadly accept modernity but have doubts about some parts of it). We may think of the relation of the three traditions diagrammatically in the following way,

Individualism

Egalitarianism   Limits

with liberals at the individualist point, conservatives at the limits one, and egalitarians including socialists at the egalitarianism one. Thinkers who tend to the 'individualist' pole emphasise the need for individual liberty and autonomy, those at the 'egalitarianism' one the need for equality while those at the 'limits' pole stress the extent to which the ability of humans to do things by conscious design is limited by ineluctable features of the human and natural world. Most actual political thinkers and movements in the modern world are found in between the various extreme points because of the trade-offs involved in emphasising one of these over others. The reason why analysts persistently tend to place political positions along a single line or spectrum rather than a triangle is because of a tendency when viewing things from any one point of the triangle to see the other two points as equally opposed to ones own position and therefore as identical. So conservatives tend to see both liberals and socialists as hubristic rationalists who ignore tradition, liberals see both conservatives and radical egalitarians as authoritarians who slight liberty, and egalitarians see both conservatives and liberals as people who accept inequality and hierarchy.

Alongside this was a fourth set of ideas, which was both independent and also found to some degree or other among all three of the traditions, although it was initially a minority perspective in each case, albeit an influential one. This was the idea, alluded to in the previous chapter, of rational administration in the general public interest, in other words of modern government. This does not necessarily imply a large government, in the sense of one that consumes a large share of total production (although it may) but it does imply a kind of public administration with a wider remit and range of concerns than the traditional political order. It was however in the first instance a thesis about the nature of government rather than its extent. This was the kind of argument first articulated by German Cameralists and later in Britain by Bentham and his followers. Although it never commanded wide popular support it was very influential, not least because of its appeal to ruling groups.

Before 1860 arguments within the pro-modern camp tended to be over matters such as the rapidity or degree of reform, the extent of the franchise, the form, nature and content of education, and foreign policy. One question that proved increasingly divisive was that of nationalism and the extent to which nationalist movements were a part of the modern movement (and therefore progressive and to be welcomed) or retrograde and regressive (and therefore to be deplored). The very interesting point is that before the later nineteenth century the classic left was generally hostile to state power and looked forward with eager expectation to its steady diminution or even disappearance. This was even or perhaps particularly the case with those in the egalitarian part of the pro-modern camp. The reason for this was the widespread acceptance of the idea that it was political power that was the source and origin of inequality and privilege, which derived from parasitic groups using government to enrich themselves at the expense of the majority, the 'industrious' classes as they were called. Given this, to the extent that progress meant a reduction in unjustified inequality and privilege it must mean a decline in the size of government, while it would be wrongheaded to expect to use the source of privilege to attack it.

Further Transformations Before 1850

The social and economic changes that got under way in the eighteenth century and the victories of those who supported them meant that the first half of the nineteenth century saw massive and unprecedented change. The most obvious were the economic and demographic, the unprecedented rise in population, increasing urbanisation and the appearance of something quite new in the industrial city from Manchester onwards, the slow but steady rise in the standard of living, and the progressive transformation of economic life by technological innovation and the reorganisation of production, in a word by the appearance of modern capitalism. Or indeed of capitalism as such: we can reasonably say that most of the world had a market economy by 1600 or that Song China had one in the twelfth century, or that markets were an important feature of economic life in many parts of the world from the ancient world onwards but it would be hard to identify capitalism in any of these times and places without stretching the meaning of that term to a point where it ceases to be useful. It makes sense rather to think of capitalism as a specific kind of market economy, one that first appears in the period between 1750 and 1850 and has such features as a true capital market, the increasing organisation of production through firms with limited liability and tradable stock, a labour system based upon free wage labour, and sustained and systematic technological innovation.

Alongside these economic and demographic transformations we can already by 1850 see at least three other of the key features of modernity. One, already alluded to, is a change in the nature of government. As well as a change in the way government was thought of and in what was seen as its purpose and function there was a marked shift in the way it was organised, in its composition and recruitment. In traditional premodern societies government was often household based, one particular large and extended household (the monarch's) was responsible for affairs of state. Politically, society was thought of as a federation of families or households (which was indeed the reality in many ways) with some families and households having a particular public role assigned to them by one means or another, which was governance and the exercise of public authority.

Empires and large states always needed more than this and thus had something more like a public administration of the kind that we are familiar with. However the scale of these administrations was always very small by modern standards, even for large states such as the Chinese, Roman or Ottoman Empires for example. Moreover, recruitment to the administration was typically through patronage and clientage with public position being given out as a reward for political support. The main alternative was for public office to be sold for cash, sometimes in the shape of an upfront payment, sometimes in the form of a recognised share of the public revenue (as in the paradigmatic case of tax farming).

In either case it was universally accepted that public office was a way to enrich oneself, ones family and dependents. In fact to not use public office in this way was often thought to be morally questionable since loyalty to and support for ones family and dependents (which included clients) was thought of as a moral imperative. There was also a persistent tendency for public office to become hereditary, which led to the creation of new positions to do the work of heritable ones where the inheritor was incapable or uninterested in the functions of their post. The major exception in theory was the Chinese mandarinate, recruited by competitive examination, but even in China the recurring pattern towards the end of each dynasty was for public administration to become a means of family advancement. Corruption, far from being an incidental phenomenon or a perversion of the correct way of doing things, was an essential, core feature of pre-modern government.

The military revolution had led to a growth in the size of government everywhere along with the appearance of some of the basic elements of modern public administration, such as division by defined function (this had been around for a long time in some places such as China). The persistence of military competition in Europe led to further pressure to make administration more cost effective and to eliminate many of the traditional features of government such as the existence of sinecures. Consequently the period after 1750 witnessed a slow but steady movement in the direction of the modern, Weberian state, with public administration clearly separate and distinct from the political, policy making aspect of government and carried out by a full time salaried bureaucracy recruited by an objective method such as examination, organised in a hierarchy divided by function and area of responsibility, and operating according to definite and clearly stated rules which precluded treating people differently because of some social connection such as kinship, friendship or political allegiance. The changes in this direction were almost always the result of wars. Thus the first major move in Britain came as part of William Pitt's reform of the public finances after he inherited a totally bankrupt treasury in 1782. The most important changes, because they became a model for those adopted elsewhere, were introduced in Prussia by Stein following the defeat by Napoleon at Jena in 1806. In Britain the final decisive move was the adoption of the recommendations of the Northcote-Trevelyan Report in 1854, much assisted by the impact of the Crimean War.

Acceleration After 1850

We may say that by about 1850 the breakthrough into modernity that had started in Britain and had spread to other parts of the world by then, had become consolidated. It was no longer possible to stop or simply reverse it in the way the early Ming emperors had overturned the developments in Song China. After 1850 however the pace of change in every area picked up significantly. To use a metaphor, there was a sudden but clear change of gear. If the period before 1750 had seen developments in first gear and there had been a shift to second after that date then the years after 1850 saw a rapid shift through third into fourth. The years between 1850 and 1914 were truly revolutionary and saw more change of a more profound nature than in any other period of human history. All of the transformations just set out suddenly accelerated and other changes under way for even longer (since the seventeenth century in the case of scientific investigation for example) also began to happen at a far more rapid rate than before. It was this period that actually created the world most people now alive have been born into and which finally swept away the remnants of the old world order that had been created in the aftermath of the fourteenth century. Indeed so profound were the changes of those two generations that they can be truly said to have drawn a line under several thousand years of history, marking the decisive break between the traditional societies created by the invention of agriculture and the modern world.

The period after 1850 and particularly the years between 1870 and 1914 is often known as the 'Belle Epoque', a name given to it by contemporaries. It saw a process of increased interconnection between the various parts of the planet that have led economic historians to speak of a 'first globalisation'. It saw an unprecedented rise in global living standards, not only in Europe and North America but also in many other parts of the world. It was the age of Strauss and Offenbach, a time of apparently unbounded optimism and also of innovation and exploration in the arts. However it also saw an accelerating arms race and a dramatic revival of imperialism – this was another great 'Age of Empire' – and the appearance of nationalism as a major political force, along with a dramatic rise in xenophobia and the articulation and widespread adoption of racist ideas and policy. It also saw acute class conflict in many parts of the world and culminated in the catastrophe of 1914-18 and the long world crisis of 1914 to 1948.

One of the most important features of those years was the sudden flowering of the central institution of capitalism, the modern business corporation, with many of the modern world's major business enterprises founded at this time (e.g. Shell, Exxon, Unilever, Mitsubishi). This transformation of business organisation is often called the 'Chandlerian revolution in business management', after its greatest historian Alfred D. Chandler. The central element in this was the appearance of the modern giant, multi-divisional business enterprise with a clear hierarchical organisation and run increasingly by professional managers rather than owners. This first appeared in the American railroad business but soon spread to other sectors. It made investment, production and distribution possible on a scale that had previously been unimaginable and brought about a huge increase in productivity and decline in costs. This meant it was associated with the appearance of mass production and the assembly line and also mass marketing and consumption – and also advertising and public relations. The modern business corporation was central to the sudden acceleration in economic growth and technological innovation described earlier and also played a large part in the social and cultural changes, particularly those affecting the family. It also completed a huge shift in the nature of work, with a movement away from small scale or artisanal forms of production to mass employment under standardised working conditions in large establishments.

It was one of several institutions of this kind to emerge at this time – others were the kind of modern government described earlier and the modern university – but it was the one that had the greatest impact on the social structure. This was because it not only changed the daily life and work experience of the great mass of people employed in industry and commerce. It also played the main part (because of the number of people involved) in the appearance of a new profession – management – and a new class or social formation, one that has gone on to become the dominant one in the contemporary world. This was the managerial class. Intellectually the key phenomenon was the development of 'scientific management' or 'Taylorism' (after its inventor Frederick Winslow Taylor), i.e. the application of theoretical analysis such as time and motion study to all kinds of work and production and the defining of a new kind of activity – management. The people who carried out the task of managing and directing the large scale integrated productive and distributive processes made possible by the new kind of business, went on to become the new dominant group in developed societies, supplanting not only the older elites of landholding aristocracy and clergy, but also the property owning business class – the 'bourgeois episode' when merchants and capital owners had been truly influential and powerful proved to be just that, an episode. One of the groups to initially benefit most from the advent of modern management were unskilled workers because things such as time and motion study led to a big increase in their marginal productivity and a corresponding rise in wages.

The new kind of business organisation was just one reason for a sudden increase in the underlying rate of economic growth after 1850. In the eighteenth century this had been about one to one and a half per cent per annum. By the 1850s it had risen to about two and a half per cent. After 1870, there were annual growth rates five per cent or even (in pre-World War I Russia) of nearly ten per cent. Growth of this kind was simply historically unprecedented – it had never happened before. Even though the proceeds of this growth were not shared evenly, to put it very mildly, the result was an unprecedented rise in the living standards of ordinary people. In Britain for example average real earnings more than doubled between 1850 and 1914. There were also losers however, above all the agricultural populations of large parts of the planet who were caught by the collapse of much traditional agriculture in the new world economy.

The feature of the Belle Epoque that most strikes contemporary economic historians was increased economic integration, which leads many to speak of a 'first globalisation', driven by a number of factors such as new technologies (the iron hulled steamship, the telegraph, the telephone, the railway), the global political order created by the British Empire (at least according to Niall Ferguson), and the creation of a worldwide money system and capital market, centred on the City of London and, increasingly, New York. The most prominent feature of this 'first globalisation' was a massive growth in world trade, both in absolute terms, and as a proportion of the GDP of most economies – in other words they became much more interconnected and integrated and the interconnections became much 'deeper', that is they involved a much larger proportion of total economic activity. The efficiency gains that this led to via specialisation and division of labour were a major force behind the economic growth of this period. Of course in one sense there was nothing new in this – there had been previous episodes of increased world trade and integration during the second century, the thirteenth century, and with the opening up of ocean trade routes in the sixteenth but these were simply not on the same scale as what happened after 1850. International trade did not reach the levels attained in the 1900s as a proportion of gross world output or the GDP of major states until the 1970s.

Another prominent feature of this 'first globalisation' was a massive movement of population, with millions of people moving from the countryside to the city and round the world – it is hard for us now to realise how open international borders were at this time. In 1914 only two European countries required passports for Entry, Russia and Turkey while Britain only abandoned a policy of completely open borders with the Aliens Act of 1905. The United States and other American countries such as Argentina also had an effective 'open borders' policy, which would last until the mid 1920s. The last one was truly dramatic flows of capital with a proportion of world capital invested outside its country of origin that we have still not got near to. In the British case for example more than half of the capital formed in the UK was invested outside its boundaries, with the greater part of the exported capital being invested outside the formal British Empire.

Modernity Spreads and Pops Up Elsewhere

Not only was there much more rapid growth, the phenomenon of sustained intensive growth began to spread ever more widely. In Europe the early birds such as Britain and Belgium were joined by Germany (after 1860), Northern Italy (after 1890), Russia (after 1895), Sweden (after 1900) and also Denmark and France (both of which modernised without becoming industrialised). Elsewhere there were breakthroughs by the United States (after 1860), Japan (after 1870) and Argentina and Uruguay (after 1870). The case of Japan was particularly significant and not only because the Japanese economy went on to be the second largest in the world. A common way of interpreting the spread of economic modernity is to see it as something exported by the already modernised 'leaders' to the not-yet developed areas of the world. There is an element of this, in the shape of capital investment from the wealthier areas, and emulation of policies and institutions that are associated with economic development but more important is the combination of participation in a global division of labour through trade and exchange with endogenous self-generated development.

Japan was the classic case of this. During the two hundred years in which Japan was isolated from the rest of the world between the 1630s and 1868 Japanese economy and society developed in the same ways as elsewhere in the world and the pressure on the existing social and economic institutions became as acute as it was anywhere. By the mid eighteenth century Edo (Tokyo) had a population of around one million while Osaka and Kyoto both had populations of around four hundred thousand. The increased commercialisation and urbanisation led to important cultural changes, especially the appearance of the culture and ideology of *chinondo* (literally 'the way of the townspeople'), a kind of bourgeois ideology. The Tokugawa shogunate sought to resist the economic and cultural changes taking place in Japan but from the 1800s onwards they faced an increasingly organised opposition. Eventually, just as in Europe, the forces of modernising change broke through. The visit of Commodore Perry should be seen as the trigger rather than the cause of this change. After 1868 Japan modernised rapidly, through being integrated into the world trading system.

The most dramatic aspect of the spread of modernity because of indigenous development along with participation in the worldwide system of trade and division of labour, which has only recently been uncovered by economic historians, was the appearance of rapid economic growth in both India and China after 1870. In India this was despite the way British imperial policy hindered economic development, through support for the indigenous 'feudal' class inherited from the Mughals and the disastrous effects of British monetary and trade policy. In China this was in spite of the incompetence and weakness of the Qing dynasty by this time (although we should not overemphasise this – the Chinese state, like the Ottoman Empire, showed an impressive capacity for internal reform and renewal at this time). Both China and India were showing significant economic growth by the last years of the nineteenth century, driven largely by internal capital (as in the case of the famous Tata company in India for example).

By 1930 between thirty and forty per cent of India's population and between twenty and thirty per cent of China's were involved in non-agricultural occupations. The degree of economic development such areas saw at this time is often downplayed by pointing out that it was concentrated in a few specific regions. However, political units such as states or empires are not the appropriate ones for economic analysis as the units and structures of economics and politics frequently fail to coincide. Moreover, the origins of economic modernity in Europe were precisely a matter of development in particular regions, not in entire states much less the whole sub-continent. Interestingly, the areas of India and China that saw the most rapid and intensive development before 1930 were precisely those that had been most involved in the world trading system since the 1450s and are also the areas at the forefront of renewed globalisation after 1990.

Earlier, the first half of the nineteenth century saw a number of what we may call 'failed modernisations' in which the attempt to bring about modernity did not succeed. Typically these involved an attempt to create a modern economy with sustained intensive growth while preserving a traditional system of governance and social order. As such they involved a form of top-down modernisation or neo-mercantilism in which the state (or actually the rulers) played an active part in trying to stimulate or guide development. The other characteristic policy was one of protectionism, amounting in some cases to near autarchy. One important example, which was to prove influential, was that of Paraguay under its dictator Dr Francia who ruled from 1814 to 1840. Another case was that of Egypt under Mehmet Ali and his successors between 1805 and 1879. Neither of these succeeded in the longer run and both either involved or led to wars between the modernising state and its neighbours.

The Great Age of Innovation

The second half of the nineteenth century was also the great age of technological innovation and saw the appearance of systematic and organised innovation and scientific R & D. The results were striking. Most of the key technologies that have created the world we live in were invented at this time (e.g. internal combustion engine, diesel engine, manned flight, turbine, electric generator, electric motor, synthetic fertiliser, mechanical data processing and the computer, refrigeration using electricity, steel fabrication and the elevator, radio, electric lighting, and many more) as were many of the central elements of modern science (thermodynamics, the General and Special Theories of Relativity, Maxwell's equations which united magnetism and light, modern medicine thanks to the work of people such as Koch and Pasteur, genetics thanks to Galton and Mendel, and, not least, Darwinism). In fact, contrary to common supposition, the twentieth century was not particularly innovative, and most of what happens after 1914 is simply the working out and application of technologies and principles discovered in the nineteenth century.

This period also saw major developments in art and culture. These included the appearance of modernism in literature and the production of many of the great works of modern literature such as the works of Joseph Conrad, Henry James, Edith Wharton, Herman Melville, Emile Zola, Gustave Flaubert, Tolstoy, and Dostoevsky and also the appearance of the first kinds of 'modern' art with movement such as Impressionism, Symbolism, and Futurism and many of the great works of music by composers such as Wagner, Mahler, Stravinsky, and Rachmaninov. It also saw the first appearance of new forms and media such as photography and the cinema, which would go on to transform popular and elite culture in the twentieth century. In popular culture there was the appearance of modern organised professional sport, now one of the central parts of contemporary popular culture.

The Dark Side of Modernity

However there was also a dark side to the Belle Epoque. One was the sudden (and unexpected) revival of imperialism. There had been a critique of colonialism and imperialism from many of the supporters of modernity from the time of Adam Smith onwards and in the early to mid nineteenth century empires and colonies were widely thought to be a waste of time and money and there were actually efforts to get rid of them. However after the 1860s they became fashionable again (Disraeli's making Queen Victoria Empress of India was perhaps a turning point, as was the new imperial policy of Napoleon III). By the time of the Berlin Conference of 1884, which carved up Africa, an empire had become a necessity for any self-respecting state. The United States joined the rush with the Spanish American War in 1901 and the subsequent conquest of the Philippines (which led Kipling to pen "The White Man's Burden"). This went along with a dramatic upsurge of militarism and an international arms race that by 1900 had made Europe into an 'armed camp'. There was also a naval arms race after 1898, sparked by the German decision to establish a 'blue water' navy to challenge the British. The Boer War of 1900-1902 also saw the appearance of guerrilla warfare and the response of both scorched earth tactics and concentration camps by the British, marking the first real appearance of something that would become a regular feature of war in the twentieth century and beyond.

At the same time there was a dramatic upsurge of nationalism, often with associated xenophobia and racism – another notion that gained wide acceptance at this time as an 'advanced' and 'scientific' idea along with the related idea of eugenics. There was also a revival of protection and a move towards a new kind of development strategy, based upon the ideas of the German economist Friedrich List. This was in many ways a revival of the policies pursued earlier by Dr Francia in Paraguay. List published these in his work *The National System of Political Economy* in 1841. He argued that the basic units of the world economy were not individuals but nations. The goal of economic policy was to promote the wealth and power of the nation as a collective entity. This involved protection to foster the growth of 'infant industries' and direct action by government to promote economic development through such things as the provision of infrastructure and compulsory state education. Part of the argument was the notion that manufacturing was a higher form of development than services or the production of primary products.

When List first published his ideas he had little impact and he died in 1846 thinking that his arguments had failed. After his death however they began to gain support firstly in the US where there was a tradition of this kind of thinking going back to the earliest days of the Republic and the policies of Alexander Hamilton – in fact List had formed his theories while living in Pennsylvania where he came into contact with the leading exponent at that time of the 'National System', Henry Charles Carey. Contrary to the idea of a prophet not finding honour in his own country, his ideas also became influential in Germany, which abandoned free trade and adopted economic nationalism in 1878. List himself was a liberal in domestic affairs and his programme may be described as 'capitalism in one country' but it proved to have a natural affinity with various kinds of authoritarian politics.

Perhaps the darkest aspect of the Belle Epoque was the global crisis of rural economies in the 1890s and 1900s. This led to massive famines that struck large areas of India, China and Africa in those decades. These are described by Mike Davis in his book *"Victorian Holocausts: El Nino Famines and the Making of the Modern World"*. He sees them as being the outcome of both a deliberate policy and the workings of the capitalist world economy. The reality was no less grim but slightly yet significantly different. These famines were caused by the combination of a natural phenomenon (El Nino) and two other factors.

The first was the development of the world economy and in particular the way its operations radically undermined the traditional agricultural systems of large parts of the world. In many areas of the world population continued to grow within the traditional kind of economic and agricultural system. This growth was partly sustained by the growth of the world economy as a whole that is it continued for longer than it otherwise would have done. Another factor was the way certain crops made it possible to feed a household on the produce of a small area of land while another factor was a decline in death rates due to things such as improved sanitation. The result was severe overpopulation of certain rural areas with large numbers of people living in an essentially subsistence based agricultural economy that could no longer sustain the level of population that had now come into existence. This meant that the whole system was highly vulnerable to any kind of natural interruption to the food supply such as a drought (or in an earlier example of the same phenomenon, a blight such as the one that affected the Irish potato crop in the 1840s).

The second factor was the political order of European and particularly British imperialism. The only real solution to the growing crisis of much of the world's rural economies by the 1890s was what had happened earlier in Europe – a sharp rise in agricultural productivity and a massive shift of population from rural areas to cities and from agriculture to manufacturing and in many cases from one part of the world to another. (The Russian state did move to such a policy after 1905, mainly in the interests of self-preservation). However the imperial powers were very resistant to applying this kind of policy to their colonies for a number of reasons, not the least of which was the way their rule depended on the support of local elites whose position would be undermined by an economic revolution of that kind. The result was the death of millions of people and a huge blow to the traditional economy and social order of large parts of the planet. Davis argues that this was an avoidable result of a world capitalist system. However it was arguably unavoidable by the 1890s, given the growth in world population by that time. It was undoubtedly seriously exacerbated by the policy of the British in particular however.

The key point is that, contrary to the popular theory on the subject, there was not a straightforward causal relation between capitalism and imperialism. Imperialism was not 'the highest stage of capitalism' – if anything the reverse was true and the revival of empire after 1850 was a reaction against the move towards economic openness between 1750 and 1850. So also were the revival of mercantilism and economic nationalism and the influence of the ideas of List and the upsurge of interest in such ideas as the theory of race. All of these were simultaneously modern and yet anti-modern. They were essentially the response to modernity of groups both elite and non-elite that disliked and feared the way the world was going yet realised the transformation that had begun in the eighteenth century could no longer be halted or reversed but only diverted. They were also in many ways a pragmatic response to the socially disruptive effects of the 'great transformation' that more and more of the world underwent with the spread of modernity.

Friedrich List and the New Mercantilism

However the most important things about ideas such as the economic nationalism of List and the policies of imperialism was that they were adopted by ruling classes, above all the traditional ruling elites of countries such as Germany and Russia. By the 1860s it had become clear that for states and the elites that controlled them to survive they had to allow or encourage a process of economic and technological modernisation. (The alternative, of separating oneself off from the world was not viable as the cases of Japan and Madagascar showed). Imperialism was the form that competition between ruling classes took at the global level, just as it had been in earlier epochs, but it was now linked to a justificatory ideology such as 'the civilising mission' or 'the spread of democracy' rather than being straightforwardly and openly about power and the control of resources.

The problem for elites was that of how to retain control and to justify their own continued existence while encouraging profound change. The kind of programme of state led industrialisation advocated by List offered a way of doing this. It also offered a way of dealing with the social disruption produced by modernisation, which tended to produce a popular reaction just as it had centuries earlier in China. Along with protectionism and state encouragement of economic modernisation went compulsory state education and government insurance and welfare transfers and radical modernisation of government. Thus economic modernisation went hand in hand with a process of state building or more precisely nation-state building.

One of the most significant parts of nineteenth century history was a fundamental change in the way that political authority was legitimised, from arguments based upon tradition and prescription (usually divine) to ones about popular sovereignty. This naturally raised the question of who were 'the people'. Increasingly the answer was that 'the people' were those who belonged to a nation, defined as a group of people with a common conscious identity that was the product of shared language, territory, historical experience or religion or some combination of these. This proved to be an enormously powerful and effective argument as it connected people's political identity to their sense of personal self so that they came to see the government they lived under as an expression or outgrowth of their self, as 'their' government in a way that had not been true before. It was this closer identification that made possible the much higher levels of taxation that became a feature of modern states from the 1900s onwards and also made possible the mass participation in war that became a feature of world politics between the 1850s and the 1960s. This was also however a cause as much as an effect, as was compulsory state education, which was both a consequence of the creation nationalism and nation states and a means by which national consciousness was created and modern nation states built. In contrast to the earlier, failed, state led modernisations such as those of

Paraguay or Egypt the policies followed in places such as Germany after 1878, the United States after the 1860s and Russia after the 1890s all appeared to be highly successful – at least for a while

The reappearance of mercantilism and imperialism and the appearance of such ideas as racism and nationalism were all parts of a realignment or reshuffling of the political argument that took place after the 1870s, during the Belle Epoque. The two driving forces behind this were the realisation, already mentioned, that it was now impossible to restore or even preserve the Ancien Regime and a redefinition of the key notion of progress so that the kind of change that was viewed as progressive became different to what it had been before. The classical left became increasingly divided over the role and place of government from the 1870s onwards. Some became ever more enamoured of government as an agent of progress while others adhered to the more longstanding classic left view that government power would decline with progress.

The first group were those who took on board the arguments of those advocating rational administration and came to believe that the nature of government had been transformed in such a way that it could now act as the genuine expression of the collective will and purpose of society as a whole rather than as the instrument and cause of a special privileged class interest, or that it could become that. (This assumed of course that there was a real collective interest and identity). Their opponents denied the existence of such a collective identity and continued to argue that government power was both inefficient and the cause of privilege, and that an increase in the scope and size of government along with such phenomena as imperialism and militarism was a retrograde tendency, a reversal of progress in fact and a reversion to a pre-modern kind of social order. This debate within the pro-modern camp took the form of an argument between self-styled 'Individualists' and 'Collectivists'. The Collectivists won the debate – in the sense that they were able to define their own position as the 'progressive' left wing one. In other words the concept of progress was redefined to mean a movement towards greater collectivism and a more active role for government whereas until the 1880s the opposite had been the case. In terms of politics and policy this meant that what was defined as 'left' politics after about 1890 was such movements as social or 'radical' liberalism, social democracy, socialism, and (after 1917) communism.

Meanwhile the response of the classical anti-modernist right to the realisation that traditional conservatism no longer had a viable political project was to divide. Some responded by articulating what Jeffrey Herf calls 'reactionary modernism'. This was a politics that accepted many aspects of modernity such as urbanism, technological innovation, and the modern economy but tried to combine it with the traditional anti-modern critique to produce a society that combined a modern technology and economy with a traditional political and social order. The label often given to this kind of politics by its own advocates was that of the 'Third Way' meaning that it was an alternative to the choice within modernist politics between capitalism and socialism. The movements that can be grouped under this rubric are many and diverse. Thus it found expression in much of the politics of Whilhelmine Germany and in movements such as the *Action Francaise* in France and later on in fascism and National Socialism. However it also included movements such as the Agrarian politics that was influential in Scandinavia and Eastern Europe before and after World War I, Distributism, and the early forms of Christian Democracy.

Other elements of the traditional right (typically the more moderate ones) meanwhile came to terms with modernity and combined with those elements of the classic left that had lost the internal debate described above and were still suspicious of state power for one reason or another (this was most of those at the limits point of the triangle and a majority of those at the liberty point). The common points were scepticism of government and, increasingly, support for the institutions and practices of 'actually existing' capitalism as these had come to be by the 1920s at the very latest. These now formed the modern post 1890s right, which included such political tendencies and movements as democratic conservatism, classical or 'moderate' liberalism, and the later forms of Christian Democracy. Thus politics after the 1890s are initially three cornered with arguments between the newly redefined left and right with the left favouring an increase in the size of government and a greater role for the state in economic life and the right being sceptical of this and favouring a reliance on market forces while 'third way' movements argued for a modern but not capitalist economy and a resistance to the modernisation of other areas of life such as the family and the political order. After World War II this third option was effectively eliminated and political argument became a debate between the redefined left and right or in terms of economic organisation, capitalism and socialism. It is important to realise that this was entirely an argument *within* modernity – it was essentially all about how to organise a modern economy and society and what place government should have in this.

The Detour of the Mid-Twentieth Century

The Belle Epoque came to an abrupt and tragic end in August 1914. This was the product and outcome of the kinds of elite competition and state building described earlier, which brought about what we may call the first great crisis of modernity. After 1870, while the world experienced the kind of unprecedented growth and scientific and technological discovery described earlier, there was also the countertrend, of a revival of mercantilism and a rise in militarism, imperialism and competition between national elites to try and control the world economy that had come into being with the 'first globalisation'. Simultaneously, the social disruption that was an inevitable part of the rapid change meant that there was widespread popular resistance, which found expression in a number of ways. This would not have mattered so much however were it not for the activities of ruling groups. The policies of protectionism and nationalism had two very damaging effects. The first was that, just as in the eighteenth century, they led to a struggle to control large parts of the world, to bring them within one 'fence' rather than another so that exchange could be monopolised by people from one part of the world. This obviously led to political conflicts, both inside and outside Europe itself. Secondly, they led rulers to see the world in a distorted way that inclined them to decisions that were ultimately disastrous. Crucially the German elite became increasingly panicked by the rapid economic development of Russia. Instead of seeing this as an unmitigated blessing and an opportunity, not least for German producers, they saw it as a threat – which it was for them since it threatened their power given what they had chosen to base it on. At the same time the policies that both ruling groups were following meant they both aspired to gain economic and political control over certain areas so as to exclude the other, above all in the Balkans and the Middle East. A similar clash of elite aspirations led to war between Russia and Japan between 1904 and 1905.

Moreover, by about 1910 the formerly successful programme of state led modernisation in Germany had begun to run into difficulties, including an increasingly severe fiscal problem caused by the combination of an inadequate tax base, with rising public spending and a growing problem of over investment due to the distortion of the investment market produced by such things as protection (which created an artificially high price for certain products) and government backed soft loans for investment (which artificially lowered the cost and raised the return on investment). By 1914 it was clear that the German state or rather its elite would have to make a major shift in policy, involving amongst other things a sharp cut in naval expenditure. Faced with this they saw the crisis that broke out in the summer of 1914 as an opportunity to destroy the threat (as they saw it) of Russia and took the insanely risky decision to fight a war on two fronts. The British decision to join the war made it truly global (although this was not the first true world war – that title belongs rather to the Seven Years War of 1756 – 1763).

The Great War of 1914 to 1918 was one of the great disasters of human history. Most obviously it involved the death of millions of people and an enormous amount of suffering. It also led directly to the appearance of totalitarian states in the shape of Nazi Germany and Soviet Russia that went on to kill millions of their own and other people. The peace that arrived in 1918 proved to be only a truce and a second even more terrible war followed that killed even more people and devastated most of Europe and much of Asia. It also undermined the transnational order that had developed in the nineteenth century and had persisted despite the move back to more protectionist policies after about 1880:

in particular it drastically undermined the stable world monetary system that had been created after 1815. There was an attempt to recreate the nineteenth century world economic order in the 1920s, with some success but this ended with the Great Depression.

This was the most severe and prolonged economic crisis since that of the mid seventeenth century, and like that one it affected the entire planet. Its best known and most studied effects were on countries such as Britain, Germany and the United States but its effects were if anything even more severe in places such as India and China. The trigger for the Depression was not simply the stock market crash of 1929 as is commonly supposed but rather a series of disastrous policy mistakes by the monetary authorities of various states, above all the Federal Reserve in the United States. By expanding the supply of money excessively in the 1920s the Fed sparked an asset bubble in things such as land and shares. When they corrected this they went much too far in the other direction and reduced the money supply in the United States by almost a third. The result was a huge contraction in economic activity and a wave of bank failures, caused by the way the Fed's policy played out in the highly regulated American banking system (Canada, where the latter did not apply, did not see a single bank failure at this time).

Not only was the Depression unprecedentedly severe, it lasted for a very long time. Nineteenth century depressions had typically been intense but short, lasting for about eighteen months with a recovery over a further three years or so. By contrast, the decline in economic activity that started in 1929 lasted until around 1948 (the idea that it was ended by the war in 1939 is a myth, particularly when one looks at things from a global perspective). The middle years of the twentieth century saw what we may call a general crisis of modernity. The kinds of process that had been going on since the early nineteenth century either stopped or went into reverse. Thus the growth of world trade went into reverse and actually shrank as a share of global output. No new modern economy emerged and in parts of the world such as India and China the incipient modernisation of the 1880 to 1930 period was turned back, as was also the case in Argentina. The kind of rapid fundamental breakthroughs in science and technology that had been such a feature of the years after 1850 also ended – what happened was mainly a working out and application of the earlier discoveries. Everywhere there was a move away from integration and in the direction of localism, autarchy and self-sufficiency. This reflected and came from the domination of public debate by anti-modernist movements, and reactions against modernity and the elements of the pro-modern side that favoured state action.

After 1948 however there was a recovery. This took a long time however – although economic growth resumed in the countries that had been modern in 1914 the spread of modernisation did not resume until the 1960s and in the cases of India and China the 1980s. (This was mainly due in the latter two cases to mistaken policy and additionally in the Chinese case their misfortune in being ruled by a complete psychopath for much of the period after 1949). World trade revived as did the process of economic integration but even after the 1960s trade was much more regulated and controlled than had been the case in the nineteenth century and the efforts by powerful interests to control economic activity have been a constant feature of life. At the end of the 1980s however the processes of the Belle Epoque seemed to have resumed and the following years saw an unprecedented episode of sustained growth in almost every part of the planet. Once again, the pressure for change brought about by the interactions of millions of people was able to subvert the efforts of rulers to control and check it, although their attempts to guide it may yet have more disastrous results. In retrospect the years between 1914 and the later 1980s appear to be a kind of pause or detour in which the growth of modernity was checked or held back before it resumed with full force. However the challenges that this process threw up in the later nineteenth century have now resumed.

One part of the events of the years after 1948 was the continuing debate within the pro-modernity side between the camps that had come into being at the end of the nineteenth century, between capitalism and socialism as it is commonly described. By 1989 this ended in a decisive victory for one side. Since the collapse of the Soviet Union the consensus has been that a modern society must be essentially a capitalist one, that is a market economy of the modern kind that came into full flower after 1850. However, since the late 1990s (or even earlier according to some) that kind of economy has faced increasing challenges, most notably increasing difficulty in sustaining intensive growth without some kind of credit driven bubble and environmental problems. This came to a head in the financial crisis of 2008 and its aftermath.

As a result the argument that began in the 1880s has in some ways resumed. As well as continuing argument over what kind of capitalist modernity there should be there are also signs of a revival of the older debate over whether modernity itself is a good thing or even something that can last. A crucial difference is that this time around the critics of modernity and also those who accept modernity but think it should have some organisational principle other than industrial capitalism do not have a clear or worked out notion of what the alternative should be. It may well be that there is now a political realignment going on like the one that happened after 1880. In this case the realignment is centred around a division between the national or territorial state on the one hand as opposed to a transnational or more global system of governance on the other, together with a division about the nature of identity. This seems to be leading to a realignment of politics as massive as the one of the late nineteenth century and in some ways a reversal of it.

The Argument Today

The real issue that is coming into focus is that of whether modernity is sustainable: can it continue? Will the wealth explosion go on, continuing onwards and upwards or will the history of the last two to three hundred years prove to be only the most spectacular of the efflorescences that have occurred in the course of human history, and end in the same way as previous ones, with a radical simplification episode? The case that we are experiencing what is no more than a particularly dramatic episode of the kind that has happened before (e.g. under the Song) has two main supports.

The first is that the transformative process of modernity depends upon, and is driven by, innovation. A number of authors have made the case that the great age of innovation was the later nineteenth and early twentieth century and that since about 1950 the pace and significance (or impact) of innovation has declined to the point where it has now effectively ceased, or reverted to its historic norm. The argument is that this is an inevitable process and that in a very real sense most of the truly impactful innovations have already been made. If this is correct then, given the centrality of innovation to modernity, the wealth explosion and its effects will peter out.

That does not mean that after the transformative effects of the three hundred years of modernity we will go on living in the world the wealth explosion has created – there will not a step change after which the world will stabilise and then continue at the new, more affluent and comfortable level. In practical terms that would be impossible because sustaining and maintaining the infrastructure of modern society requires continued increases in productivity and efficiency, which means sustained effective innovation. Instead there will be a simplification process, lasting about a hundred to a hundred and fifty years, after which the world will end up at something like the historically normal level and pattern of wealth and everyday experience. There will be a reversion to the norm, just as there was after previous episodes of intensive growth and cultural innovation.

A slightly different version is that the social and political conditions that led to sustained innovation (competition between elites and cultural openness to innovation and exchange) will disappear. In that case there will be nothing inherently or structurally necessary about the end of innovation and modernity, it will rather be the result of actions and policy. It would in other words be the story of Ming and Qing China writ large. How you would feel about that will depend on the view you take of the modern world.

The second reason for thinking that modernity may prove to be a passing phase concerns natural resources and above all the key one of energy. The argument of the first chapter was that our ancestors lived in a world in which Malthus's diagnosis was correct because there were fundamental and almost immoveable resource constraints on human civilisations, and that we had escaped this through sustained innovation and consequent intensive growth and social transformation. It is possible that the ability of innovation to deal with the progressive exhaustion of natural resources has limits (due to diminishing marginal returns primarily). This applies to a number of key resources for which there are no readily available substitutes. One of these is fresh water but the main one is energy, above all fossil fuels. A number of historians (such as E. A. Wrigley) argue that the crucial factor that makes the modern world possible is the increased use of energy. Diminishing energy returns (caused by the fact that it takes increasing amounts of energy input to get a given amount of useful energy) mean that this process is going to end sooner rather than later. One key element to this argument is that so-called renewable energy is not an effective substitute for fossil fuel based energy, mainly because it is typically too diffuse.

The result if this is correct will be a reversion to a lower level of energy capture and use and a consequent decline in the complexity and dynamism of human societies. Once again there will be a simplification and a move from a complex and extremely wealthy civilisation to something much simpler and more historically normal. In this case it does not matter if innovation continues so long as innovation is unable to resolve the challenge of the declining rate of return on energy and some other non-substitutable resources. None of this is inevitable however. The other possibility is that the process of innovation will continue (absent a modern equivalent of the Ming emperors) and will continue to keep the human race ahead of resource constraints. The key innovation here would be a breakthrough in energy storage and compression, which would make renewable energy a true substitute for fossil fuels.

In that case we or our descendants will be able to look back at the wealth explosion of the mid-eighteenth through mid-twentyfirst centuries in the same way that we now think about the advent of agriculture in the Fertile Crescent several thousand years ago, as a transformative period that saw the human experience and relation to the natural world move from one mode to another. In that case we may even as some have speculated see the process of the last three hundred years culminate in a 'singularity' a truly abrupt change after which things will have changed so much from all previous human experience that we will inhabit a state of existence that is post or trans human.

What all this leads to finally is the question of how to place the present world into a longer historical perspective, to locate it in the kind of story this book has told. What is the world we now live in and how are we to understand its place in history and its relation to classic civilisations, above all Western civilisation?

Further Reading

Among books that consider the consolidation and successful defence of modernity in the first part of the nineteenth century are C. A. Bayly *The Birth of the Modern World 1780 – 1914* (Blackwell, 2004), Robert B. Marks *The Origins of the Modern World: A Global and Ecological Narrative from the Fifteenth to the Twentyfirst Century* (Rowman & Littlefield, 2006). One famous and hostile account is Karl Polanyi *The Great Transformation: The Political and Economic Origins of Our Times* (Beacon Press, 2001; 1st published 1944). Another critical perspective is provided by Stephen E. Toulmin *Cosmopolis: The Hidden Agenda of Modernity* (Chicago University Press, 1992). A recent and outstanding study of the way economic life was transformed is Joel Mokyr *A Culture of Growth: The Origins of the Modern Economy* (Princeton University Press, 2018)

The best and clearest account of the persistent and repetitive themes of anti-modernism is Ian Buruma & Avishai Margalit *Occidentalism: A Short History of Anti- Westernism* (Atlantic Books, 2004). Another work that points out these persistent themes is Stephen Holmes *The Anatomy of Anti-Liberalism* (Harvard University Press, 1996). The Counter-Enlightenment has not attracted as much attention as its opponent but there are good introductions and surveys in Christopher O. Blum (ed.) *Critics of the Enlightenment: Readings in the French Counter-Revolutionary Tradition* (ISI Books, 2004), Darrin McMahon *Enemies of the Enlightenment: The French Counter-Enlightenment and the Making of Modernity* (Oxford University Press, 2002), and Graeme Garrard *Counter Enlightenments: From the Eighteenth Century to the Present* (Routledge, 2005). For Rousseau's position as by far the most important critic and opponent of the Enlightenment see Graeme Garrard *Rousseau's Counter- Enlightenment: A Republican Critique of the Philosophes* (SUNY Press, 2012).

The later forms of radical anti-Enlightenment thinking, which involved an embrace of some aspects of modernity while rejecting others are the subject of the classic work of Jeffrey Herf *Reactionary Modernism: Technology, Culture, and Politics in Weimar Germany and the Third Reich* (Cambridge University Press, 1986). Other works that examine this continuing phenomenon are Fritz Stern The *politics of Cultural Despair: A Study in the Rise of the Germanic Ideology* (University of California Press, 1974), and Richard Wolin *The Seduction of Unreason: The Intellectual Romance With Fascism from Nietzsche to Postmodernism* (Princeton University Press, 2006). Allan C. Carlson. *Third Ways: How Bulgarian Greens, Swedish Housewives, and Beer-Swilling Englishmen Created Family-Centred Economies – and Why They Disappeared* (ISI Books, 2007) looks at more benign forms of this kind of sensibility and agenda.

The original work of economic nationalism is Friedrich List The *National System of Political Economy*. (Lippincott, 1856. Facsimile reprint by University of Michigan University Library Historical Reprints). A recent work that argues powerfully for the centrality of nation states and nationalism in economic development is Liah Greenfield *The Spirit of Capitalism: Nationalism and Economic Growth* (Harvard University Press, 2001). The positive case for empire as the framework of a global economic order is found in Niall Ferguson *Empire: The Rise and Demise of the British World Order and the Lessons for Global*

Power (Basic Books, 2004), and Deepak Lal *In Praise of Empires: Globalization and Order* (Palgrave Macmillan, 2004). These should be read alongside John Darwin, *After Tamerlane: The Rise and Fall of Global Empires, 1400 – 2000* (Penguin, 2007). A study of the British Empire during the consolidation of modernity is C. A. Bayly, *Imperial Meridian: The British Empire and the World 1780 – 1830* (Longman, 1989). The phenomenon of globalisation and its recurrence as a feature of world history is the theme of the collection by A. G. Hopkins (ed.) *Globalization in World History* (Pimlico, 2002). The so called 'First Globalisation' of the Belle Epoque is described in the first part of Martin Wolf *Why Globalisation Works* (Yale University Press, 2005) and in Christie Davies "The Rise and Fall of the First Globalisation" *Economic Affairs* 25 (2002) 55 – 57. The arguments and developments of the twentieth century are surveyed in Daniel Yergin & Joseph Stanislaw, *The Commanding Heights: The Battle For the World Economy* (Simon & Shuster, 2002).

The great revolution in business organisation in the second half of the nineteenth century was first identified and analysed in the great work of Alfred D. Chandler, most notably in his trilogy of works *The Visible Hand: The Managerial Revolution in American Business* (Belknap Press, 1977), *Scale and Scope: The Dynamics of Industrial Capitalism* (Belknap Press, 1990), *Strategy and Structure: Chapters in the History of the American Industrial Enterprise* (MIT Press, 1990 1st pub. 1962). Also worth reading is Alfred D. Chandler, Franco Amatori, & Takashi Hikino (eds.) *Big Business and the Wealth of Nations* (Cambridge University Press, 1997).

The thwarted economic development of many parts of the world in the later nineteenth and early twentieth century is the subject of Alexander Woodside, *Lost Modernities: China, Vietnam, Korea and the Hazards of World History* (Harvard University Press, 2006), while Thomas C. Smith *Native Sources of Japanese Industrialisation, 1750 – 1920* (University of California Press, 1989) looks at the Tokugawa roots of Japan's successful transition. John Steele Gordon *An Empire of Wealth: The Epic History of American Economic Power* (Harper Collins 2004) is a popular and well written account of American industrial growth. The tripartite division of political discussion that I set out was something I first discovered from Jacob T Levy and it underlies the analysis he presents in *Rationalism, Pluralism, and Freedom* (Oxford University Press, 2014). An outstandingly perceptive work that looks at the way politics changed in the later nineteenth and early twentieth century is Sheri Berman *The Primacy of Politics: Social Democracy and the Making of Europe's Twentieth Century* (Cambridge University Press, 2006).

The great demographic crisis of the 1890s and 1900s in many parts of the world is the subject of Mike Davis *Late Victorian Holocausts: El Nino Famines and the Making of the Third World* (Verso, 2002). The Great Depression has a virtual library of books devoted to it. One survey that looks at the contemporary response is John A Garraty *The Great Depression: An Inquiry Into the Causes,*

Course, and Consequences of the Worldwide Depression of the Nineteen-Thirties, As Seen By Contemporaries (Anchor Books, 1987). Of the many books written subsequently the work of Barry Eichengreen gives the best survey of the current state of play and in particular of the centrality of monetary explanations for the unprecedented severity and longevity of the contraction: see *Golden Fetters: The Gold Standard and the Great Depression, 1919 – 1939* (Oxford University Press, 1992). For an account of more recent economic turbulence see Adam Tooze *Crashed: How a Decade of Financial Crises Changed the World* (Allen Lane, 2018).

The question of whether we will continue to see the kinds of levels of innovation that have marked the world since the mid-nineteenth century at least (or as I would argue, the later eighteenth century) was raised quite a long time ago by Jean Gimpel in *The End of the Future: The Waning of the High-Tech World* (Adamantine Press, 1995) but has become fashionable recently with the publication of Jonathan Huebner "A Possible Declining Trend for Worldwide Innovation" *Technological Forecasting and Social Change* 72 (2005) 780 – 786. Two more recent works that argue the case for a decline in innovation and consequent slowing of economic growth are Tyler Cowen *The Great Stagnation: How America Ate All the Low-Hanging Fruit of Modern History, Got Sick and Will (Eventually) Recover* (Dutton, 2011) and Robert Gordon *The Rise and Fall of American Growth: The US Standard of Living Since the Civil War* (Princeton University Press, 2017) while Matt Ridley *The Rational Optimist: How Prosperity Evolves* (Fourth Estate, 2010) puts the contrary case.

Are We Still Living in Western Civilisation?

T HE world today is profoundly different from the way it has been for most of recorded history. There are still continuities with the past, obviously, but in all sorts of ways we are moving ever more rapidly away from the world and life of our ancestors. The last two hundred and fifty years have seen enormous change but there is even more to come. How and why though did this transformation of human experience come about? The narrative of this book tries to answer this question but inevitably raises others along the way. One of these is that of inevitability. How far was the appearance of modernity something that was inevitable, in the sense that it was something that was bound to happen sooner or later? There are all kinds of reasons for rejecting the idea that the modern world was the goal or target of historical development or that it was somehow implicit in human society and was gradually brought into full realisation by a process of historical evolution. However that does not mean that the appearance of the modern world was completely accidental and adventitious.

Instead, the plausible and persuasive position is that the modern condition, if we may call it that, was a potential or possibility for a considerable time in human history and became more likely at certain times. For much of human history there was no realistic chance of a recognisably modern society and economy appearing anywhere because certain necessary conditions were not in place. These would include a sufficiently large population, a sufficient population density in a significant part of the planet, and a system of trade and division of labour that covered a large enough portion of both the planet's surface and its population and integrated and coordinated a high enough proportion of total economic activity within that area. (Arguably another candidate is access to an adequate supply of easily usable and accessible energy but that is less clear). However these are only necessary conditions and not sufficient ones, so even if all three were met the development of a modern economy and society would not follow automatically. Also, it does not seem plausible to argue (as Julian Simon does for example) that one of these is independent of the others and the one that drives or determines the rest.

What is missing from the list just given (or rather hinted at in the reference to trade and labour) is the role of human action, in particular the part played by freely chosen cooperation and exchange of both products and ideas. It is this which is the dynamic factor in history and it is the relative freedom allowed to them that accounts ultimately for the difference between the modern world and what has gone before. Other things, such as technology are rather the consequences of this. However this leads on to a further conundrum and is that answer to that particular puzzle that is the central theme of the narrative given in the preceding chapters. As Eric Jones has argued, intensive growth is historically rare and short lived before the advent of modernity. However, growth of this kind is the natural and inevitable outcome of trade and exchange, economic integration and the division of labour, all of which are natural social phenomena that appear in almost every human society since the end of the last Ice Age. Open ended intellectual development and discovery is likewise the natural outcome of free discussion and the exchange of ideas. In contemporary terminology the kind of things that are the predominant features of modernity are the default setting for human experience, they should arise naturally and spontaneously and become self-sustaining once the three minimum necessary criteria set out above are in place.

One answer therefore could be that it was only by the second half of the eighteenth century that the necessary conditions were in place for these natural processes to achieve a self-sustaining existence. When we look more closely at the evidence however this seems doubtful, as Jones himself has observed. In particular there is the problematic case of Song China (although there are possibly others). On all the evidence there was no difference between China in the thirteenth century and Western Europe in the eighteenth that would account for an emergence of modernity in the second case but not the first. It may be that the difference lay in the relatively greater development of the world as a whole by 1750 but that also seems unlikely.

The answer then would seem to be this. Once certain necessary conditions were met the natural outcome of certain spontaneous processes that are a constant feature of human life should have led to a shift into an economy and society marked by the main features of what we now call modernity. That this did not happen shows that there was some kind of countervailing or contrary force that checked these kinds of developments and prevented this from happening. There are a number of possible candidates for this. One is the pressing need until the later eighteenth century for a large majority of the population to be involved in agriculture and the extreme difficulty of moving enough of the labour force out of that sector. Another undoubtedly important factor is the existence in all agricultural societies of what we have come to call the 'moral economy' This was a set of institutions, practices, laws and conventions, and attitudes and sensibilities that collectively checked and limited innovation while at the same time providing security and protection for people in a largely zero sum and non-dynamic economy. However the most plausible force to explain both the stability of traditional society and the way this was finally upset is the role of power and domination in human affairs, the opposite in other words of free association. This combined with moral economy to make innovation and discovery either very slow and piecemeal or episodic. It is the role of power and the actions of classes that have it however that is the active agent.

All human societies since the advent of agriculture have seen a division between ruling groups that gain income and status from the exercise of power on the one hand and the productive classes who create wealth through trade and production on the other. Of course the division is not so clear cut but that does not make it any the less real. The central argument of the narrative of this book is that on several occasions, most notably in China, the dynamics of power and the need on the part of rulers to control the spontaneous processes of social and economic change, when combined with the other phenomenon (which took the form of popular resistance to innovation), led to the choking off of the process that would otherwise lead to the appearance of modernity. In the later eighteenth century this recurring pattern of force meeting object had an outcome that had not occurred before. Instead of power checking development it was the force of free exchange that triumphed, with ruling groups either actively encouraging this or seeking to turn it to their advantage rather than to suppress it. This is explained by the way that in the years between roughly 1580 and 1690 political, intellectual and military events had a particular outcome in Europe that was not found elsewhere or before and was this combination of events (largely driven by chance) that so changed the balance of social forces in Europe and the incentives facing its ruling groups that the outcome of the crisis of the later eighteenth century took the form that it did.

The narrative and historical explanation given in the body of this work and presented in compressed form just now still leaves certain issues that we need to consider. One is that of whether in the contemporary world the condition of modernity is not so much inevitable as inescapable. The answer must surely be that as long as it persists it is indeed inescapable, that the chance to stand aside from modernity has passed. The obvious comparison is with the impact of agriculture. Once agricultural civilisations had become established hunter-gatherer societies were doomed in the long run to absorption and conquest, transformation into agricultural societies, or confinement to the most marginal parts of the planet. Similarly, once modernity became established by the middle of the nineteenth century there was no long term future for traditional social orders and ways of life as long as the condition of modernity persisted.

This in turn raises the question of whether this is regrettable or to put it another way of whether the 'deal' of modernity is a good one. There have been, and continue to be, many who argue it is not, that on the contrary modernity is a Faustian bargain in which the higher things in life are traded for base comforts and mere knowledge – a mess of pottage in the Biblical terminology. Even if this argument is rejected (which is my own position) it is inescapably true that some forms of human good and excellence are lost forever as a result of the modern world and its nature and this has to be simply accepted as an inevitable cost. Some would argue that modernity is ultimately incompatible with human nature, with what it is about us that defines our nature or kind. If this is so, then to continue on the path of the modern is to cease to be human and to become something else. This may happen gradually or it could happen very suddenly, in a matter of a few years in what has come to be known as a 'technological singularity', possibly because of the advent of superhuman artificial intelligence, possibly because of radical breakthroughs in biological and medical science. In that case modernity will have been a transitional period, from the greater part of human history where we as a species were constrained by our biological nature and the physical constraints of the material environment that we inhabited, to a future where our mastery of both would make us posthuman or transhuman.

All of this depends of course on modernity and its features being sustained. Above all it assumes that intensive growth and intensified innovation will continue. There is a widely held view that this is not true. In this view we are at the latter part of a three hundred yearlong episode in human history that is unique and will not be repeated. The kind of state of affairs described in the first chapter, which we call modernity, will just be an episode and once it has concluded (quite soon according to most people making this argument) the conditions of life for human beings will revert to what they have been for most of human history. In the most extreme version of this thesis (known as the Olduvai Hypothesis) it is the entire history of agricultural civilisation that is the aberrant episode, with modernity merely its climax, and after some longer time we will revert to the conditions of out hunter-gatherer stone age ancestors. (Duncan, 2007) The case for this view, of the modern world as an unsustainable episode rather than a decisive break, rests upon two arguments. The first is that the crucial factor in the sudden rupture that created modernity was none of factors described in the second chapter but simply human beings having suddenly gained access to large reserves of cheap and highly concentrated energy in the shape of fossil fuels. As these become depleted and the energy cost of extracting them gets ever greater (so that the positive return in energy that you get is reduced) so it becomes ever more difficult to sustain a modern civilisation. The result will be another of the simplification episodes observed in previous history, in which a complex and elaborate civilisation collapses and becomes much simpler.

The rejoinder of course is that what really matters is not energy per se but the process of innovation that became self sustaining in the later eighteenth century in North-Western Europe. In this view, as long as the innovation continues solutions will be found to challenges such as energy supply and the process of modernity will continue.

This brings us to the second argument in favour of modernity only being an episode, which is that the innovation that we say in the nineteenth century in particular was itself a one-off and has already declined. The argument here is that most of the innovations that can realistically be made and above all the ones that lead to intensive growth have already happened. People making this case argue that we have already seen a sharp slowdown in meaningful innovation, or at least innovation that raises productivity and leads to intensive growth. If this is correct then there will be a period of economic stagnation followed by the gradual decay of modern civilisation and a reversion to the historical norm (the immediate reason being that in the absence of continuing productivity growth brought about by innovation it becomes impossible to maintain the existing stock of capital goods which therefore gradually break down). The response is that if anything we are in the early years of another episode of radical innovation, which promises to be as dramatic and significant as the one that happened in the later nineteenth century. We may experience a troublesome few years but in the medium to longer term we can expect the innovative process to continue, even if it is not as transformative as the transhumanists expect.

This in turn leads to yet another question, that of whether the modern condition is irreversible. Even if it is unavoidable in the sense that traditional human societies cannot simply resist it and exist alongside it, and even if we grant that it will continue, could it be that with effort the modern world might be rolled back? At first sight this seems simply impossible, a fantasy. However the evidence of the past and particularly the history of China, suggests that it may not be. It may well be that a deliberate and conscious policy could reverse many of the social and economic changes of the last two hundred years, eliminate a great deal of the technology that has developed, and restore an older intellectual order, just as the early Ming emperors did. In other words there could be an anti-modern revolution. However the cost of this would be enormous in terms of the conditions of daily life and range of options and choices available to most people. Above all it is impossible to imagine how anything like the world's present population can be sustained in such a case and so reversing modernity must mean accepting the death of several billion people. This need not happen suddenly but it would mean having a period of around fifty years in which death rates would be higher than birth rates and this almost certainly would involve several severe 'mortality episodes' as they are euphemistically called.

However the real problem with the scenario of an anti-modern revolution of the kind effected by the Ming and Qing emperors is that it would now have to be global in scope. The Chinese elite could carry through their policy because the world at that time was not as integrated as it is now and, most importantly, because the elites of other parts of the world, particularly Europe, had not then fully gone down the road of encouraging innovation. Even so, the longer term results of policies such as the scrapping of China's long distance maritime capability was that China ceased to be the centre of the world economy and experienced a century of harassment and exploitation by European imperial powers. No one elite group, no matter how much of the planet it controls, can hold back or even reverse innovation without suffering a serious loss of power and status relative to other elites unless all of the other groups follow the same policy. The global situation for ruling classes is now the same as the one that faced European ruling groups after the Treaty of Westphalia, a competition in which the rewards will go to the group that most embraces innovation.

The final question that this account of our historical origin leaves us with is one that has already been touched on in the introduction to this work. How are we to define or name our own position and identity? Or, as the title of this section puts it, are we still living in Western civilisation? The account presented in this book leads to the conclusion that we are not. Traditional Western, Christian civilisation ceased to exist as a living social and intellectual order sometime between the 1850s and the 1940s. We no longer have or inhabit a Christian civilisation that would be recognisable to anyone from our past, in the way that a time traveller from twelfth century Europe would recognise the same continent in the seventeenth century as being occupied by the same civilisation as the one he had left, despite the undoubted changes that had taken place. Our position now is perhaps analogous to that of a cultivated landowner in Gaul in the late eighth or early ninth century. Although such a person would have been aware of the traditions and inheritance of the old classical civilisation of Greece and Rome they were no longer living in that civilisation but in a new one that had grown out of it and supplanted it. The same comment can be made for the other identifiable traditional civilisations such as the Islamic and Confucian. They exist as a heritage and body of ideas and practices but the historical continuity has been decisively broken.

We are now living in fact in at least one new civilisation, one that will increasingly draw upon the inheritance from all of the traditional ones while developing its own forms, symbols and ways of life. In terms of historical periodisation it makes sense to think of our own times as 'Early Modern' (certainly not as post-modern) and the era usually given that label should rather be thought of as 'Late Western'. As time passes the world of our ancestors becomes ever more distant and strange to us and our descendants, like a coastline slowly fading into the distance and its details blurring as we move on into an unknown and unprecedented future.

Further Reading

For those who wish to look at the argument about whether modernity can continue, one side is given elegantly and forcefully in Matt Ridley *The Rational Optimist: How Prosperity Evolves* (Fourth Estate, 2010). The idea that the modern is about to lead into a total transformation of our existence into a transhuman condition is examined in Damien Broderick *The Spike: How Our Lives Are Being Transformed By Rapidly Advancing Technologies* (Forge, 2001). The view that we have reached a Malthusian limit and will soon experience a collapse was first put clearly in William R. Catton *Overshoot: The Ecological Basis of Revolutionary Change* (University of Illinois Press, 1980). Its best contemporary exponent is John Michael Greer, in a number of works with a good introduction being *The Long Descent: A Users Guide to the End of the Industrial Age.* (New Society Publishers, 2008). Another example is James Howard Kunstler *The Long Emergency: Surviving the end of Oil, Climate Change, and Other Converging Catastrophes of the Twenty-First Century* (Grove Press, 2007).

Index